How To Do Critical Discourse Analysis
Analysis

A Multimodal Introduction

David Machin and Andrea Mayr

Los Angeles | London | New Delhi
Singapore | Washington DC

First published 2012
Reprinted 2013

SAGE Publications Ltd
1 Oliver's Yard
55 City Road
London EC1Y 1SP

SAGE Publications Inc.
2455 Teller Road
Thousand Oaks, California 91320

SAGE Publications India Pvt Ltd
B 1/I 1 Mohan Cooperative Industrial Area
Mathura Road
New Delhi 110 044

SAGE Publications Asia-Pacific Pte Ltd
3 Church Street
#10-04 Samsung Hub
Singapore 049483

Library of Congress Control Number: 2011936661

British Library Cataloguing in Publication data

A catalogue record for this book is available from the British Library

ISBN 978-0-85702-891-4
ISBN 978-0-85702-892-1 (pbk)

Typeset by C&M (P) Ltd, Chennai, India
Printed in Great Britain by MPG Printgroup, UK
Printed on paper from sustainable resources

Contents

Introduction: How Meaning is Created

In Media and Cultural Studies, at whose scholars and students this book is in the first place aimed, there has been a growing interest in the particular set of tools for analysing texts and spoken language that is called Critical Discourse Analysis (CDA), a loose combination of approaches founded in linguistics, associated for the most part with a number of key authors (Kress, 1985; Fairclough, 1989; Wodak, 1989; Van Dijk, 1991; Van Leeuwen, 1996; Caldas Coulthard, 1997). There has been an increased sense of there being value in carrying out more thorough and systematic analysis of language and texts than is permitted through content analysis-type approaches or the more literary style interpretation of Cultural Studies. Guided by linguistic expertise, such detailed analysis can allow us to reveal more precisely how speakers and authors use language and grammatical features to create meaning, to persuade people to think about events in a particular way, sometimes even to seek to manipulate them while at the same time concealing their communicative intentions. The aim of this book, on the one hand, is to present a set of tools often used by critical discourse analysts and show how these can be used to analyse a range of media texts.

On the other hand, this book presents a set of methods for more precisely analysing visual communication. Among linguists and discourse analysts there has been a corresponding increase in interest in analysing the way that meaning is communicated not just through language, but through visual language (Hodge and Kress, 1988; Kress and van Leeuwen, 1996; Kress, 2010). Many of the texts linguists analyse can also communicate through their visual features, which they had formerly been overlooking through their desire to understand language, which these authors began to argue was problematic as much of the way meaning was communicated was being missed.

While visual analysis has more traditionally been the domain of Media and Cultural Studies, linguists such as Kress and van Leeuwen (1996, 2001), O'Halloran (2004) and Baldry and Thibault (2006) have begun to develop some of their own models for analysis that draw on the same kinds of precision and more systematic kinds of description that characterised the approach to language in CDA. These authors began to look at how language, image and other modes of communication, such as toys, monuments, films, sounds, etc., combine to make meaning. This has broadly been referred to as 'multimodal' analysis. Not all of this work has adopted the kind of critical approach used in CDA, where the aim is to reveal buried ideology. As with linguistics in general, the aim has often rather been one of description, of simply documenting patterns. The aim of much of linguistics has, after all, been to explain the nature of languages. But what this kind of visual multimodal analysis can also offer Media and Cultural Studies is a more precise set of tools that, like those offered for the analysis of language, encourage more systematic analysis of (media) texts.

Critical linguistics

Critical Discourse Analysis arguably has its origins in 'critical linguistics', which appeared in the late 1970s in the work of Roger Fowler, Robert Hodge, Gunter Kress and Tony Trew at the University of East Anglia in the UK. This can be found in their classic publication *Language and Control* (Fowler et al., 1979). Critical Linguistics sought to show how language and grammar can be used as ideological instruments. Texts can be studied for the ways that they categorise people, events, places and actions. Analysts can look for what kinds of events and persons are foregrounded and which are backgrounded or excluded altogether. Different kinds of choices can affect the meaning of texts. Close analysis of texts, therefore, can reveal the underlying ideology of the texts. Kress (1989), for example, was able to show how in school geography books certain agents and actions would be suppressed in order to background capitalist motives for 'assessing the productivity' in a particular region. For example, if we find in a text explaining the development of a particular region in Africa:

> The large size of the farms is needed because of the land's poor carrying capacity.

This sentence is typical of the text as a whole. We are not told who here does the 'needing'. Who it is that requires the area to be productive is never mentioned. The land is often described in terms of what it is bad for, in this case having a poor carrying capacity. But the text focuses entirely on what the land is bad for and not what it is good for. The land is not assessed in its own right, for its beauty, for its ability to support countless wildlife and small-scale communities, but only for its ability to yield produce and resources. What is never mentioned in the text is that the assessment of the region is basically about economic exploitation. What is the key for Critical Linguistics here is that these things are never communicated directly in the text but can be revealed by looking for absences.

What authors like Hodge and Kress (1988) went on to argue was that language is a form of social practice. Language is intertwined with how we act and how we maintain and regulate our societies. Language is part of the way that people seek to promote particular views of the world and *naturalise* them, that is, make them appear natural and commonsensical. Through language, certain kinds of practices, ideas, values and identities are promoted and naturalised. Institutions such as schools become one site where such knowledge becomes disseminated and regulated. What we think of as our culture is inseparable from language.

A more contemporary example from British politics can illustrate how we can best think about these ideas. Leading up to the general election in Britain in 2010, Conservative Party leader David Cameron launched a criticism of the opposition party in terms of the way they were failing to protect 'family values'. He targeted the way young girls are becoming too mature sexually due to their exposure to popular culture. The speech began like this:

> Premature sexualization is like pollution. It's in the air that our children breathe. All the time. Every day.

What we can see here is that Cameron does not speak about specifics. He does not identify precisely what comprises the process of 'sexualization'. He does not define what 'sexualization' is nor at what point it can be said to be 'premature'. Rather than speaking about specifics, Cameron makes a comparison to environmental pollution. By taking this step, he is able to create a great sense of menace and easily attribute blame to the society created by the existing New Labour government without stating exactly what he is accusing them of doing. General listeners may realise that little in concrete is being communicated here. But Critical Linguistics would want to identify some of the specific language choices that allow combinations of ambiguity and strong commitment. It would want to identify what kinds of definitions of events are being promoted here and what kinds of ideas, values and identities.

Cameron's language strategy here makes the problem appear to be one that we would all agree upon. After all, who would want 'children' to be breathing 'pollution'? What Critical Linguists would have pointed out is that this language is inseparable from the way that we build our societies and the way that we act in them. When ideas like 'premature sexualization' become naturalised, they can come to comprise ways that we go on to socialise and control our children. They can become a part of the way we organise our institutions how we teach about the body and identity. Sexuality is not something in the first place that young people need to explore, but from which they should be protected.

Critical Linguistics would point to the assumptions that a text makes yet which remain implicit; in other words, things that are communicated but which are not directly 'present' in the text – in this case, that there is indeed an identifiable and isolatable thing called 'sexualization' that has an agreed upon appropriate timing, that we only really worry about this as regards girls and not boys.

As well as looking for what is absent from the text, Critical Linguists would also look for assumptions and taken-for-granted concepts. We can see in Cameron's statement that there is an assumption, what they would call a 'presupposition', that there was a previous time when the air was not polluted and that we can therefore return to this former condition. It is a well-trodden Conservative Party view that aspects of the world should and can be returned to a former glorious era characterised by a mythical family and safe, supportive and crime-free communities. None of this is specified here in what Cameron says, but this underlying assumption is certainly present. Analysis of even this short statement can go much deeper. But for now we wish to give a sense of the aims of Critical Linguistics that were later taken up and modified by Critical Discourse Analysis.

Critical discourse analysis (CDA)

One of the main criticisms of Critical Linguistics has been its lack of development of the nature of the link between language, power and ideology (Fairclough, 1992). Critical Discourse Analysts sought to develop methods and theory that could better capture this interrelationship and especially to draw out and describe the practices and conventions in and behind texts that reveal political and ideological investment. Critical Discourse Analysis is also openly committed to political intervention and social change (Fairclough and Wodak, 1997: 258). For example, a number of analysts are politically active against racism, exposing racist stereotypes and ideologies in media and other institutional discourses. However, this is often viewed negatively by other linguists who hold on to the idea of objectivity in their own work. We discuss this matter towards the end of the book where we evaluate CDA from a number of perspectives.

CDA has been mainly associated with the ideas of Norman Fairclough, Ruth Wodak and Teun van Dijk, although as Critical Discourse Analysts themselves point out, there is no single, homogeneous version of CDA. Rather, what we find is a whole range of critical approaches which can be classified as CDA (e.g. Gee, 1990; Scollon, 1998; Rogers, 2004; Jeffries, 2007; Richardson, 2007). And many of these authors emphasise the need for analysis to draw on a range of (linguistic) methods to research things like the production and reception of texts (Wodak and Meyer, 2001; Richardson, 2007). But importantly, what all these authors have in common is the view of language as a means of social construction: language both *shapes* and *is shaped by* society. CDA is not so much interested in language use itself, but in the linguistic character of social and cultural processes and structures.

CDA assumes that power relations are discursive. In other words, power is transmitted and practised through discourse. Therefore, we can study 'how power relations are exercised and negotiated in discourse' (Fairclough and Wodak, 1997: 272).

The word 'critical' has been central to CDA, as it was in Critical Linguistics. In the same way, CDA points to a departure from the more descriptive goals of linguistics and discourse analysis, where the focus has been more on describing and detailing linguistic features than about *why* and *how* these features are produced and what possible ideological goals they might serve.

CDA typically analyses news texts, political speeches, advertisements, school books, etc., exposing strategies that appear normal or neutral on the surface but which may in fact be ideological and seek to shape the representation of events and persons for particular ends. The term 'critical' therefore means 'denaturalising' the language to reveal the kinds of ideas, absences and taken-for-granted assumptions in texts. This will allow us to reveal the kinds of power interests buried in these texts.

For Critical Discourse Analysts like Fairclough and Wodak (1997: 258), the primary focus is on how power relations are exercised and negotiated in discourse. So analysis can show how the kinds of power relations involved in racism are maintained through news texts and political speeches. Analysis can show how politicians such as David Cameron seek to promote conservative ideologies of 'family values' in order to create the kinds of enemies in society that distract from the actual forces that create concrete inequality and poor life experiences.

Fairclough (1989: 5) sums up the idea of 'critical' language study as the processes of analysing linguistic elements in order to reveal connections between language, power and ideology that are hidden from people. When a researcher draws on CDA for the first time, what they will realise is that it is often in the smallest linguistic details where power relations and political ideology can be found. In texts we may be aware of *what* the speaker or author is doing, but not so much *how* they are doing this.

For example, in a speech by former British Prime Minister Tony Blair given in 2010 to the World Faith Foundation, we can begin to explore how the ideology in this text may be found, particularly at the level of linguistic and grammatical choice. We find this in the line:

> Religious understanding is key to defeating hostilities threatening the world.

Throughout this speech Tony Blair talks about 'understanding' and 'knowledge' as things rather than as processes. In other words, he represents them as nouns rather than verbs. This means that he never has to specify exactly *what* it is that we will need to understand or know in order to defeat hostilities, nor *who* will have to demonstrate 'understanding'. Following on from this, he states:

> What needs to be globalized is knowledge and understanding. ... It is knowledge that gives us foresight and helps people realize what they have in common.

We can see here that rather than saying 'we need to understand' a particular thing or 'we need to know about' a particular thing, Blair simply states that we need 'knowledge' and 'understanding', and that these need to be 'globalized'.

It would be reasonable to suggest that the problems to which Blair refers involve fundamental differences in world-view. Different religious and cultural belief systems can hold clashing views as to how we should organise our societies, whether we should allow global capitalism to rule, whether consumerism and its associated identities should be permitted to spread unhindered around the planet or simply who should have control over world trade. And certainly some hostilities in the world, while they may involve different religious groups, are also rooted in territorial matters in which the Western superpowers have some responsibility. In both these cases, what it is that we need to 'know' and 'understand' about each other that will prevent such hostilities remains unclear. In the speech Blair never explains what these things are. Nevertheless, through these linguistic and grammatical strategies (nouns and nominalisations), he is able to use the words 'knowledge' and 'understanding' which suggest humanity, tolerance and openness. The speech appears to be one filled with hope and certainty yet at the same time is able to avoid actual concrete examples of how it is to work. Fairclough and Wodak (1997: 273) argue that such language reflects and reproduces power relations in society. By revealing these linguistic strategies we can better understand, expose and challenge these power relations.

In this book, providing many more examples, we explain much more about such language processes, looking at some of the tools offered by CDA for identifying and explaining how they work. We deal with these in turn and individually so that those less familiar with this kind of analysis can build up their own set of tools. But this book is not only about linguistic choices but also about the visual mode. We now look at how this very specific approach to analysing visual communication emerged in relation to Critical Linguistics and Critical Discourse Analysis.

Multimodal critical discourse analysis

In the late 1980s and 1990s a number of authors who had been working in linguistics began to realise that meaning is generally communicated not only through language but also through other semiotic modes. A linguist might, for example, be able to provide a thorough and revealing analysis of the language used in an advertisement. But much of the meaning in this advertisement might be communicated by visual features. The same would apply to a news text that was accompanied by a photograph or a textbook where an exercise was part linguistic and part visual.

Of course in many disciplines there are long traditions of analysing the meaning-making processes in visual communication, such as in Media and Cultural Studies, Film Studies and Semiotics. But as with much of the interpretative type of analysis of texts often found in Media and Cultural Studies, so too theorists like Hodge and Kress (1988) and Kress and van Leeuwen (1996) felt that much visual analysis also lacked the kind of toolkit that could facilitate more precise, systematic and careful description that would in turn allow more accurate analysis. These authors believed that some of the principles of linguistic analysis found in the systemic functional theory of Halliday (1978), also used as the basis of much CDA, could be equally applied to visual communication. What was needed, Kress and van Leeuwen (1996) argued, was a set of tools that would allow us to study the choices of visual features just as CDA allowed us to study lexical and grammatical choices in language. Kress had been one of the pioneers of Critical Linguistics and took the same set of concerns to visual communication – what Kress and van Leeuwen coined 'Multimodal Analysis'. Other researchers, also drawing on a Hallidayan framework, took up the same challenge (e.g., O'Toole, 1994; O'Halloran, 2004), although without the same critical stance and with less of the wider knowledge of other visual theories possessed by Kress and van Leeuwen.

Figure 1 Woman in *Cosmopolitan* magazine (19 July 2010)

Kress and van Leeuwen (1996, 2001) began to work on a number of concepts and tools that would allow the analyst to describe not only the features and elements of images, but also how these worked together. How much images can be described as working like language is something that has been challenged. But nevertheless, the toolkit provided by these authors does enhance our ability to describe more systematically what it is that we see.

The image on page 7 accompanies a text on '7 easy fitness tips' from the women's lifestyle magazine *Cosmopolitan* (19 July 2010). The text tells the reader about 'fitness tips for bikini body confidence'.

Easy at-work fitness tips!

Time for change

Start the week off by changing all those old habits. Neil Dimmock, master trainer at TenPilates, gives us his expert tips on how to keep fit while you're at the office. With these seven easy steps, you'll be sporting that flat tummy in no time!

Don't expect too much too soon

Small and frequent activities help you attain bite size goals. Briskly walking for a short while each day will increase your metabolism. Duration is less important at the beginning. Think of it as teaching your body. When you learn something, it needs to be done on a regular basis.

Check back every day for TenPilates' daily fitness tips for bikini body confidence.

On the one hand, we could analyse the language used in the text. We could look at strategies by which the author makes the advice appear fun, practical and authoritative, as will be the subject of a later chapter. But this analysis alone would miss the way that the image too contributes to this process of meaning-making here. As regards the *Cosmopolitan* image on page 7, this would mean describing the intricate details of features such as colour, lighting, articulation of detail, 'rhyming' in the image, where colours, shapes and forms repeat within the composition, positioning of elements, etc. In the very brief look above at the way analysis of linguistic details can reveal more about the buried meanings and ideologies in a text, we saw the value of such attention to detail. The same kind of detailed analysis can be just as useful in the case of images.

In the case of this particular image, to give a sense of how this kind of analysis works, the background appears out of focus, the textures of the model's clothes appear flat and the colours are saturated. There is also extensive colour coordination in the image, between the model's clothing and the setting.

Lighting is very bright and it is difficult to isolate individual light sources. The image appears almost over-exposed.

In later chapters this kind of analysis will be broken down and presented more gradually. But for the moment we point out that these visual choices indicate that this is clearly not an image intended to document a case of a real woman at work, but one that *symbolises* a particular kind of lifestyle. One the one hand, of course, this is a pretty obvious observation. But on the other, the detail of these observations, as in a Critical Discourse Analysis of language choices, allows us to show exactly *how* this happens. Again we need to emphasise that it is the first stage of complete and accurate description that then permits more complete and accurate analysis.

In this image, the workplace is clean, spacious and glamorous, suffused with an optimistic light, free of all the actual features and associations of most work settings. We can imagine the difference had the text shown a photograph of a real woman standing next to her cluttered desk with a range of bored or busy colleagues around her at their desks, all with clothing that does not coordinate with props in the setting. Immediately, this would have made the fun and confident language of the text appear much less feasible. In such magazines the aim is, after all, to sell advertising. It is important that they create a 'can-do', glamorous, lively world where features and advice always sit easily next to acts of consumerism. Doing exercise at work looks pretty much like the world you might find in a fashion advert.

What is important in such cases is that images can be used to say things that we cannot say in language. The text cannot say 'you work in a glamorous modernistic office'. But the image can be used to foreground this kind of idea, to distract the reader from the absurdity of many of the tips provided.

In Multimodal Critical Discourse Analysis (MCDA) we are interested in showing how images, photographs, diagrams and graphics also work to create meaning, in each case describing the choices made by the author. We want to place these meanings next to those we have found in the accompanying texts. Later in the book we will see how it may be the case that an image accompanying a news story may not actually depict what is in the story yet is able to contribute to some of the meanings communicated by the text, helping to background others that the text also seeks to conceal. Both text and image can be thought of as being composed of communicative choices by authors that seek to do certain kinds of work for them. The job of Multimodal Critical Discourse Analysis is to identify and reveal these choices through a careful process of description guided by the tools provided. But what is central to Multimodal Critical Discourse Analysis is the sense of being critical, as described by Fairclough and Wodak (1997). Texts will use linguistics and visual strategies that appear normal or neutral on the surface, but which may in fact be ideological and seek to shape the representation of events and persons for particular ends. So in Multimodal Critical Discourse Analysis we will also seek to 'denaturalise' representations on other modes of communication. We will reveal the kinds of ideas, absences and taken-for-granted assumptions in the images as well as the texts which will also serve the ends of revealing the kinds of power interests buried in them.

Also in common with CDA, MCDA views other modes of communication as a means of social construction. Visual communication, as well as language, both *shapes* and *is shaped by* society. MCDA therefore is not so much interested in the visual semiotic choices in themselves, but also in the way that they play a part in the communication of power relations.

We would like to point out that the Multimodal Critical Discourse Analysis approach we adopt and employ in this book is only one of a number of different possibilities. Here we draw mainly on the work of Gunter Kress, Norman Fairclough, Ruth Wodak and Theo van Leeuwen. Other (linguistic) approaches CDA has built upon are discussed in the final chapter of the book.

We also want to point out that the toolkit we present in this book is suitable for allowing us to observe how texts, both linguistic and visual, are composed. But we emphasise that these tools only allow us to show what semiotic resources have been used in texts, what meaning potential these have. We cannot say from the application of these tools how readers will receive these texts nor make any conclusions about the intentions of authors. In the case of the *Cosmopolitan* image, a reader may find it simply trivial and silly, although this by no means excludes the possibility that its message still gets through to them, rather than simply taking on the values it communicates. There is a long tradition in Media and Cultural Studies of considering the way that audiences deal with texts in may different ways, influenced by their own personal dispositions and cultural baggage (see three classic studies in Hall, 1973 and Morley, 1980, and Kitzinger, 2004 for an overview), although in Linguistics and Critical Discourse Analysis this has been much less attended to. In the same way, there is, in Media and Cultural Studies, a long tradition that emphasises the need to study processes of the production of texts to avoid imposing our own assumptions of the intentions of authors and text producers (again see two classic studies in Tuchman, 1978 and Fishman, 1980). We will discuss the subsequent criticisms of CDA and MCDA in this context in the conclusion to the book. But we emphasise that such criticisms should not distract from the kinds of tools we explore in this book offer in terms of enhancing our ability to describe the semiotic choices found in texts. They allow us to show more clearly *how* they make meaning as well as *what* they mean. In Media and Cultural Studies there has often been a tendency to hasten to the interpretative stage of the 'what' rather than the 'how'.

Chapter contents of the book

Chapter 1 introduces some of the main theoretical concepts that underpin the approach we take in this book. The form of Multimodal Critical Discourse

Analysis we use in the present volume draws heavily on the work of M.A.K. Halliday (1978, 1985). This provides a particular approach to language that regards it as a set of resources and, as such, is therefore concerned with describing what these are and identifying what meaning potentials (how they have a range of meanings that can be 'activated' in contexts) they have and then showing how these are used for specific purposes in social settings. We look at the concept of 'discourse', which is a term that has been used to describe the broader ideas shared by people in a society about how the world works. Discourses are comprised of ideas, values, identities and sequences of activity. In Multimodal Critical Discourse Analysis we look at how semiotic choices used by speakers, authors and in visual communication are able to signify these broader discourses, the way that they can signify ideas, values, identities and sequences of activity even though these are not specifically identified. We look at a number of texts that illustrate this process. We also look at the way that we can find these same processes not only in public texts and speeches, but also in everyday social interactions as speakers attempt to convey identities and ideas not overtly but indirectly through certain kinds of language and fashion choices.

Chapter 2 considers basic lexical analysis of a range of texts. It explores the idea of lexical fields that can be used to signify meanings not made explicit in speech and texts, and how we can look at the way that these can be used to foreground and background different kinds of discourses and associations. We can look at what is missing from texts. Are any kinds of participants, settings, actions or elements not present that should be? We move on to look at how lexical choices can set up structural opposition in texts or indicate different genres of communication. In the latter we look at the way more formal and informal genres can be mixed in order to carry out particular kinds of persuasive work. We also look at the less easy task of applying CDA to texts that we may ideologically agree with. The chapter then moves on to begin to consider the use and analysis of individual visual semiotic choices in texts. Here we look at the iconography of attributes or objects placed in images and settings. We look at how individual objects and places can signify wider discourses that include ideas, values, identities and sequences of activity. We consider the way that visual semiotic choices are useful for communication because they carry different meaning potentials or affordances from linguistic resources.

Chapter 3 deals with semiotic resources for representing the attitudes of speakers. It begins by analysing quoting verbs. These are simply the words used to describe the way people speak in texts or speech, such as 'Jack *grumbled* about his coursework'. There is no objective measure of 'grumbling', as it is an interpretation. But in this case we see that this evaluates both Jack's complaint as being perhaps simply an unjustified one and also Jack himself as someone who perhaps should not be taken so seriously. What we find in this chapter is the way that careful attention to the different categories of quoting verbs and the way that they are used is one way we can reveal the way that a speaker or author encourages us to evaluate a speaker and what they say. Whole events, kinds of assertions and issues can be shaped in texts simply by the attribution of certain kinds of quoting verbs, as our case studies show. The chapter then moves on to look at the representation of the attitude of speakers through visual semiotic recourses. Here we look first at the meaning of gaze in photographs. How are the participants depicted as looking? Do they look out at the viewer or not? If not, where do they look? All of these choices carry important meaning potential. We also consider the meaning potential of poses, drawing again on iconographical analysis.

Chapter 4 looks specifically at the linguistic and visual semiotic resources available for representing people. In language and visual communication there are a range of available semiotic choices through which we can foreground and background different aspects of identity, through which we can encourage and discourage either alignment with or against that person that can place them within broader discourses that can serve to legitimise or deligitimise them. These naming strategies should be seen also as resources for conveying power or the lack of it, and for making certain agents subtly disappear from texts. This means that certain participants in texts or images can be evaluated not on the basis of what they do, but through how they are named. We look at how, through language and image, some participants are individualised or collectivised, made specific or generic, personalised or impersonalised, objectivated, anonymised, aggregated and suppressed.

Chapter 5 deals with the linguistic and visual semiotic resources for representing what people do. This is the study of transitivity, or verb processes. The words and images chosen to represent what people do will signify discourses that can shape the way that we will perceive participants, events and circumstances. These choices too can align us alongside or against participants without overtly stating that this should be the case. How we perceive people is shaped not only by the representational strategies we saw in the previous chapter, but also by the representation of action. As we shall see, there are several resources available for representing the same action in very different ways and for either highlighting or concealing who is the agent, who is responsible, and who is the person affected by this action. Analysis in this chapter is based in the first place around Halliday's six categories of verb processes (Halliday, 1985). We can ask if some participants are represented as always engaged in actions that have a material outcome, whereas others are always engaged in mental-type processes that may suggest that they are more thoughtful and humane or, on the other hand, simply less able to act. We also look at the importance of the grammatical positioning of actions, the use of adjuncts that modify verbs, and where actions are represented through abstraction.

Chapter 6 deals with metaphorical tropes in discourse. There is a widely held assumption that metaphor is about flowery language and is associated

with things like poetry. But linguists have shown that metaphor is fundamental to human thought and that metaphor is not so much the opposite of
truth, but a basic part of the way we describe and think about the world. We
continually think about things through reference to other things in order to
help us to understand them. Of course metaphors, as well as allowing us to
throw light on things, also serve to highlight some aspects of that thing and
background or silence other aspects. In this chapter we look at how different
kinds of metaphors and other rhetorical tropes are used in different contexts
to attempt to shape understandings and also to avoid certain kinds of details
for the convenience of political manoeuvring.

Chapter 7 deals with nominalisation and presupposition in language. Both
of these draw our attention to certain kinds of linguistic strategies of concealment. The first of these is simply the process whereby verb processes are
replaced by nouns. This can be important for obscuring who carried out the
verb processes, exactly what was done and when this took place. The second of these is one skilful way in which authors are able to imply meanings
without them being overtly stated, or to present things as taken for granted
and stable where they are clearly contestable. We begin by looking at eight
effects of nominalisation and therefore how these can be used strategically
by speakers and writers. We then look at how these are used in a number of
case studies. We then move on to presupposition, looking at a number of classic examples and how these can be used, particularly in political speech and
other kinds of texts.

Chapter 8 deals with modality and hedging in texts and visual communication. Modality is about commitment to levels of truth in language and images.
In language, modality can also tell us something about people's own sense of
perceived status and can be used to convey deliberate ambiguity about this.
In cases of visual communication, modality can tell us precisely in what ways
aspects of images are more or less than real and what different kinds of truth
claims this allows them to make, whether naturalistic truth, scientific or sensory truth. These can be usefully combined with linguistic semiotic resources
in order to introduce different levels of signification of discourses. A text
might contain low modality whereas an image has high naturalistic modality
but regarding a domain that may be only linked to the text by certain isolated
lexical features. Hedging is the use of language features that allow a speaker
or writer to avoid coming cleanly and quickly to the point, to avoid being specific and therefore possibly providing 'padding' to the consequences of what
they do say. At the same time, this hedging can serve to give the impression of
in fact being precise and detailed.

The conclusion to this book looks at a number of criticisms of CDA and
Multimodal CDA. Here we find that there are issues in the way that texts tend
to be more arbitrarily selected so that meanings are largely attributed to the
texts by analysts rather than by asking the readers what they make of them,
and there have been calls for CDA to make more effort to connect analyses to
processes of production. Such additions to text analysis will better allow us

to understand the way that discourses have lives in society. If we really want to reveal power processes through language in order to challenge them, then they must be understood not only at the level of text, but also in how they are assembled often in institutional contexts and how they take on and are used by people in everyday life.

1

Making Active Choices: Language as a Set of Resources

Introduction

In this chapter we lay out some of the basic principles and concepts that form the basis of the Multimodal Critical Discourse Analysis that we present in this book. We begin by explaining what we mean by a Social Semiotic view of language that we take in this book, which emphasises the way that we should see all communication, whether through language, images, or sounds, as accomplished through a set of semiotic resources, options and choices. It is because of this that we are so concerned to emphasise that analysis should be based on a first stage description of the semiotic choices found in talk, texts and images. We ask what options communicators use, why they use them and what the consequences of these choices are.

The chapter then moves on to look at the way that semiotic choices are able to signify broader sets of associations that may not be overtly specified. A choice of word or visual element might suggest kinds of identities, values and activities due to established associations. We think about this in terms of power relations, since CDA has traditionally been concerned with exposing ideologies that are hidden within language, whether these are produced by authorities, ruling groups, institutions or in individual face-to-face situations. The idea has been that revealing these power relations can play an important emancipatory role.

Finally we look at the way that language choices, signification, discourses and power feed into our everyday identities. Broader discourses and widely shared social meanings are played out both in the official language of politics, the news media, our major institutions, such as schools, entertainments media, but also in everyday mundane contexts.

Communication through a system of choices

In linguistics there have been a number of positions regarding the relationship between language and thought. It is important that we consider these briefly here as this provides us with a clear foundation for the theory of language and visual communication that we use in this book, where we see communication as being done through using a system of choices that are used by humans. It is one that is interested in the means for making meanings which is always subject to social, cultural and economic situations.

Linguistic determinism

One of the best known positions on language use is based on the Sapir-Whorf hypothesis, named after the American linguists Edward Sapir and Benjamin Lee Whorf. They argued that humans do not live in an objective world, but rather that this world is shaped for them by the language that has become the medium of expression in their society. Language is therefore not just a way by which we describe the world, but rather comes to comprise what we think of as 'the real world':

> According to this view, different languages will shape the world differently. So the worlds different language speakers inhabit are not simply ones with different labels but are therefore distinct worlds. (Sapir 1929/1958: 69)

Edmund Leach (1964) reflects this view in a frequently cited passage:

> I postulate that the physical and social environment of a young child is perceived as a continuum. It does not contain any intrinsically separate 'things'. The child, in due course, is taught to impose upon this environment a kind of discriminating grid which serves to distinguish the world as being composed of a large number of separate things, each labelled with a name. This world is a representation of our language categories, not vice versa. Because my mother tongue is English, it seems evident that bushes and trees are different kinds of things. I would not think this unless I had been taught that it was the case. (Leach, 1964: 34)

In its extreme form, this is what we would call *linguistic determinism*, where our thinking is determined by our language. In fact, few linguists accept this strong view, but rather think about how the way we see the world might be *influenced* by the kind of language we use rather than be *determined* by it. They would also see this as a two-way process so that the kind of language we use is influenced by the way we see the world. Linguists have also focused on the importance of social context in language use, that we use certain types of language in certain settings due to social pressures rather than through linguistic determination. What is considered as appropriate language use exists both in everyday conventions and in institutionalised or specialist ones. For example, in news reading or in the university classroom we find there are certain rules and expectations as regards language use.

Until the 1970s, Structuralist views of language deriving from the work of Saussure ([1916] 1983) were prevalent and still are popular today. The idea here is that we can study the features of language, the lexical and grammatical choices, as building blocks. Communication in language is based, as in the Sapir-Whorf model, on the idea that everyone agrees to use the same words to mean the same thing. These words have no natural relationship to the world out there – the word 'tree' has no natural relationship to the thing in the world – but are arbitrary. Language is seen as a kind of code whose parts are therefore relational rather than referential. In other words, they have meaning by their difference from each other rather than their similarity to objects and phenomena, such as in early hieroglyphics. Saussure argued that language could be studied in terms of its use, which he called *parole*, and which would allow us to establish the underlying system, which he called *langue*.

A Social Semiotic theory of communication

This approach to language is slightly different as it is interested particularly in the way it is used in social context and the way we use language to *create* society. What is perhaps the key to this theory is the shift away from looking at language as a *system* to one where we think about language as a set of *resources*. Here we are less interested in attempting to describe a system of grammatical rules of communication, but rather are more interested in the way the communicator uses the semiotic resources available to them, either in language or in visual communication, to realise their interests. A Social Semiotic approach to communication is interested in describing the available choices of signs, but in the first place, so that we can understand what it is that people are doing with them. And Multimodal Social Semiotics is interested not just in the means for making meanings, but in what these means are, so whether we choose to use language, images, gestures, sounds, etc. (Kress, 2010).

Individuals are aware of the way words and visual elements have particular affordances or potentials to mean. They will be aware that certain words can carry particular potentials, such as Blair's use of 'knowledge' discussed in the Introduction to this book, as can certain visual elements and features, as in the use of the high-key lighting in the *Cosmopolitan* image also discussed previously. They will be aware that different modes of communication offer different kinds of affordances or different means for communicating meanings. In other words, as in the case of the *Cosmopolitan* image and text, they will have a sense of the way that an image can communicate something about the broader ideas about the lives of women, in a way not so conveniently accomplished by language.

This approach to communication and society draws on the work of M.A.K. Halliday (1978, 1985). He thought that language creates dispositions in people while at the same time allowing the possibility of more open interpretations of the world. Halliday argued that speakers can see through and around the words and concepts that they have in language. This is why we are able to explain what we mean to people if they do not initially understand what we say and can argue over definitions.

Halliday was first and foremost concerned with the social uses of language. When we code events in language this involves choices among options which are available in grammar. Kress (1985) points out that all such choices can be viewed as ideologically significant. For example, it is important which terms we use to describe people or the processes (actions) they carry out. Are women described as 'wives' and 'mothers' in the press, whereas men are not described so often as 'husbands' or 'fathers'? Why might we want to emphasise that a British soldier is a 'father' and 'husband' but not do the same for the enemy? What if we choose the word 'bloke' over 'man'? Or we might choose to represent a process as a noun, as we saw in the Introduction in the comments made by Tony Blair. For example, 'knowledge of each other is the way to avoid conflicts'. This can change the way that a conflict is perceived and also who has responsibility and what the remedy is, by concealing what it is we actually need to know through simply stating that we need 'knowledge'. All of these language choices are political in that they shape how people and events are represented.

In the 1970s and 1980s, linguists like Fowler, Hodge, Kress and Trew (1979) began a tradition of Critical Linguistics which, drawing on Halliday sought to begin to explore the way that language can be used, therefore, not just to represent the world but to constitute it. This was also influenced by Chomskyan linguistics and work in French semiotics (Barthes, 1973). Since language shapes and maintains a society's ideas and values, it can also serve to create, maintain and legitimise certain kinds of social practices. It can become more or less common practice to think that 'knowledge' and 'under-standing' are indeed sufficient to prevent conflicts. In Britain, local govern-ments set up opportunities for children from different ethnic groups to share in 'knowledge' and 'understanding' sessions to help create multicultural cohesion. Yet what the children's knowledge and know or understanding will lead to is never specified.

A Social Semiotic view of visual communication, or of any other mode of communication, such as sound and music, is based on the same set of prin-ciples. Social Semiotics assumes that we must understand that all processes of communication are to some extent rule-based, although the nature of these rules can vary immensely (Van Leeuwen, 2005). We are more familiar with the idea that communication through language is rule-based. And it is readily accepted that we can only communicate, in other words create and understand its meanings, through language once we have mastered its rules. In a Social Semiotic theory of visual communication, we are concerned with describing and documenting the underlying resources available to those who want to communicate meanings visually and analysing the way that these are used in settings to do particular things.

In a Social Semiotic approach we are concerned with the underlying available repertoire of signs and their use in context to communicate wider ideas, moods and attitudes and identities, and we are interested in why specific means were used to create these. We would ask upon what set of available resources the creator of the *Cosmopolitan* photograph shown in the Introduction to this book has drawn. The creator would be aware of the way that manipulating the realism of textures and colours to different degrees would tend to create specific kinds of meanings, here one that would clearly tell the viewer that this image is not intended to document the activities of a particular woman at a particular time and place. The viewer is not likely to sit there wondering 'who is this woman?' or 'I wonder where she works?'. The correct visual choices have been made to communicate to the viewer that this is meant to be viewed as a symbolic image. And it is clear that the same kind of meanings could not have been accomplished through language.

In a Social Semiotic view of visual communication, then, choices of visual elements and features do not just represent the world, but *constitute* it. Like language, visual communication plays its part in shaping and maintaining a society's ideologies, and can also serve to create, maintain and legitimise certain kinds of social practices.

As in language, where we must look at the terms used to describe people, such as women being described as 'wives' and 'mothers', or the processes they carry out, so we need to look at the visual representation of women as 'wives', 'mothers' or 'glamorous career women'. Why, we can ask, are women in *Cosmopolitan* never represented or mothers or as workers who carry out any specific task?

One final point to emphasise regarding a Social Semiotic approach is its difference from traditional semiotic approaches, which addressed the way that individual signs connote or symbolise (see Barthes, 1973). In this approach we might say a flag symbolises the nation. To those who fly the flag this might connote pride and strength, although to others in might equally connote closed-mindedness and stifling exclusion. A Social Semiotic approach would be interested in the details of things like colour and shape and their interrelationship in any visual design or image. For example, a flag might carry a bold saturated red rather than a muted or diluted one. Clearly, here there is a continuum of meaning potential in the saturation–dilution spectrum. In traditional semiotics, we might describe a saturated red as connoting sensuality. But is this the case for the flag? Clearly, more saturated colours have the meaning potential for bolder passionate visual statements. A flag carrying a very pale diluted red would not signify the correct passion of the national spirit. The point here is that in Social Semiotics, in both the study of language and images, we must be able to describe and document the precise semiotic choices made and view these in the context of the observed available resources.

Discourse, semiotic choices and signification

Through the individual semiotic choices that they make, authors and designers are able to encourage us to place events and ideas into broader frameworks of interpretation that are referred to as 'discourses'. Once one of these frameworks is activated, they bring with them different kinds of associations and, as in the use of metaphor by David Cameron and the image in *Cosmopolitan* considered in the Introduction, shape how we are encouraged to think about events.

The term 'discourse' is central to CDA. Basically, 'discourse' is language in real contexts of use. In other words, discourse operates above the level of grammar and semantics to 'capture what happens when these language forms are played out in different social, political and cultural arenas (Simpson and Mayr, 2010: 5). In CDA, the broader ideas communicated by a text are referred to as 'discourses' (Van Dijk, 1993; Fairclough, 2000; Wodak, 2001). These discourses can be thought of as models of the world, in the sense described by Foucault (1980). The process of doing CDA involves looking at choices of words and grammar in texts in order to discover the underlying discourse(s) and ideologies. A text's linguistic structure functions, as discourse, to highlight certain ideologies, while downplaying or concealing others. One example of such a discourse is that 'immigrants are a threat to a national culture'. This is a model of events associated with the notion that there is a unified nation and an identifiable national identity and culture. Normally this discourse encompasses a mythical proud history and authentic traditions. We can see this discourse in the following editorial from the *Daily Mail* (25 October 2007) titled 'Britain will be scarcely recognisable in 50 years if the immigration deluge continues'. The item goes on to discuss how 'we' need to 'defend' our 'indigenous culture'. Who 'we' are remains unspecified, as does the nature of our 'indigenous culture'. In Britain's evolving multicultural make-up and the diversity of ways of life and cultural values that have long been present based around social class, regional and other groupings, so how can we pin such factors down?

In the headline of this news item, immigration is described using the term 'deluge', a metaphor that draws on the idea of masses of rainfall that overspill, creating floods and damage. While the author of this text is at pains to point out that they are not racist, everything else they say suggests that they are. Of course, in this case it is clear even after a superficial reading that this *Daily Mail* text is anti-immigration and most likely racist. But by looking at the word choices in the text we can pinpoint exactly why this is so, which is even more important in texts where the discourse is less obvious.

There are other discourses for thinking about nation and national identity. A sociologist or historian would tell us that what we think of as nation and national identity is for the most part invented, with only a relatively short history (Gellner, 1983; Hobsbawm, 1983). Here the proud history and indigenous culture under threat by immigrants is itself not factual at all. And

Marxist thinkers would point to such an emphasis of difference on the basis on national identity as concealing actual divisions in society between the rich and the exploited and poor, and therefore that nationalism is a concept serving the interests of the powerful.

Van Leeuwen and Wodak (1999) suggest that we should think about discourses as including or being comprised of kinds of participants, behaviours, goals, values and locations. We see this in our example from the *Daily Mail*. This discourse involves participants: real British people and immigrants. It involves values or an 'indigenous culture'. It specifies that 'we' must 'defend' this culture. This discourse represents a 'we' who should not see incomers as an opportunity for change and growth, nor as fundamentally the same as ourselves on many levels, but as a threat to be repelled and something that will change 'us'.

What we can see from the *Daily Mail* example of the national 'we' versus the deluge of immigrants is that discourses do not simply mirror reality but, as Fairclough and Wodak (1997: 258) point out, bring into being 'situations, objects of knowledge, and the social identities of and relations between people and groups of people'.

Fairclough (2000) explains that these discourses, such as of national unity or racial or cultural superiority, project certain social values and ideas and in turn contribute to the (re)production of social life. In other words, it is through language that we constitute the social world, or put simply, how we talk about the world influences the society we create, the knowledge we celebrate and despise, and the institutions we build. For example, if in a society the discourse that dominates our understanding of crime is that it is simply wrongdoing which requires retribution, then we build prisons and lock people away. Yet it is the case that most people who end up in prisons are from poor or more vulnerable sections of the population. Sociologists and criminologists will tell us that if we are born black in countries like Britain or America, then our life position will mean that we are much more likely to end up in prison. This is because of the complex relationship of poverty, race and inequality. Yet we do not organise our societies on the assumption that crime is associated with such factors. Nor do we tend to associate crime with the actions of global corporations or banks in Third World countries or the acts of our governments when they go to war, or reorganise society in the interests of the wealthy. It is our dominant discourse of crime that we end up targeting only the poor and least powerful members of our societies, where we build prisons, use the police in the way that we do, take particular crime prevention measures and vote for political parties that will be tough on crime, rather than creating societies where it is less likely to take place. Of course in this sense we can see that certain discourses represent the interests of specific groups. In the case of crime it will be in the interests of those who have wealth and power to conceal its relationship to factors such as race and poverty.

The following newspaper item is about drug dealing in provincial British rural areas. What we can see here is that crime issues related to things like social decline, unemployment and poverty are placed in a particular discourse about the threat to a rural idyll.

In such a report we might expect to become informed about these events through information about statistics and interviews with experts and victims. Yet this is not by any means what we find in this text. The journalist places the event within a particular set of associations that serve to transform or 'recontextualise' them.

It begins as follows:

> THE time is 7.30pm on a quiet autumnal evening in Totnes, once a fortified Saxon settlement and now one of Devon's most elegant towns.
>
> A place which, outwardly at least, seems far removed from the sordid world of drugs and dealers.
>
> But within just a few minutes of arriving in the town, a female reporter has been offered Ecstasy for one of cheapest prices ever recorded in Britain – 1.25 a tablet.
>
> What makes the transaction so shocking is that it proves Ecstasy is no longer confined to the places you would think are its natural home – music festivals, Ibiza raves and city centre nightclubs.
>
> It can be bought in the most rural and picturesque of areas across the country for the same price as a portion of chips. (*Daily Mail* October 16, 2003)

We often think of news as informing us about events in the world. Journalists are often described as the 'eyes and the ears of the public'. They tell us about important things that are going on so that we can remain informed, so that we can call upon our politicians to make the decisions necessary to make our societies operate in the best possible way. So the news might report on a particular instance of drugs problems in our society, as in the case of this news item. The public, once informed about this problem, can then vote for those politicians who offer the best solutions for correcting these problems.

In fact, sociologists of news have long established that this is rarely what news actually does, due to a complex range of factors, related to sourcing, the pressures of filling news space, the need to make events 'newsworthy' (Bennett, 2005). Rather, news is a very peculiar social construction of reality. The news item above can be seen as one case where an event has been placed in a discourse of 'enemies of society' to give it shape and meaning. This has been accomplished through the use of certain kinds of language. The opening line tells us it is a 'quiet autumnal evening' in what was 'once a fortified Saxon settlement' and now 'one of Devon's most elegant towns'. On the one hand, we could ask how this is relevant in reporting the story. Journalists do not normally preface stories with a mention of the season, or by giving a brief history of the setting. We would not expect to see 'On a lazy late spring evening in the once Roman outpost, Manchester, a man was attacked last night'.

In this text, the journalist is developing on a press release that referred to drugs problems in rural British areas, where there is often much unemployment and other related social issues. This is a phenomenon well known to local police. One of the authors lived for a while in such a village where there was a substantial unemployed, very poor section of the population, which had a strong drug culture among its youth, living in what otherwise was a pretty tourist attraction complete with beautiful sixteenth-century streets. But in this text the journalist has chosen to locate the events as if they have intruded into an otherwise perfect rural idyll. The text is filled with contrasts between the corrupt city and the innocent and pure countryside inhabited by 'communities' and 'innocent families'. What has happened here is that the journalist is encouraging the reader to understand these events not simply as a part of the social phenomenon that they comprise, but through a discourse of corruption to the rural heartlands of Britain. Drug dealing, their use and effects are one area where the British press has been extremely unhelpful in providing well-informed reporting to the public. In later chapters we will be looking at this in greater depth.

Discourse can also be signified through visual semiotic choices. In the image from *Cosmopolitan* considered in the Introduction, we can think about the broader ideas, values, identities and sequences of activity that are signified.

Developing on the ideas put forward by feminists since the 1960s, *Cosmopolitan* magazine originally emerged challenging existing representations of women as homemakers, mothers and wives. The magazine began to discuss women's sexuality and their more independent lives in the workplace. Still today the main topics are relationships, sex and work, although these sit seamlessly alongside promotions of fashion, accessories and consumer lifestyle products – although in *Cosmopolitan* it is never clear exactly what work women do, only that that work is in minimalist, modernist, designed office settings, where they can also look glamorous and sensual. In this sense, some argue that, while it is clearly not negative that women should be able to celebrate their sexuality and lives aside from motherhood, women's agency is still generally reduced to how they look and their need for a relationship with a man rather than how they act in society. Machin and van Leeuwen (2007) show that in women's magazines in Vietnam, women are depicted not in fashionable settings but carrying out actual work, for example, on projects helping homeless single women. Based on this observation, we can think about the way that the semiotic choices in the *Cosmopolitan* image signify a discourse of women as independent and having exciting lives. This suggests a life which is glamorous and interesting. But unlike the Vietnamese magazine, this is a world where the woman acts alone and in her own interest, often learning hot tips to look good, to keep her man, to have hot sex and to get on in the world. She has no broader contribution to make either to society or other women. So what is important here is to be aware of the way that semiotic choices can be used to signify identities and values associated with women's agency without fully articulating them. This means that these discourses can be manipulated precisely for the purposes of aligning such identities and values with consumer behaviour. Independence can be signified through how you look, the clothes you wear and the poses you strike, and not through the way you think or act in broader political terms.

Ideology and power

The question of power has been at the core of the CDA project. Basically, power comes from privileged access to social resources such as education, knowledge and wealth, which provides authority, status and influence to those who gain this access and enables them to dominate, coerce and control subordinate groups. The aim in CDA has been to reveal what kinds of social relations of power are present in texts both explicitly and implicitly (Van Dijk, 1993: 249). Since language can (re)produce social life, what kind of world is being created by texts and what kinds of inequalities and interests might this seek to perpetuate, generate or legitimate? Here language is not simply a vehicle of communication, or for persuasion, but a means of social construction and domination. Therefore, discourse does not merely reflect social processes and structures but is itself seen to contribute to the production and reproduction of these processes and structures. As Fairclough and Wodak (1997: 258) state, 'the discursive event is shaped by situations, institutions and social structures, but it also shapes them'. It is also important to note that power can be more than simple domination from above; it can also be jointly produced when people believe or are led to believe that dominance is legitimate in some way or other. For example, in our Western democracies, people elect politicians because they believe that they have the authority to govern a country. We also believe that doctors have the 'power' to provide us with the care we need. The point is that power, at least in democratic societies, needs to be seen as legitimate by people in order to be accepted, and this process of legitimation is generally expressed through language and other communicative systems.

Research in CDA has been mainly concerned with the persuasive influence of power, a conception of power associated with Gramsci (1971), whose concept of hegemony describes the ways through which dominant groups in society succeed in persuading subordinate groups to accept the former's own moral, political and cultural values and institutions. Within this framework, discourse constructs hegemonic attitudes, opinions and beliefs and, as we shall see throughout this book, in such a way as to make them appear 'natural' and 'common sense', while in fact they may be ideological.

The term 'ideology' is yet another central concept in CDA. Coined in the early 1800s by the French philosopher Destutt de Tracy, the concept is mainly associated with Karl Marx (1933). In its original Marxist conception, ideology is an important means by which dominant forces in society can exercise power over subordinate and subjugated groups. Over the years, the concept has developed a broader meaning to refer to belief systems held by individuals and collectives. Like discourse, it is used to capture the way that we share broader ideas about the way the world works. In CDA, ideology has been used (and without necessary adherence to Marx) to describe the way that the ideas and values that comprise these ideas reflect particular interests on the part of the powerful. So in discourses that promote being tougher on crime, where crime is identified as the relatively minor actions of the least powerful members of society, rather than those of banks and corporations who seek to reorganise society in their own interest for reasons of profit, we can ask whose interests these definitions serve.

The aim of CDA is to draw out ideologies, showing where they might be buried in texts. Drawing on Gramsci (1971), Fairclough argued that, while many institutions and forms of social organisation clearly reflect ideological interests, one place where we can observe exactly how these interests operate is in language. This is simply because language is a common social behaviour where we share our views of how the world works, what is natural and common sense. It is through language that we share the idea of things like 'British culture', 'nationalism' and what immigrants are like. People and institutions then draw on this language as it appears to be neutral and 'common sense'.

Of course ideologies and power can be found communicated through other semiotic modes and not only through language. We can ask what kinds of interests are served by the stream of visual images we find in the news media that most often represent crime not as the actions of wealthy corporate people but of the thuggish working classes, or other marginalised people, such as immigrants, often depicted as grinning at the viewer with their large families, accused of fraudulently claiming state benefits.

Ideology characterises the way that certain discourses become accepted in this way and therefore obscure the way they help to sustain power relations. According to one view of ideology, ideology obscures the nature of our unequal societies and prevents us from seeing alternatives. It limits what can be seen and what we think we can do. In present Western societies, we take it for granted or as common sense that 'business' should be at the heart of everything, that it is the lifeblood of our societies and of human existence. Such is the power of this view that alternatives are viewed with ridicule. We only have to think in this respect of how British educational institutions are run.

Ideologies can be found across whole areas of social life, in ideas, knowledge, and institutional practices. In the case of 'business', this ideology comes to dominate everything in society – even how we run schools and hospitals. Social welfare, economic equality and quality of civil life become subordinate to the logic of business 'efficiency', which in practice means profit. In Britain at the time of writing, it was becoming common to see schools being re-launched as academies, semi-privatised and apparently more attuned to work demands, often with new buildings designed in the style of the corporate head office to communicate business-style buzzwords such as 'innovation' and 'vision'.

Halliday (1978) argued that language can create dispositions within us. CDA analysts, such as Fairclough, following Foucault, believe that one way to put this is that language constitutes us as subjects (1994: 318). This is because the person who comes to think through the discourses of business is thinking of themselves, their identity and their possibilities, through this discourse. What would be important in terms of MCDA would be to identify the kinds of semiotic choices that were being used to communicate about these things. We would ask what kinds of ideas, values, identities and sequences of activity are being represented or implied. Often, as we will show, some of these aspects may be completely suppressed or concealed for the purposes of legitimising a particular ideology.

Social Semiotics and everyday identity

It is important to realise that discourses and ideologies are not simply to be found in official and media texts. Social Semiotics views the individual as embedded in networks of social relations where all of us are communicating, making signs through semiotic choices. This network will be at the same time cooperative, contested and fragmentary as we come together with different kinds of people (Kress, 2010). It is these interactions and the needs generated in and through them, which drive communication and shape the semiotic resources available. The reader of the text about the drug problems in Totnes or the viewer of the image in *Cosmopolitan* is located in a network of social relations. These individuals too are sign makers within their own social environments. They are part of the process through which signs are made, used, and remade. Of course they may not have the power of dissemination afforded to the *Daily Mail* newspaper or to *Cosmopolitan* magazine, but nevertheless they are sign users and sign makers. They too will use language and other semiotic modes in their own interests. This is an important observation as this means that we can plot the way that the ideas, identities and values that comprise discourses have a life across networks of social relations. What follows is one such example regarding the comments and behaviour of a young woman encountered by one of the authors of this book.

One of the authors was recently in a town centre bar having a beer after work with several colleagues. Three of them, all male, were leaning at the bar. Two were listening to the other who was recounting a paper heard at a recent conference. The author noticed that a group of women came into the bar dressed as school girls, with short skirts, long socks and wigs giving them all pigtails. Most of them carried hockey sticks. Those familiar with certain British cultural practices would immediately recognise this as a 'hen night', where a bride-to-be will go out partying with her female friends on the evening before her wedding. A typical theme is for them to dress in this manner, a cross between school uniforms and stripper clothes.

It was about 7.30pm and the women appeared already fairly drunk. One of them approached the author and engaged him in conversation. The author's aim, unsociably, and feeling slightly awkward with a drunk person, was to get rid of the woman. What we draw attention to in this case is the language used by the woman. This example reveals three things. One, it shows how as language producers what we want to say is not always made explicit. Two, it is a useful way to show how as analysts of language we can draw out what is and what is not made explicit, what remains slightly concealed beneath the surface of dialogue. Three, it points to the way that in social networks we share available semiotic resources which favour the realisation of certain discourses. And additionally, this is an opportunity to think about the other modes of communication the woman relied upon. The dialogue went like this:

Woman: Hey, do you like my hockey stick?

Author: Looks fine to me but I'm no expert.

Woman: (drunk mock seductive expression) Do you like to play?

Author: (shyly) More into football myself. You off to a game then?

Woman: Am I making you nervous?

Author: Well, I don't get out much.

Woman's friend (coming over): You scaring this nice gentleman?

Woman: No, he just thinks we are wild, crazy women.

Woman: Am I scaring you? Do you think we are scary?

Author: I am afraid I do.

Woman: Where are the real men? Everywhere we go we scare them to death.

Her friends then took her off to speak with some other people. The author shortly afterwards heard the women having a similar conversation with another group of men, and seemed to be keen to maintain the engagement about how 'scary' they were. Ten minutes later two of these men came to the bar to buy drinks for themselves and the women. One was remarking on their chances of developing something with the women and on the quality of the breasts of the particular woman who had approached the author. A few weeks later the author came across the woman again in her role as a shop-worker, selling him a sandwich. Here she was not speaking of being 'scary'.

In this short conversation a number of interesting features can be found. Of course, on the one hand, this is simply a group of women out having some fun, being playful and flirtatious. And a group of academics, engaged in some self-important, pompous conversation, may have seemed like a good, or safe, target for such fun. But, on the other hand, this example can tell us a lot about the way that, even in the most mundane of social contexts, we will use language in creative ways to persuade, influence and manipulate people, and most importantly to lead them to kinds of understandings that we may not make explicit but that once drawn out can give us access to the available semiotic resources for communication in a social network.

The conversation began with an innuendo about the hockey stick, which the woman later used again in subsequent conversations with the other men. But what is interesting is the fact that her being 'scary' was a theme that she repeated in her talk. The author did not find her scary, although he did feel awkward. And certainly the two men who were assessing their chances with her did not find her scary, but rather a potentially easy opportunity. Had the author been able to record the women's talk throughout the time they were in the bar, we could see that the words 'scary' and 'wild' were used strikingly often. In the kind of linguistic analysis we explore in this book, where a word or kind of word is used more than might be normally expected, this would be considered as an indication of some kind of underlying but not overtly expressed contentious social issues.

So what is going on here is that the women are interacting exclusively with men in bars as they move through the town centre, flirting with them through sexual innuendo, dressed in a playful manner that appeals to traditional ideas of male sexual fantasy, telling men that they are, as a collective, being 'scary'. So what exactly is the contentious issue that is being indicated by the use of the word 'scary'?

Some researchers have explained that women represented in women's lifestyle magazines are often depicted as being 'naughty' through breaking the taboos of traditional domestic sexual behaviour (Caldas Coulthard, 1994). As noted above, since the late 1960s, British society, although to some extent in the mass media only, has seen a change in representations of women, challenging the traditional idea of the woman as homemaker, whose sexuality belongs in the domestic environment and is associated with marriage and motherhood. Later forms of feminism, taken up by *Cosmopolitan* and seen also in the television series *Sex and the City*, represented women's blatant use of their powers of seduction over men as a form of agency. Here we can see the meaning potential of, and discourses signified by, the word 'scary'. The behaviour and language of woman in the bar might therefore be interpreted as telling the author and the other men that she is powerful. Dressing in an overtly sexual fashion could be viewed as 'transgressive' and 'naughty' in the manner described by Caldas Coulthard (1994), although the woman to some extent fulfils a male fantasy. And importantly, the use of language overtly reminds men that they should be intimidated by this transgression and this taking of control.

The extensive use of the word 'scary' is evidence that this is an issue that is still considered to be contentious and far from settled. Those in society who really have power do not need to ask others if they find them scary. Had the author walked up to a woman in a bar and said 'Are you scared of me?', or 'I think you find me scary', this would have appeared odd, and indeed as scary. And a man who was overheard to spend the evening telling everyone how scary he was or how scary 'we' were, referring to him and his friends, would be viewed as rather silly.

This example shows that a closer look at the language used in everyday conversation reveals how people tell us things about themselves that are not made explicit. We could say that people, through such talk, are encouraging us to see them as having particular kinds of identities and are engaged in particular kinds of activity without actually stating this. The woman in the bar was saying something like: 'since you expect women to act in ways appropriate to a domestic model of gender roles and behaviour, our actions shock and intimidate you'. This is not said explicitly, but is signified. Put another way, in her network of social relations this woman shares semiotic resources for communication from which she chooses, aware of their meaning potential. Of course in this case the academic she encountered was not from her more usual network of social environments and the meaning potential was taken differently. But it is important to remember that all social interaction is to some extent like this, and as Kress (2010) points out, is that which provides the dynamic force that drives communication and the need to work with semiotic resources. If everything was simply fixed in meaning, there would be no sense in semiotic production. As we considered when we looked at Halliday's Social Semiotic theory of language, it is important that we view all uses of semiotic resources as evidence of people having, to some extent, an awareness of the work that they can accomplish through their choices and being aware of how to best make such choices in the context of the prompts that are provided in every social interaction.

Conclusion

In this chapter we have seen that we should think of all communication, whether through language, images or sounds, as being accomplished through a set of semiotic resources, options and choices. Such semiotic choices are able to signify broader sets of associations that may not be overtly specified. A choice of word or visual element might suggest kinds of identities, values and activities. It is because of this that we are so concerned to emphasise that analysis should be based on careful detailed description of the semiotic choices found in talk, texts and images. We ask what options communicators use, why and what are the consequences of these choices? And crucially, we must think about these choices in terms of power relations. How do the choices we find serve the interests of authorities, ruling groups, institutions or even individuals in face-to-face situations?

2

Analysing Semiotic Choices:
Words and Images

Introduction

In this chapter we begin to introduce the toolkit for analysing the way that people make semiotic choices in language and visual communication in order to achieve their communicative aims. Here we look at the simplest form of analysis by considering how authors make choices in individual semiotic resources, in terms of individual words and individual visual elements and features. Each of these kinds of resources can allow the author to set up a basic shape of a social and natural world through their speech, text or image. It allows them to highlight some kinds of meanings and to background others. These authors will use combinations of visual and linguistic elements, depending upon their affordances, to best accomplish what they wish to communicate. Through this process, those meanings they wish to convey may not be communicated so much overtly but in a more subtle way that requires analysis to be careful in order to reveal its precise nature.

One of the most basic kinds of linguistic analysis carried out in CDA is a lexical analysis. This means simply looking at what kinds of words there are in a text. In other words, we ask what vocabulary an author uses. Do they tend to use certain kinds of words and avoid others?

A number of writers have described the significance of this kind of analysis showing that different lexical, or word, choices can signify different discourses or set up different 'lexical fields'. These discourses or fields will signify certain kinds of identities, values and sequences of activity which are not necessarily made explicit.

Van Dijk (2001) describes CDA precisely as the study of 'implicit or 'indirect meanings' in texts. These are the kinds of meanings that are alluded to without being explicitly expressed. He explains this implicit information 'is part of the mental model of ... a text, but not of the text itself. Thus, implicit meanings are related to underlying beliefs, but are not openly, directly, completely or precisely asserted' (Van Dijk, 2001: 104). The study of simple word content, the highlighting of a lexical field, is, as we shall see one way we can begin to reveal these underlying beliefs.

A lexical field, Fowler (1991) points out, is like the map an author is creating for us. A map is a 'symbolic' representation of a territory. The signs it uses indicate areas of interest, areas of salience where on the actual terrain there may be none. Maps made for different purposes will carry different features, so a map for geological features will differ from those made for motorists. A map maker may include political boundaries that may be largely ignored or resented by the people who live there. So the map maker in each case is foregrounding some features and suppressing others. What exactly is included and excluded, how areas are defined, what is shaded and not, where boundaries are placed is a matter of the interests of the map maker. The point is that '[t]he meaning and structure of the map are not governed by the physical characteristics of the landscape, but by the structural conventions appropriate to figuring the territory for a specific social purpose' (Fowler, 1991: 82). We can think of the lexical choices used by an author or speaker in the same way, governed by certain types of preoccupation or specific social purposes.

This observation can apply equally both to texts and images. One of the simplest kinds of analysis carried out in Multimodal Critical Discourse Analysis is iconographical or iconological analysis. This means we explore the way that individual elements in images, such as objects and settings, are able to signify discourses in ways that might not be obvious at an initial viewing. We ask which visual features and elements are foregrounded and which are backgrounded or excluded.

However, it is important to note that in visual communication semiotic resources are used to communicate things that may be more difficult to express through language, since images do not tend to have such fixed meaning or at least the producer can always claim that it is more suggestive and open to various interpretations. In news reports, for example, it is possible to show a photograph of a Muslim woman in traditional clothing, wearing a veil next to an article on Muslim-related issues. But it is not possible to say 'All Muslims look like this'. Visual communication, by its nature, tends to be more open to interpretation, which gives the author some degree of manoeuvre not permitted though language use. They can use the image of the Muslim woman in traditional clothing to place the story in a broader discourse about clashes of culture and values. But this is done implicitly through visual semiotic resources.

Visual and linguistic semiotic resources have different affordances. In other words, they are more suitable for different kinds of purposes. For example, in the previous chapters we considered the photograph that was part of an article in *Cosmopolitan* magazine. In this case, we can ask how it was that the setting and colours helped to encourage the viewer to think about certain kinds of identities and values in a way that language could not have done. How did these choices contribute to the mapping out of women's lives and identities that were being created for the reader which were different from that of language? As with the image of the Muslim woman, discourses are communicated implicitly. We are not told 'this is what you will look like at work', but the image serves to bring particular associations of glamour and modernity to bear on the story. Being able to analyse the work done by semiotic choices, such as props, setting and lighting, allows us to be more specific about exactly what is communicated and how.

Van Leeuwen (2000), drawing on the work of Barthes (1977) and Panofsky (1972), has also shown the value of looking at images for the way that individual elements and features can communicate implicit or indirect meanings and that they too can be thought of as mapping out a terrain driven by certain preoccupations. Later in the chapter we will be looking at a set of tools for analysing the way that those who produce visual discourses are able to draw our attention to certain aspects of images.

In this chapter, we first look at studying lexical choices in language. In the second part we look at visual choices, returning to some of the same texts to consider how these two modes communicate together.

Word connotations

To begin with we can analyse the basic choice of words used by a text producer. Simply, we ask what kinds of words are used. Is there a predominance of particular kinds of words, for example? In this process we assume that, since language is an available set of options, certain choices have been made by the author for their own motivated reasons. For example, if I choose to call where I live a 'building', 'an address' or a 'family home', it immediately brings certain sets of associations. What if a news item headline was one of the following?

'Youths attack local buildings'

'Youths attack local addresses'

'Youths attack local family homes'

In the last of these sentences, the lexical choice suggests something much more sacred than the first two, something much more personal. The words 'family' and 'home' suggest something safe and stable that is cherished in society. Of course families are not necessarily something so wonderful. Families can also be demanding, overwhelming, oppressive and destructive. But combined here with 'home' it signifies a discourse of the family as something safe, stable and common to all of us. It communicates something that should be protected and therefore produces greater moral outrage than the first headline. Without making the case overtly, the discourse created signifies associated identities, values and likely sequences of action. The writer has not commented overtly on the morally outrageous behaviour of the youths, but this is signified through the associations of home and family since these words tend to carry particular connotations in a particular culture. So these connotations help to place these events into particular frameworks of reference or discourses.

We can see the way that lexical choices place events in discourses in the following extract taken from an East Midlands Development Agency (EMDA) document. EMDA is one of a number of regional organisations set up in Britain by the former New Labour government to 'regenerate' parts of the country that were suffering from a number of issues, such as poverty, unemployment, urban decay and interracial tensions. We can ask what kind of discourse the words we find in the text realise, what kind of world they constitute and what kinds of interests they serve.

EMDA 'mission statement'

The vision is for the East Midlands to become a fast growing, dynamic economy based on innovative, knowledge based companies competing successfully in the global economy.

East Midlands Innovation launched its Regional Innovation Strategy and action plan in November 2006. This sets out how we will use the knowledge, skills and creativity of organisations and individuals to build an innovation led economy.

Our primary role to deliver our mission is to be the strategic driver of economic development in the East Midlands, working with partners to deliver the goals of the Regional Economic Strategy, which EMDA produces on behalf of the region.

I am committed to ensuring that these strategic priorities act as guiding principles for EMDA as we work with our partners in the region and beyond to achieve the region's ambition to be a Top 20 Region by 2010 and a flourishing region by 2020.

When we read reports by these developmental agencies it is rather difficult to get any concrete sense of what they actually do. But maybe this is not the point of these texts.

A lexical analysis of the text reveals a predominance of words such as 'dynamic', 'innovation', 'competing', 'creativity', 'strategic', 'ambition', 'challenges', 'goals' and 'strengths'. When discussing what might seem like straightforward matters of unemployment or poverty, there is no mention of these things nor is there a mention of how they are to be addressed. And the actual social actors involved are also absent, i.e. the unemployed, the poor, those appointed to develop solutions and those who will bring these into fruition. Rather, we find 'partners' and 'stakeholders'. Reading more of the texts on the EMDA website, we find that these in fact seem to refer to the poor, council workers and businesses as a collective, although the poor are never overtly named.

These kinds of terms, Chiapello and Fairclough (2002) point out, come from the language of business rhetoric, which they describe as the empty rhetoric of corporate-speak. The result of referring to issues such as poverty as a 'challenge', the poor as 'stakeholders' and solutions in terms of 'creativity' and 'innovation' can conceal what the actual problem is and therefore what the solution could be. What these terms do instead is connote a sense of business-like activity and 'drive'. Words like 'stakeholders' connote that those taking action are those who have a vested interest in the outcome or those that control it, although exactly who will do something, who actually has responsibility, is concealed. For Fairclough (2000) this language serves to conceal where the actual responsibility lies, which is with the government and the fundamental nature of social organisation.

In fact, poverty and unemployment in the East Midlands is partly due to changes in economic policies pushing Britain into the global economy and allowing industries that formerly created employment to shift to other parts of the world where labour is cheaper (Levitas, 2005). In certain areas, whole sections of the population live in families where there have been no workers often for three generations. While terms like 'creativity', 'innovation' and 'knowledge economy' sound exciting and active, they will not help us to deal with fundamental structural issues. And calling them, along with the local councillors and businesses who are to provide solutions, 'stakeholders' further obscures power relations. By constantly using terms like 'stakeholders', it becomes unclear as to who will act, and at the same time gives a sense that it is the poor who must take shared responsibility and action. This mixture of rights and responsibilities was a key part of New Labour discourse (Levitas, 2005). Of course, as Fairclough (2000) explains, this is precisely the point, as we are distracted from real causes and necessary solutions. It is simply by looking at the kinds of words found in a text that we can draw out the discourse that is being communicated. In this case, regional authorities are represented through a discourse of corporate businesses, although this is not openly stated.

These kinds of lexical choices are now typical of the way that any private or public organisation will position itself. Most universities, health authorities, hospitals and schools now have a 'vision' or 'mission statement'. The very fact that such organisations feel required to declare they have a 'vision' rather than simply an 'identity' or a 'role' indicates the pervasiveness of corporate-business language. The term 'vision' connotes 'ambition', 'looking ahead' and 'lofty ideas'. In former times it would have been sufficient for a university simply to state that it was concerned with ideas, to celebrate, disseminate and push the boundaries of knowledge and science, and simply to educate, thereby playing a part in a better and more sophisticated society. Even in the 1980s there was a sense in Britain that universities were simply essential to the functioning of a healthy democracy. We can see something of the way this has disappeared in the opening paragraph of Loughborough University's mission statement:

> Loughborough University is a dynamic, forward looking institution, committed to being a centre of excellence in teaching, learning and enterprise. We have much to be proud of – surveys in the media

constantly rate Loughborough as a top university. In June 2006 the Times Good University Guide ranked Loughborough University the sixth highest university in the UK. (Loughborough University website)

We can see in this case that the university is marketing itself in terms of being 'dynamic' and 'forward looking'. What is interesting in terms of CDA is to ask why these terms have become so universally accepted. In the previous chapter we asked why a young woman in a bar used the word 'scary' to speak about herself. We thought about the way this reflected changes in the role of women yet also a lingering need for her to express her sexual agency. In CDA it is assumed that language and society are deeply intertwined. They are not to be thought of as separate entities. Linguistic activity is social practice. Language use should be treated as part of social processes. Why did this young woman not want to go around boasting about being 'responsible' or 'compassionate'? These two terms both sound like very good qualities to have. But these are not, as far as the woman is concerned, part of the discourses that have become widely shared for indicating that women have desirable and credible levels of agency and personality.

We can ask what the consequences would be in a society where certain concepts of identity become valued over others, where identity categories of compassion and responsibility gain negative connotations as opposed to 'independence' and 'scariness'. Machin and van Leeuwen (2007), in an analysis of women's lifestyle magazines, show how women always act alone and strategically, whether it is in relationships or at work. They appear to have no ties of interest to any kind of wider community, apart from their shared strategic solutions to getting a man or winning prestige socially or at work. They certainly appear to have no responsibility for anyone apart from their own pleasure and status. Machin and van Leeuwen suggest that these are ideal identities for aligning women to the interests of consumerism.

We can say the same about the way Loughborough University is described. Why should 'dynamic' and 'forward looking' be desirable qualities? Both connote movement and lack of stasis. So 'change' is clearly regarded as positive, whereas 'stability' appears to be less so. Likewise, in our contemporary society, 'speed' is also highly prized. Things that are done quickly and technology that allows more urgency are presented as good in themselves. But why should this be the case? If we are always 'forward looking', does this mean that we are not attending to the present? If we do things quickly, again does this mean we are not attending to the actual process of doing it or doing it haphazardly? If 'innovation' is good, does this mean that what we already know should always be quickly discarded? This trend appears to be reflected in the way that Human Resources run training programmes in businesses and in public sector organisations. In our experience, employees at their annual appraisals are encouraged to think about their training requirements, often by those who have no idea about the jobs that these people do, whereas before it was those who had considerable experience in a profession who were seen to have the expertise.

We can see a similar set of lexical choices on the homepage of a British National Health Service website:

Vision and Values: Heart of England NHS Trust

As a large Trust, with four hospitals and a number of satellite units, we have the power to make a real difference to the lives of patients and our fellow workers. As part of the Organisational Development programme, staff from across Heart of England met and discussed values for the Trust going forward. These are the values by which we already live and work in the Trust; the values that help us achieve our mission:

To improve the health of people by pursuing excellence in healthcare and education

To achieve this mission, the Trust lives by five values:

Cherishing

Excellence

Finding a Way

Innovation for Advancement

Working Together

We see terms such as 'innovation', 'excellence', 'vision', 'power' and 'values', but none of these terms is explained. One of their values is 'excellence', but what does this mean? What is the Trust excellent in? The main question we can ask here is why should a health Trust need this language? Does a hospital not simply have to make people better? And why should we want to worry about staff 'working together'. If we are ill, we just want to be offered the best possible healthcare.

The linguistic and visual semiotic choices, which we analyse later, used on the Trust website need to be understood in terms of the broader changes in the British health system, which was established as a state-run, free-to-use healthcare system. Pollock (2006) has documented the way that the emergence of 'Health Trusts' was part of a trend to cut state funding and the corresponding influx of private finance and the need to generate profits. The health service is being effectively privatised and broken up into hundreds of competing companies where a vast range of companies provide finance, buildings, maintenance, repairs, laundry, catering, portering, nursing, etc. Hidden behind all the lexis of vision concepts, the health service is being dismantled and privatised with corporations cherry-picking the most lucrative areas and pushing the balance of care in the direction that is most profitable. Pollock

(2006) describes the increasing loss of equal access and common universal standards and shrinking services.

As the health services become run increasingly on business models, so the language through which they communicate becomes characterised by empty business rhetoric. Changes are concealed behind the language of 'vitality', 'excellence', 'vision' and 'cooperation'. Later in the chapter we will be looking at the way that these kinds of organisations also use visual resources to communicate the same set of ideas.

Overlexicalisation

Another way of describing what is going on in the EMDA text, with its seeming overemphasis on terms that connote movement and change, is 'overlexicalisation'. Teo (2000: 20) explains that overlexicalisation 'results when a surfeit of repetitious, quasi-synonymous terms is woven into the fabric of news discourse, giving rise to a sense of overcompleteness'.

Overlexicalisation gives a sense of over-persuasion and is normally evidence that something is problematic or of ideological contention. So in our analysis of a text, we would find overlexicalisation where there was an abundance of particular words and their synonyms. This would point to where the persuasion was taking place and the area of ideological contention. Two simple examples are:

Male nurse

Female doctor

We can ask why these job titles require elaboration in terms of gender. In this case, of course, it signals a deviation from social convention or expectation. But these are always cues to the dominant ideology. In other words, it is still expected that men are doctors and women are nurses.

Achugar (2007) gives a typical example of the way that enemies can be overlexicalised:

Certainly our Armed Forces victorious in the battle against the unpatriotic forces of Marxist subversion were accused of supposed violations to human rights. (*El Soldado*, April 1989)

Here the Armed Forces are battling against '*the unpatriotic forces of Marxist subversion*'. Such overlexicalisation, or excessive description, indicates some anxiety on the part of the author. Here it appears necessary to justify the 'supposed violations of human rights' by the Armed Forces.

In the case of the EMDA text above, we can see that there is an overlexicalisation of words that communicate deliberate and energetic action, such as 'dynamic', 'innovation', 'competing', 'creativity', 'strategic', 'ambition', 'goals' and 'strengths'. This overuse suggests that something is problematic here. In this case, the aim is to connote a sense of vibrant activity where in fact little is being done at all to combat the structural problems, with EMDA given the impossible task to solve these. Unemployment, inequality and poor social inclusion can only be dealt with by major policy changes at a central government level that would involve changing the way our society is organised in relation to the economic context of global capitalism.

Suppression or lexical absence

As we can find overlexicalisation in texts, we can also find suppression, where certain terms that we might expect are absent. Below there are two short texts. The first is an international news agency feed received by a news organisation, Independent Radio News (IRN). The second is the text after IRN had reworked it for broadcast for one of their clients, based on knowledge of their client's listeners through the need to prove that they are able to target specific consumer groups for advertisers. Since we have the original text we can more easily show what the journalist has decided to remove or suppress from the text. We can ask, therefore, what are the main changes of discourse in the rewrite?

> APTN feed as received by IRN, 18 September 2003:

> One of the few suspects to express remorse over his alleged involvement in last year's bombings on Indonesia's Bali island arrived at court on Thursday to hear his sentence. Ali Imron is facing a possible death penalty, but prosecutors have asked that he receive 20 years in prison because he has shown regret and cooperated with investigators. Imran's older brother Amrozi bin Nurhasyim, and another key defendant, Imam Samudra, already have been sentenced to face firing squads for their roles in the attack, which killed 202 people – mostly foreign tourists.

> IRN rewrite:

> A man's been jailed for life for helping to plan and carry out the Bali bombings. Twenty-six Britons were among more than two hundred people killed in the attack in October last year. Ali Imron was spared the death sentence handed down to other suspects because he expressed remorse and co-operated with the Indonesian authorities.

IRN has, of course, simplified the story in order to reduce ambiguity. Such stories in radio news have to be delivered in very short bursts. But it is revealing to look at how the one above has been changed. This has been done in a number of ways, but for the present we can attend specifically to a number of important lexical changes or omissions. In the original text we find many legal terms, such as 'alleged', 'prosecutors', 'defendant'. These have been removed from the rewrite. In fact the original text has been generated from a court report, as is standard in news gathering of crime. But the rewrite has omitted all legal reference. The journalist may have believed that listeners to this particular radio programme would not be interested in legal information. But the effect is that we are no longer required to think about *whose* court or under *whose* jurisdiction this event is taking place. This becomes one more story in the war on terror, where the journalist has inserted information about the number of Britons killed – a story about evil-doers being caught. Clearly, on the one hand this could be explained through the needs for simplicity and for ease of understanding. But on the other it is nevertheless important and revealing to ask what has been left out or added and what ideological work this does.

In the IRN example we conveniently had the original text so that we could show clearly what had been deleted. But in the case of any text we can ask what lexical items are missing that we might expect to be included. In the example of the Heart of England NHS Trust text, there is no mention of illness, of caring or of medicines. Instead of caring for people we have terms such as 'make a real difference to the lives of patients' and 'cherishing'. If we are ill, will our first concern be to be 'cherished' or for someone to 'make a difference' to our lives? Would we not rather want to be reassured that there are enough facilities and staff to make us better quickly? If there are absences in terms of activities, elements or participants, then we can think about why it was the case that the text producer did not want us to think of these. Of course where services are being privatised and expensive ones being closed down, where there are money-saving job freezes and ward closures, more ambiguous claims couched in a more positive-sounding language need to be made.

Structural oppositions

Halliday's (1978, 1985) theory of Social Semiotics explains that words mean not only on their own but as part of a network of meanings. Vocabulary also makes distinctions between classes of concepts. So we find structural oppositions in texts. This is an important part of understanding this kind of language analysis and it also underpins much of the visual toolkit we present later in the book.

In language, these oppositions are opposing concepts such as young–old, good–bad, or democracy–communism. Often only one of these may be mentioned, which can imply differences from qualities of its opposites without these being overtly stated. Or this particular word can bring with it associations from its related clusters of concepts. So if a particular participant in a news text is described as a 'militant' or an 'extremist', we can fathom that such a person acts in the opposite manner expected of a 'citizen' or a 'member of a community'. As in the case of 'youths attack local family homes', a set of ideas around what 'youths' are and are not can be activated.

When such oppositions are more overtly included in a text, we can talk of 'ideological squaring' (Van Dijk, 1998), which means that opposing classes of concepts are built up around participants. This may not necessarily mean that the participants are overtly labelled as 'good' or 'bad', but rather that this is implied through structuring concepts. We can see how this use of oppositions, both overt and implicit, works in the following item from the British newspaper *The Sun*. In this text we are never told why the events take place, nor are the participants overtly evaluated as 'good' or 'bad'. Evaluation takes place through the oppositions. The image here is also very important and plays a crucial role in setting up oppositions. This will be analysed below and in more detail in the remaining chapters.

Figure 2   On patrol ... British soldier in Helmand province

Our boys blitz Taliban bash (*The Sun*, 31 December 2007)
BRITISH commandos launched a devastating blitz on the Taliban – as the evil terrorists held a party to celebrate Benazir Bhutto's murder.

The dawn raid was staged after messages were intercepted about the sick knees-up in Afghanistan's Helmand province.

Royal Marines crept into position as the fanatics partied the night away just hours after Ms Bhutto was killed in Pakistan.

The bash was being held in ruined compounds a few hundred yards from Our Boys' remote base in Kajaki.

Ragtag Taliban sentries tried to hit back with machine gun fire – but stood no chance against the heroes of 40 Commando's Charlie Company.

Bloodthirsty

The terrorists were pounded with mortars, rockets and heavy machine guns.

Two bloodthirsty revellers trying to creep towards Our Boys in a trench were spotted by thermal-imaging equipment – and targeted with a Javelin heat-seeking missile.

The £65,000 rocket – designed to stop Soviet tanks – locked on to their body heat and tore more than a kilometer across the desert in seconds.

Troop Sergeant Dominic Conway, 32 – who directed mortar rounds – grinned: "It must have had quite a detrimental effect on their morale."

Sgt Conway, from Whitley Bay, Tyneside, said of the Taliban lair: "It used to be their backyard and now we've made it ours."

In this text we find very different sets of word choices used to represent the two sides, the British commandoes and the Taliban. At no point does the text overtly state who is good and bad or why this is. But the structural oppositions or 'ideological squaring' clearly indicate how the participants should be evaluated.

The British soldiers are described as 'our' side: 'British commandos', 'Royal Marines', 'Troop Sergeant', 'heroes of 40 Commando's Charlie Company' and on three occasions 'Our Boys'. These are described in terms of professional rank and organisation in ways that connote pride: 'our boys' and 'heroes'. In contrast, the Taliban are referred to as 'their' side: 'the Taliban', 'evil terrorists', 'fanatics', 'Ragtag Taliban sentries' and 'bloodthirsty revellers', 'animals' who are based in a 'lair'. These connotations are of disorganisation, through terms like 'Ragtag' and 'revellers', and of irrationality, through terms like 'fanatics'. What often lies behind such stories are local people who oppose the occupation of what they perceive as their territory. Western armies are often present in part to protect economic and strategic interests of Western governments. Yet here we are provided with no political or social context, only good and bad participants.

The lexis which is used to describe the actions of the two sides is also of the same order. The British soldiers 'carry out a dawn raid', 'staged an attack', 'crept into position', 'spotted', 'targeted', 'designed', 'locked on to' and 'directed'. All these terms suggest precision, careful focus and organisation. In contrast, the Taliban are described thus: 'held a party', 'sick knees-up', 'partied the night away' and 'bash'. This is to emphasise their inappropriate and unprofessional attitude to killing, although at the end of the text we find that Troop Sergeant Dominic Conway, 32, himself takes a somewhat callous attitude to the deaths where he is described as grinning and gloating "It must have had quite a detrimental effect on their morale." There is also a clear sense that the British are described as being decisive as they 'launched a devastating blitz', 'spotted by thermal-imaging equipment'. In contrast, the Taliban are twice described as only 'trying': 'tried to hit back with machine gun fire' and 'trying to creep towards Our Boys'. They are clearly represented as incompetent.

At no point in this text are we told overtly how we should interpret this conflict, yet this is clearly indicated through lexical choices which create an opposition between the professional British soldiers on the one hand and the inhumane, savage, irrational Taliban on the other. We are certainly never told why the soldiers are fighting. Why exactly is the British army killing these people and who exactly are they? What is the overall aim? In the case of this story we can say, therefore, that there is a suppression of information at the level of motives, of broader values and sequences of activity. There is also a suppression of the brutality of war, of the mutilating effects of the weapons used by these soldiers on the bodies of their enemies. Instead, there is an overlexicalisation of terms for precision combat.

Lexical choices and genre of communication

Often texts can use lexical choices to indicate levels of authority and co-membership with the audience (Fairclough, 1995a). Authors will often seek to influence us through claims to having power over us. This may be through legal or hierarchical means or through claiming specialist knowledge. In the first case, a text might simply tell us we cannot act in a particular way because of the law. In the second, a scientist might tell us that we should understand the world in a particular way due to their knowledge of facts. They will use specific, official-sounding terms that help to convey authority. We often see this in advertising for cosmetics, where technical-sounding terms are used to connote 'science' and 'specialist knowledge' where in fact there might be none. Drugs marketing companies are aware that products often have to carry brand names that connote science, for example that carry lots of 'x's and 'y's. So a cough medicine might be named 'txylxyn'. It seems that consumers are much less likely to buy the same product if it is called something more literal like 'smooth cough'. Other texts might try to influence us through claiming to speak through a language common to the readership or listener, by using more colloquial and everyday language, hence giving the impression of being like us (Leitner, 1980).

In the following text extract we find two sets of lexical choices used to convey different kinds of authority at the same time. This text is supposedly about drug problems and young people, but it is vague about facts and is little more than a sensational piece. It reveals nothing about the actual numbers of young people taking drugs. Drug-use researchers often comment on how the press continually serves to distract the public from the reality of drug problems through its moral outrage stance (Manning, 2007b). Instead of rational debates that would inform the public about the potential long-term damage of prolonged ecstasy use, 'news construction reinforces moral evaluation' (Manning, 2007b: 163). In this sense, the drug debate is more of a self-perpetuating witch hunt; a 'call for the "evil" individual seeking to lead innocents astray' (Manning, 2007b: 162). Much research on drugs use now emphasises that millions of people take recreational drugs in a 'normalised' way, which is not characterised by addiction, but rather periodic use (Parker et al., 1998, 2002). Only a small percentage of drug users fall into the hard use/hard drugs category – groups associated with poverty and marginalisation and prior connections with crime and the 'irregular' economy (Seddon, 2008). Yet media reporting tends to focus on drugs as something sordid and deviant, and merges all drug use into the same discourse, where innocent victims are in grave danger from a shadowy world.

The really innocent victims of our drugs explosion (*The Sun*, 10 October 2002[1])

Emma Jones

WHEN I was a kid, one of my mum's worst fears was me accidentally swallowing bleach. It was the health scare of the moment. There were public information adverts on telly and campaigns for child-proof tops.

For modern mums there is a more hidden and sinister danger – ecstasy tablets and illegal drugs.

This week Sadie Frost and Jude Law's two-year-old daughter, Iris, swallowed part of a discarded E tablet she found on the floor at a children's birthday party.

She was robbed of her innocence (after most likely suffering hallucinogenic effects) and nearly her life.

Iris survived – but others haven't.

In July this year ten-year-old Jade Slack became the youngest person to die from ecstasy after taking five tablets she found.

Dangers

A week later, three-year-old Brandon White, from London, was rushed to hospital after swallowing ecstasy he mistook for a sweet.

In June, a 20-month-old Swansea girl suffered the same fate.

In another incident a 19-month-old nearly died after mistaking the killer drug for mints.

And it's not just ecstasy.

In 1999 a three-year-old girl from Newcastle swallowed cocaine powder she thought was sherbet after finding it in her garden.

The charity DrugScope warn one of the biggest dangers is the heroin substitute methadone because of its green colour and sweet taste.

Dozens have accidentally drunk methadone thinking it was pop and some have died.

---

[1]Thanks to Will Hall for this text.

These tragedies may seem like a series of unrelated, freak accidents.

Sadly, they are not.

The phenomenon is a sign of the times, giving us a shocking insight into how drugs have swamped our country and spilled over the hands of our children.

Drugs have become so cheap and freely available that they can be found nearly EVERYWHERE. Iris Law found the E tablet at Soho House, one of Britain's poshest private members' clubs.

No longer are ecstasy tablets confined to the sleazy dance clubs and cocaine to showbiz parties.

Drugs are so cheap and plentiful that people routinely buy them in bulk and have them lying around the house in cupboards, handbags and coat pockets – places where curious kids will root them out.

What we do not find in this text is an account of the facts of ecstasy use and users. In the following table we have placed the formal and informal lexical items in different columns. In the right-hand column we find terms that connote what Fairclough (1995a) call a 'discourse of information', a sense of imparting facts.

In the left-hand column we find a much more informal lexis. This too serves to provide authority, in that the newspaper speaks 'our language'. Commentators on language use and communication have long observed the technique of using conversational style to bring a sense of informality to the conversational mix (Scannell and Cardiff, 1991; Bell and van Leeuwen, 1994). Conversational style is both private and suggests dialogue between equals. For this reason it is a useful strategy for politicians, advertisers and, here, journalists. Technical language can be used to connote 'facts and information'. But this can be delivered in a way that suggests equality. So in this text we find the opening sentence sets this theme with:

When I was a kid, one of my mum's worst fears was me accidentally swallowing bleach.

In terms of the connotations of this lexis, we also find nostalgic references to an idealised family life through 'my mum', 'kid', and the mundane everyday

Table 1   Genre indications in drug explosion text

Informal lexical choices	Formal lexical choices
Kid(s)	Public information adverts
Mum(s)	Ecstasy tablets
Telly	Hallucinogenic effects
Modern mums	Heroin substitute methadone
E tablet	Independent Drugs Monitoring Unit
Green colour/sweet taste	Cocaine, heroin, amphetamines
Poshest private clubs	Decriminalisation
Sleazy dance clubs	Criminal enterprises
Mates	Reformists
Sweets in a playground	Traditionalists

Figure 3   Career woman from *Marie Claire* (Jupiter images)

(www.marieclaire.com/career-money/advice/tips/promotion-recession-work)

fear of the dangers of bleach. This is used to contrast with the connotations then used for the information discourse: 'there is a more hidden and sinister danger – ecstasy tablets and illegal drugs'.

Fairclough (1995a) explains that mixing these two lexicons in this way helps to infuse official discourse with a populist voice. The newspaper does nothing to explain problems with drugs in society, whether or not they are related to unemployment and other social problems. Rather, we might say it serves to distract the reader from these. Again, we find suppression of facts and participants and foregrounding of moral outrage.

The writer uses this juxtaposition throughout, as in the sentences:

Dozens of children have accidentally drunk methadone thinking it was pop and some have died. These tragedies may seem like a series of unrelated, freak accidents. Sadly, they are not.

The formal descriptive term, 'methadone' is here contrasted to the informal 'pop'. Fairclough (1989: 184) describes this process as 'simulated equalization' – whereby the text producer appears on an 'equal footing with the reader through choices of expressions readers may make themselves'.

The following extract is from a careers advice section of the women's lifestyle magazine *Marie Claire* (2010). Here we find a different set of genre indicators:

Yes, it is still possible to scale the corporate ladder in spite of layoffs. Here, Bob Calandra, co-author of *How to Keep Your Job in a Tough Competitive Market*, offers advice for gingerly negotiating a title bump:

- **Act like the boss.** If your manager gets canned, set up a meeting with her supervisor right away. Calandra's no-fail script: "I'm not looking to be promoted, but I also recognize no one wants chaos. I know the ins and outs of my boss's job, so feel free to tap me for any of her work while we're in this transitional phase." To come off a hero, you can't appear as if you're expecting anything in return.
- **Pollyanna gets the corner office.** Be a relentless cheerleader for the company, even if it means irking co-workers. Your manager is bound to pick up on your positive outlook and use you as a model.
- **Mind your alliances.** If watercooler gossip reveals your cubemate is on management's hit list, publicly align yourself with the office hotshot, even if it makes you feel like Tracy Flick. Appearances matter — and you can always commiserate with your axed colleague over cocktails later (your treat).

In this text too we find the conversational genre which can be seen from the extensive use of personal pronouns: 'your', 'you' and 'I'. This is one device which creates a sense of dialogue between equals. We also find this in terms of lexical choices as in 'If your manager gets canned', and 'negotiate a title bump' and 'tap me for any of her work'. Machin and van Leeuwen (2005) point out the way that lifestyle magazines often use a lexis of 'street' vocabulary by using a sprinkling of the latest slang expressions used by the young and trendy. This is an important aspect of lifestyle as both the goods the magazines sell and the identities and values that are aligned with them must always appear to be up to date. Much of this is accomplished through marketing and focus groups.

In this text we also find the inclusion of fictional genres. 'Tracy Flick' and 'Pollyanna' are from a movie and a children's story. Both are assertive and ambitious, although they feel the weight of this from others. But importantly both are slightly comical and the tales are lightweight. The text is able to draw on these references for their connotations of playfulness. And particularly 'Tracy Flick' is played by Hollywood actress Reese Witherspoon.

Alongside the conversational and street styles we also find the style of the expert. The key characteristics of this are the use of a more formal vocabulary often with more technical terms, such as 'competitive market', 'corporate ladder', 'this transitional phase', 'positive outlook' and 'publicly align yourself'.

In our 'lifestyle society', authority depends not so much on tradition and established professionals but on role models and the 'expert'. Here we see the expert using lots of directives: 'set up a meeting with her supervisor', 'Be a relentless cheerleader for the company', 'publicly align yourself with the office hotshot'. Directives are where sentences start with a verb to give a command. These are from what we would call the imperative mood in language.

The indicative mood simply states something. An example would be 'The book is on the table'. The interrogative mood, which is used for seeking information, would be 'Where is the book?' So the advice about publicaly aligning with the office hotshot could have been conveyed through the indicative mood also: 'It is a good idea to align yourself with the office hotshot'. Or it could be done through the interrogative: 'Why not try aligning yourself with the office hotshot?' The point is that the magazine positions itself as a voice of expertise through the use of imperatives. In fact, as Machin and van Leeuwen (2005) point out, across different kinds of content in these magazines, whether features, advice or advertising, we find an overlexicalisation of imperative verb forms. In part, this brings a sense of energy and forthrightness and above all confidence and authority.

What is also notable about the *Marie Claire* text is what is suppressed. 'Be a relentless cheerleader for the company' is an abstraction. What it specifically means is not explained; nor is it clear from the text. Likewise we are not told what actual role the woman has in this text, nor the nature of her company, apart from the fact that it is an 'office'. This means that the text addresses all kinds of workers as being able to play this strategic game.

Notably, women in these lifestyle magazines do not work in factories, shops or kitchens, nor are they on casual contracts. Nor does the text explain any of the characteristics of the woman herself. Getting on at work has nothing to do with personal characteristics, educational qualifications or connections. What these kinds of texts clearly do not deal with are real social and personal issues. Their role is simply to signify a discourse where women can be in control of themselves and be fashionable through the way they dress and speak.

Critically analysing texts that reflect our own ideology

What can be most difficult in carrying out Critical Discourse Analysis is the critical analysis of texts that we agree with, which are in accord with our own ideological viewpoint. The following text from the British newspaper *The Guardian* is critical of government funding cuts in the university sector. The authors' views align with that of the text. In such a case the lexical choices can tend to appear as neutral to the analyst. But a closer look at these choices nevertheless helps us to reveal the way the author selects from a range of possible language choices to represent the situation.

Thousands to lose jobs as universities prepare to cope with cuts
(*The Guardian*, 7 February 2010)

Universities across the country are preparing to axe thousands of teaching jobs, close campuses and ditch courses to cope with government funding cuts, the Guardian has learned.

Other plans include using post-graduates rather than professors for teaching and the delay of major building projects. The proposals have already provoked ballots for industrial action at a number of universities in the past week raising fears of strike action which could severely disrupt lectures and examinations.

The Guardian spoke to vice-chancellors and other senior staff at 25 universities, some of whom condemned the funding squeeze as "painful" and "insidious". They warned that UK universities were being pushed towards becoming US-style, quasi-privatized institutions.

The cuts are being put in place to cope with the announcement last week by the Higher Education Funding Council for England (Hefce) that £449m – equivalent to more than a 5% reduction nationally – would be stripped out of university budgets.

The University and College Union (UCU) believes that more than 15,000 posts – the majority academic – could disappear in the next few years. Precise funding figures for each university will be released on 18 March.

The chairman of the Russell Group of elite institutions, Professor Michael Arthur, vice-chancellor of Leeds University, warned that budgets would be further slashed by 6% in each of the next three years. Last month he described the cuts as "devastating".

To begin with, the author of this text has chosen words that connote ruthlessness to describe the instigation of the cuts, using 'axe' and 'ditch'. This could have been written in a more neutral language such as: 'Universities will have to *reduce* teaching posts' or as 'Universities will need to operate more efficiently and balance staff–student ratios'.

The lexical choices used to describe the financial changes describe universities being 'stripped' and budgets being 'slashed'. Such terms do not sound like they are the result of measured activity, but suggest violence and lack of reasonable measure. Again, more moderate terms such as '*reduced*' could have been used.

We are told there are plans for the 'delay of major building projects'. Yet what constitutes 'major' projects is not explained and nor is the extent of the delay. These might appear as minor details but as van Leeuwen and Wodak (1999) explain, where actual facts and processes are replaced by abstractions and generalisations, this is a sign that there is ideological work being done.

The proposals themselves are described as 'provoking' and 'raising fears' and 'severely disrupt'. Again this could have been written: 'The proposals have been followed by ballots which may *result in* strike action'. The word 'provoke', of course, suggests conflict. Clearly, opposition to the action is favoured by the author. The text states that the proposals are 'raising fears of strike action'. However, who has these fears is not stated. Fairlough (2003: 136) argues that where participants are excluded from a text we need to ask why.

We can also see here that the author of the text has chosen to include quotes from what looks like more than 25 sources in the form of two single words 'painful' and 'insidious'. How are we to take such quotes? Such disembodied words tell us little of the context in which they were used. The author also states 'some of whom condemned the funding squeeze'. Yet the term 'funding squeeze' does not appear in quotation marks so it is again a lexical choice made by the author.

Finally, we find the word 'warned' appears twice in the text to account for the opinions of the interviewees. The author could have used more neutral terms, such as '*said*' or '*commented*'. We look in more detail at these 'verbs of saying' in the next chapter. But here it is clear that such lexical choices indicate the ideological work done in the text and the clear stance of the author.

Visual semiotic choices

The texts we come across often communicate not only through word choices but also through non-linguistic features and elements. Even this very text you are now reading, which contains no image as such, communicates partly through choice of font type, colour of font, line spacing and alignment of text. Would it be read differently were it written in a comic font using a broad palette of colours, or were it printed on parchment paper? Here we want to think specifically about the images that accompany some of the texts we have been analysing so far.

In the last chapter we looked at the image from *Cosmopolitan* magazine of the woman leading against a desk. We thought more broadly about the way it communicated. Here we show how we can analyse this and images like it much more systematically by asking a sequence of specific questions. We then return to a number of the texts analysed in this chapter looking at the way the images contribute to meaning making.

Iconography

We begin with the widely known semiotic theory of Roland Barthes (1973, 1977) and his account of how images can denote and connote. But here the emphasis normally given to the two levels of analysis is switched.

On one level, images can be said to document. In other words, they show *particular* events, *particular* people, places and things. Or in semiotic terminology, they *denote*. So asking what an image denotes is asking: Who and/or what is depicted here? So a picture of a house denotes a house. In the case of the photograph from *Cosmopolitan* we could say that it denotes a woman, a desk and a computer.

Other images will still depict particular people, places, things and events, but 'denotation' is not their primary or only purpose. They depict concrete people, places, things and events to get general or abstract *ideas* across. They use them to *connote* ideas and concepts. So asking what an image connotes is asking: What ideas and values are communicated through what is represented, and through the way in which it is represented? Or, from the point of view of the image maker: How do I get general or abstract ideas across? How do I get across what events, places and things *mean*? What concrete signifier can I use to get a particular abstract idea across? We can see how this is relevant in the case of the *Cosmopolitan* photograph. The image has been chosen as it connotes certain kinds of identities and practices. While it denotes a women and a desk, these are not an ordinary, everyday women and desk. Rather, the image communicates a particular set of values about glamour, excitement and women's identities. So for any image we can ask what discourse is communicated that includes kinds of persons, attitudes, values and actions.

Of course we could argue that there is no neutral denotation, and that all images connote something for us. For example, an image of a large house can connote wealth and excess. But considering what is denoted, arguably, is what is often undervalued in semiotic analysis. Students often look at an advertisement for a car, for example, and immediately speak of what is connoted in terms of 'energy', 'style' and 'modernity'. But here they are jumping a step. They are saying *what* is connoted but not exactly *how* it is connoted. When we listen to a political speech we might be aware that the speaker has managed to give a particular spin on a set of events, but it may take the kind of language analysis done throughout this book, which emphasises careful attention to the detail of the way that language is used, to show exactly how they have done this. This is why we need to be attentive to denotation.

So in the case of the *Cosmopolitan* image we need to describe the desk carefully, that it is very clean and shiny with polished surfaces. We need to describe what clothes the woman is wearing, what is placed on her desk and what kind of wider setting we find. In this case, there is very little in the image in terms of objects. What we would need to ask here is: What is the meaning of all this space in a setting that would in normal life be characterised by lots of items related to work activities, such as files, papers, pens and pencils, personal photographs, drinking mugs, etc.? We will think more about this shortly.

There are a few other points of relation between denotation and connotation that we also need to make. Again, the importance of these will become clearer shortly. First, the more abstract the image, the more overt and fore-grounded its connotative communicative purpose. In the *Cosmopolitan* image we can see that the high key lighting has the effect of making the scene appear slightly fuzzy or softened. This means that there is reduced likelihood that this image was intended to show us something about a particular place at a particular time, but rather that it has a symbolic value. We will be dealing more with how we assess levels of abstraction in images in Chapter 8.

Secondly, whether the communicative purpose of an image is primarily denotative or connotative depends to some extent on the context in which the image is used. An image of a mother and child in a war-torn street could be used to denote the experiences of these particular people in a news report.

In another news report, the same image could be used to symbolise suffering through war in general, where motherhood and childhood signify innocence.

Thirdly, what an image connotes may, in some contexts, be a matter of free association. But where image makers need to get a specific idea across, they will rely on established *connotators*, carriers of connotations, which they feel confident their target audiences will understand (whether consciously or not). In *Cosmopolitan*, where it is advertising revenue that is at stake, a range of established connotators will be used to signify women as having a life that is fun and glamorous and certainly not bound by the tedium of domestic life. But these connotators must allow a fit with consumer activities. So we would not find connotators of discourses where women found agency outside consumer society.

While the concept of connotation is one we use in our analysis, we also use the term 'meaning potential'. In language we have a range of communicative resources that we can use in contexts to communicate. For example, we might choose one word over another. We therefore have a range of choices that we can use to create particular meanings. However, these meanings can change depending on the context in which they are used. For example, if we put the words 'You must' at the start of sentence in place of 'Can you', it changes the meaning of the sentence from imperative to interrogative – in other words, a demand rather than a question. The words that follow therefore are part of a different meaning. So words have meaning potential that can be realised in different contexts and which is sensitive to that context. Visual semiotic resources also have the potential to mean that is realised in specific contexts. The term 'meaning potential' has the advantage over 'connote' as it suggests not something fixed, but a possibility, and it encourages us to consider specifically how any visual element or feature is connected to and used with other visual elements, which may serve to modify its meaning. Why this is important will become increasingly clear.

Barthes listed a number of important connotators of meaning: poses, objects and settings. We will look at objects and settings here, leaving the meaning of poses for the next chapter. We will be discussing in much more detail how to analyse the representation of people themselves in Chapter 4.

Attributes

Here we are concerned with the ideas and values communicated by objects and how they are represented. What discourses do they communicate? When carrying out analysis of objects, the meaning of every object should be considered. In the *Cosmopolitan* image, for example, there are a number of objects, such as the computer, the clean empty desk, the handbag under the table. We can also turn our attention to the woman's clothing, such as the high-heeled shoes, the scarf around her neck, her hair and other clothing.

Images like the one just described are typical of *Cosmopolitan*, with an emphasis on clingy fabrics, loose lavish hair, high heels and heavy lipstick. At the heart of *Cosmopolitan*'s brand, of its representation of women in non-domestic settings, is glamour and seductiveness through traditional female attributes. The scarf flying loose around the woman's neck would in many ways be impractical, unless looking glamorous was high on the agenda. The placing of the handbag in a prominent place in the image draws our attention to accessories and high fashion. As a rule, the women in *Cosmopolitan* images are model-beautiful. Their sexy clothes draw on traditional notions of female sexuality and male desire: short skirts, revealing tops, high heels, shiny red, sensuous lipstick. Women's sexuality is the source of their power over men and appears to be linked to their success in the workplace. Much of this is never explicitly mentioned in the magazine texts, but it is signalled clearly enough in the images, through the things the women are doing and the interactions they engage in.

The computer is also important in that it is a PC computer. Often women are shown with laptop computers which suggest mobility and independence. This computer suggests work where the woman is tied to the desk. But most remarkable in the image is the lack of everyday objects that can be found in work environments. We discuss this under the next heading.

In the *Marie Claire* photograph, accompanying the text regarding work previously discussed in the chapter, we find a woman holding a notebook or agenda and a pen, whose clothing is less glamorous and informal and perhaps 'creative', complete with hippy beads. This suggests a kind of work which requires an agenda or somewhere to write down ideas, therefore suggesting a kind of job that does not have a daily, repeating routine. The clothes too suggest no formal regimentation, as might be characteristic of a faceless bureaucratic job, but someone who can choose their own clothing, importantly, someone who has the power to do so. While the text communicates a cynical self-interest by using trendy language and confident directives along with technical business terms, the image appears much softer, creative and pleasant.

Settings

We can also look at the way that settings are used to communicate general ideas, to connote discourses and their values, identities and actions. In the *Cosmopolitan* photograph, as in the *Marie Claire* photograph, the settings only hint at office work, where only a few attributes stand for work in an abstracted way. In the *Cosmopolitan* image the woman is not really using the computer. There is no evidence of any activity at all in fact. The emptiness of the setting suggests the luxury of space, as is often found in corporate entrance halls. We could imagine the opposite effect, were it made to look like she was in a very small cluttered space. In the *Marie Claire* image too there is clearly a luxury of space with very large windows and a high ceiling.

Important in both of these photographs is the use of high key lighting, which suggests optimism. In both of these photographs the setting serves to symbolise work rather than documenting it. What is signified is glamour, modernism, optimism, creativity and excitement. In the *Cosmopolitan* text, the topic was doing exercise in the workplace. In *Marie Claire*, it was the cynical getting ahead while your colleagues are losing their jobs. In both cases, photographs of real women in real work settings would have made the texts appear very odd and may have revealed their silliness. But these symbolic images load the texts with the above values and therefore allow them to signify discourses of women's agency. These abstracted settings are one way that these women's lifestyle magazines create a fantasy world through the use of symbolic images, which allow a particular kind of agency that is suffused with women's ability to seduce and the glamour of fashion, and to signify power. For the producers of *Cosmopolitan*, a 'brand' is a set of representations and values that are not indissolubly tied to a specific product.

What *Cosmopolitan* sells to its readers are not magazines, but connotators of independence, power and fun. In sum, these representations of women are not realistic, an aspect which some critics of women's magazines have pointed out. Women's lives are presented as playful fantasies. Thus, the heritage of 1960s' feminism, with the idea of the woman as independent from the domestic situation, as fully able to enjoy her own sexuality, has become to some extent intertwined with consumerism (Irigaray, 1985).

Below we see the homepage from where the text analysed earlier in the chapter for the vision the Heart of England Health Trust was taken. We compare this with the homepage from the North Glamorgan Trust to draw out the particular choices used. What is important here is to think about what is being foregrounded and what backgrounded, as this terrain is mapped out for us visually.

Earlier we described the way that in terms of language choices the Trust represented itself and its aims through abstractions: 'Cherishing', 'Excellence' 'Finding a Way', 'Innovation for Advancement', 'Working Together'. We considered the way that this was part of the empty corporate business language that has come to dominate public institutions and backgrounds actual concrete matters about facilities, staffing and treatment. Looking below and comparing the two Trust homepages in terms of the visual semiotic choices, we can see that the Glamorgan page contains real settings with its photographs of actual hospitals, whereas North Glamorgan itself appears to be represented in the banner bar through a cartoon of countryside which links with a graphic of a heart-rate monitor.

Somewhat like the *Cosmopolitan* image described above, this serves to idealise North Glamorgan. In contrast, the Heart of England homepage displays settings only in terms of abstracted spaces like those found in *Cosmopolitan*. The iconography that connotes medicine is the stethoscope around the neck of the man at the front of the image in the banner. Also important in the image is the headset worn by the woman to the right of the image. This is to signify 'communication', presumably part of the mission value of 'Cherishing' and 'Working Together'.

What is important in this image is the gaze of the participants. Three of them engage with the viewer, smiling warmly and striking relaxed poses. The woman with the headset looks off into the distance thoughtfully, presumably engaged in friendly chatter with a person requiring treatment.

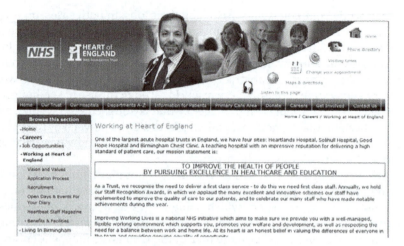

Figure 4   Heart of England Health Trust homepage

Just as the language serves to conceal the changes through a vibrant lexis, so visually we find semiotic choices not to document practices but to symbolise 'communication' and 'caring'. More will be said about these two homepages across the following chapters.

Salience

Salience is where certain features in compositions are made to stand out, to draw our attention to foreground certain meanings. Such features will have the central symbolic value in the composition. There are a number of ways that salience can be achieved in images. We list these below. But we must be aware that different principles of salience may be more or less important in each composition and that they will work together in different ways often to create hierarchies of salience.

- *Potent cultural symbols*: Certain elements carry much cultural symbolism. It is a good idea to scan the composition for such elements. In the Health Trust image above it is important that we see the stethoscope to signify medical practice, but also the clear importance of the woman communicating and the fact that everyone is smiling. If we had a broken leg, would we care if everyone was smiling or would we want them to simply treat us? And quite simply, the Heart of England page includes only people and not settings, as does the Glamorgan page.
- *Size*: This can be used to indicate ranking of importance, ranging from the largest to the smallest. On the Heart of England page we can see that the doctor is slightly larger than the other employees, although only slightly

Figure 5   North Glamorgan Health Trust homepage

so. He is therefore the most important but in other ways only part of the 'team', of the 'we' who speak through the language as 'having values' and as 'cherishing you'. In contrast on the North Glamorgan page, it is the hospitals themselves that are given salience in terms of size. We might view this as being more indicative of a discourse from a former era where there is some remaining attempt to document actual services rather than signify 'values'.

- *Colour*: This can simply be the use of striking colours, rich saturated colours or contrasts. Less salient elements may have more muted or less saturated colours. We can see the use of richer colours for salience on the North Essex Health Trust webpage on page 99 in Chapter 4. The warmth of the faces of the two people stands out against the colder blue and white. Without these, this page would look very barren. Here salience is given to the pleasure brought to the service users. Again the emphasis is on her being pleased not with treatment, but with the broader way was she dealt with in terms of communication.
- *Tone*: This can simply be the use of brightness to attract the eye. Advertisers often use brighter tones on products themselves to make them shine. On the North Essex webpage we can see that the faces of the two people are glowing with highlights. This helps them to literally shine off the page.
- *Focus*: In compositions different levels of focus can be used to give salience to an element. It can be heightened to exaggerate details, or focus can be reduced. In the Helmand province story earlier in this chapter, we find the soldier in the foreground is in focus, whereas the civilian fades into the setting. He serves only to foreground the experience of the soldier. At this point in this conflict there was considerable effort to gain public support for the presence of the troops, not by explaining the reasons for the war, but by stressing how brave and dedicated they were.

- *Foregrounding*: Simply, foregrounding creates importance. Elements that are further back may become subordinate. In the photograph accompanying the Helmand province story, the British soldier is given greater salience due to foregrounding. We could imagine the difference if the civilian in the background were brought to the front. This would have made the story more about the civilian experience when, as it stands, it is about 'our boys' as heroes. In the *Marie Claire* image, we find the woman herself considerably foregrounded in close shot. This serves to foreground her individual experiences and diminish the context and setting. We can imagine the difference here had her colleagues, who were to lose their jobs, also been present in the image, or even if we were simply to have a fuller view of the workplace itself. In this case, the consequences of the actions recommended in the text would have been brought to the foreground rather than being suppressed.
- *Overlapping*: This is like foregrounding since it has the effect of placing elements in front of others. This gives the impression that the element is in front of others. On the Heart of England webpage, we find the doctor overlaps the other social actors. But at the next level we find the nurse and the telephone operator at the same level. Care and customer service through 'communication' here appear to be ranked at the same level.

Conclusion

In this chapter we have begun to look at the way we can more systematically analyse some of the basic semiotic choices found in texts both linguistically and visually in ways that allow us to draw out the broader discourses being communicated and hence to reveal the ideology communicated. Basic choices in words and iconography can be used to create a field of meaning. This can serve to both foreground and background, or even suppress, some meanings or to connote and symbolise others. This mapping proves an ideological interpretation of events and social practices, which imply identities and actions even if not overtly stated.

What we have shown is that much of this meaning lies at the implicit level. It is only through attention to linguistic and visual detail that we can reveal just what these implicit meanings are. We saw that we can look for the kinds of oppositions that texts set up and the importance of looking for words that are overused. We also found that there can be important differences between what is communicated through words and through visual elements. What follows in the remaining chapters are ways to breakdown the analysis of word and visual semiotic choices into more specific categories.

3

Presenting Speech and Speakers: Quoting Verbs

Introduction

Whereas in the previous chapter we dealt with a broader lexical content analysis, in this chapter and those that follow we begin to provide tools for the analysis of more specific language and grammatical and visual features. Our first step is to look into the importance of carefully describing and analysing the way people are represented as speaking both in language and images. Here we find some important language and visual resources for evaluating social actors, for signifying broader discourses, ideas and values that are not overtly articulated. We begin with the representation in language and then in the second half of the chapter move on to visual representations, looking at gaze and interaction, and poses.

Quoting verbs

In both texts and in speech it is extremely revealing if we look closely at the words chosen to represent how someone has spoken. For example, you are having a conversation with Jane, who says:

My house mates simply don't do enough cleaning.

You then report this conversation to someone else. You might quote Jane exactly. But you will also have to choose a word to express that it is something she said. So you might say simply:

Jane <u>said</u>, 'My house mates simply don't do enough cleaning.'

Or you could say

Jane <u>whinged</u>, 'My house mates simply don't do enough cleaning.'

The first case, using 'said', sounds much more neutral. But in the second case, the word 'whinged' creates much more of an impression on the person you are telling this to as to the mood, attitude or even character of Jane, and therefore to the credibility of her comments. Such choices of quoting verbs can, in this way, lead you to make evaluations of the situation she explains, on the likelihood of it being true or whether we may more easily dismiss the complaint as just more of Jane's whinging nature.

This section deals with the way that these simple word choices, describing how someone has spoken, can have a considerable impact on the way that authors can shape perceptions of events. In the above case, both sentences simply state what Jane has said. Neither passes any judgement on what Jane said explicitly, whether it is true, exaggerated or otherwise. But quoting verbs can be used to provide such information implicitly (Austin, 1975; Caldas Coulthard, 1994; Fairclough, 1995a).

Consider the difference between the following two sentences:

The management <u>announced</u> that striking workers would be punished.
The workers <u>grumbled</u> about problems with conditions.

In the first sentence the management 'announced', while in the second the workers 'grumbled'. In this case, there may well have been nothing inherent in how each group spoke that warranted these word choices. The word 'said' could have served in both cases. So

The management <u>said</u> that striking workers would be punished.

The workers <u>said</u> there were problems with conditions.

In this case, what is said is not evaluated. But in the case where 'announced' and 'grumbled' are used we are encouraged to make particular interpretations of the events. Those who 'announce' things appear to have power and legitimacy. Those who 'grumble' appear to have much less of both. This can be brought out if we reverse the two.

The management <u>grumbled</u> that striking workers would be punished.

The workers <u>announced</u> there were problems with conditions.

Here it now appears that it is the management who are unreasonable and that the workers have a legitimate complaint that is not so much about their character but about the actual conditions in which they work. This is not stated overtly but is communicated through the connotative value of the quoting verb choices. In each case we can see how these choices communicate entire discourses. In the first place, where the management 'announce' and the workers 'grumble', we find a whole set of identities, 'scripts' and values are signified. We have a rational, organised management concerned with productivity and the well-being of the factory. In contrast, we have the selfish, much less well-organised rabble of the grumbling workers who may harm productivity.

Caldas Coulthard (1994: 305–6) offers a systematic breakdown of verbs of saying that allows us to direct our attention more precisely to the implicit evaluation and connotation that is taking place through their use. These are shown in Table 2.

What is important is that through analysis we are able to draw out more precisely just what is connoted through the use of each kind of quoting verb. Below we expand on what we view as the more salient parts of the table:

- **Neutral structuring verbs** introduce a saying without evaluating it explicitly (e.g. say, tell, ask). So if I report that Jane said 'My house mates simply don't do enough cleaning', this does not carry any particular guidance as to how we should think about this statement and about Jane herself. But often in language speakers who are represented as only using these kinds of speaking verbs can appear as disengaged or even less personalised. And as we consider in later chapters on representational strategies and transitivity, it may be important for authors to bring readers/listeners closer or further away from the thoughts and feelings of certain social actors. One way to do this is to elaborate on their thoughts and feelings or their internal mental state. So if we say that someone 'cried' and 'whispered', the reader is drawn to empathise with them much more so than with a person who only 'said'.

Table 2 The meaning potentials of quoting verbs (from Caldas Coulthard, 1994)

Speech-reporting verbs		
Neutral structuring verbs		say, tell, ask, enquire, reply, answer
Metapropositional verbs	Assertives	remark, explain, agree, assent, accept, correct, counter, announce
	Directives	urge, instruct, order
	Expressives	accuse, grumble, lament, confess, complain, swear, claim
Metalinguistic verbs		narrate, quote, recount
Descriptive verbs		
Prosodic (loudness, pitch emotion)		cry, intone, shout, yell, scream
	Voice qualifier (manner)	whisper, murmur, mutter
Paralinguistic	Voice qualification (attitude)	laugh, giggle, sigh, gasp, groan
Transcript verbs	Relation to other parts of discourse	repeat, echo, add, amend
Discourse signalling	Discourse progress	pause, go on, hesitate, continue

- **Metapropositional verbs** mark the author's interpretation of a speaker. For example: 'declare', 'urge' and 'grumble' are assertive, directive and expressive respectively. We saw this where the management were described as having 'announced', which is assertive. We can see the difference here if we said Jane <u>declared</u>, 'My house mates simply don't do enough cleaning'. This immediately appears much more likely to be a true report on events than were Jane to be depicted as 'complaining'. It also makes her appear as more assertive than a person who whinged.

- **Metalinguistic verbs** are where the kind of language used by a speaker is specified. For example, if a speaker said: 'it was really hard living with all those messy people' Jane narrated. Here this may be used for ironic effect. On the other hand, were this switched to 'Jane recounted' there is a greater sense of her simply reporting on what happened.

- **Descriptive verbs** categorise the interaction. For example: 'whisper' and 'laugh' mark the manner and attitude of a speaker in relation to what is being said. So if Jane <u>whispered</u>, 'My house mates simply don't do enough cleaning', the audience is directed more to *how* she said this. Of course, this too signifies attitudes, power relations and likelihood of truth. In this case, whispering would suggest lack of power in that she did not feel able to speak out. If workers 'whispered' that there were problems with working conditions, this would indicate something of the predicament in which they found themselves in relation to the management, for example, that anyone heard publically might not have their contract renewed.

- **Transcript verbs** mark the development of the discourse (e.g. repeat) or relate the quotation to other parts of the discourse (e.g. pause). So we might find 'Jane <u>added</u>, they are all quite lazy to say the least'. Press releases might present the person or persons they are promoting as 'he added' or 'continued' to give an impression of them offering more information when in fact it may be the same point.

All of these different verbs of saying can be used to make certain participants appear more authoritative or subservient, legitimate or non-legitimate. They can help define the roles of sets of participants or events even though these might not be explicitly stated. In the example above, 'announcing' sounds more official, formal, and is the stuff of official groups. 'Grumblings' are not necessarily well formulated, they are not coherent and therefore indicate not being official and suggest a lack of power.

Quoting verbs can also direct us to consider some participants as having a negative attitude and others as being friendly, or they can suggest levels of moderation, such as where a person is represented as 'remarking' as opposed to prosodic descriptive verb such as 'yelling'. We can see this effect in the following two sentences

Minority community leaders <u>shouted</u> that they have suffered increased levels of abuse.

> Minority community leaders <u>remarked</u> that they have suffered increased levels of abuse.

In the second case, the leaders appear moderate, in control and official through the use of a neutral structuring verb of 'saying'. In the first sentence, however, the use of the prosodic descriptive verb 'shouted' makes them appear emotional and perhaps threatening.

In the following example we see a different kind of representation created through a different verb of saying related to levels of implicitly ascribed reliability:

> Minority community leaders <u>claimed</u> that they have suffered increased levels of abuse.

Here we can see the effect of 'claim', what Caldas Coulthard would describe as a 'metapropositional expressive'. Claims are not factual but can be contested and the use of this word invites doubt. The word 'felt' would have a similar meaning. In the following case we can see how the use of the word 'explain' changes the meaning to decrease uncertainty:

> Minority community leaders <u>explained</u> that they have suffered increased levels of abuse.

In this case, the minority leaders appear to be telling us facts rather that simply their opinions, although this is not overtly stated.

By turning our attention to some concrete examples of how verbs of saying are used in actual texts, we can develop our sense of how they have been used in different ways to influence the way a reader will interpret events and persons.

Case study 1: Quoting verbs and implicitly implied guilt

The first example is a report in the British newspaper *The Daily Mail* (29 January 2010) on the enquiry into the British government's decision to participate in the invasion of Iraq in 2003, where former British Prime Minister, and New Labour leader, Tony Blair is questioned. The *Daily Mail* is traditionally hostile to New Labour, so the attitude taken in the text is not surprising. However, what CDA helps us to show is exactly how texts communicate their ideologies in ways that are not necessarily overt. And in this case, as we shall see, quoting verbs play a big role in the evaluation of social actors and the reliability of what they say. The quoting verbs are underlined.

(Continued)

(Continued)

'You're a liar and murderer': Blair booed after telling Iraq inquiry he has no regrets

© AFP/Getty Images

Figure 6   Tony Blair defends himself (The *Daily Mail*, 29 January 2010)

No regrets: Tony Blair said Britain would ultimately be able to look back on the Iraq War with 'immense pride'

Tony Blair was <u>heckled</u> today as he <u>refused to express</u> any regret for the Iraq war and <u>insisted</u> Britain would ultimately be able to look back on the conflict with 'immense pride'. There were <u>cries</u> of consternation from witnesses watching the official inquiry into the conflict as the former prime minister <u>rejected</u> the chance to note his sorrow at the loss of British lives. Chairman Sir John Chilcot <u>had to tell</u> audience members to be quiet during Mr Blair's closing comments, in which he <u>insisted</u> he stood by his actions in the run-up to the 2003 war, despite the 179 British troops killed in the conflict. 'It was divisive and I'm sorry about that,' he <u>conceded but continued</u>: 'If I'm asked whether I believe we're safer, more secure with Saddam and his sons out of power, I believe that we are.' Asked if he had any regrets at all, he <u>replied</u>: 'Responsibility but not a regret,' prompting the audience to <u>erupt and cry</u>: 'What, no regrets? Come on'. When the cameras cut off and Mr Blair readied to leave, he was <u>booed</u> and one audience member <u>shouted</u> 'you're a liar' before another <u>chimed</u> in 'and a murderer'.

In this article, we find 13 cases of quoting verbs in this short text. These are: 'heckled', 'refused to express', 'insisted' (twice), 'cries', 'rejected', 'tell', 'commented', 'replied', 'erupt and cry', 'booed,' 'shouted' and 'chimed'. Only one of these, 'replied', is a neutral structuring verb. It is clear, therefore, that the writers of this piece are seeking to shape how we are to interpret this particular set of events and its participants, especially Tony Blair. In the text there are three participants: Tony Blair, the audience, and the Chair. We can create a table to show which verbs of saying are used to describe the comments of each:

Table 3 Quoting verbs for 'No regrets' article

Blair	Crowd	Chair
Refused to express	Heckled	Tell
Rejected	Cries	
Insisted	Erupt	
Conceded	Cry	
Continued	Booed	
Replied	Shouted	
	Chimed	

What we find is that Blair's comments are represented for the most part through metapropositional verbs such as 'refused to express', 'rejected', 'insisted' and 'conceded'. All these clearly mark the author's interpretation of the speaker, i.e. Tony Blair. In all these cases he is represented as a man who is being defensive. We can see this in the following sentence:

He <u>refused to express</u> any regret for the Iraq war and <u>insisted</u> Britain would ultimately be able to look back on the conflict with 'immense pride'.

We can draw out the way that these choices of quoting verb create meaning by showing the way different choices could have been made, as in:

He <u>explained</u> that he did not feel any regret for the Iraq war and <u>suggested</u> that Britain would ultimately be able to look back on the conflict with 'immense pride'.

In the text, the fact that he 'refused to express' suggests that he should, in the opinion of the writers, express regret. Where we have substituted the quoting verb 'explain' above, he sounds much more comfortable with what he is saying. It is common in news reporting to use 'refused to comment', or 'refused to express' as an indication of

(Continued)

(Continued)

avoidance and therefore something to hide or of plain guilt. Journalists can use this strategy to avoid having to overtly claim that there is guilt, which could place them in a difficult legal situation.

Where the text uses 'insisted', in the following sentence we are given an impression of lack of confidence, of a man who lacks credibility:

> Mr Blair's closing comments, in which he <u>insisted</u> he stood by his actions in the run-up to the 2003 war, despite the 179 British troops killed in the conflict.

We can draw out the way that this quoting verb works in the following sentences:

> The pool attendant instructed that we leave immediately.

> The pool attendant insisted that we leave immediately.

In the first sentence, the attendant is represented as simply delivering instructions. In the second, the insistence suggests that they might be ignored. It suggests a level of persistence that would not be required of someone who was confident of having authority and respect.

We can draw out this meaning a little more through a further example:

> The librarian explained that the student must return the book immediately.

> The librarian insisted that the student must return the book immediately.

In the first case, we can see that the librarian appears calm and authoritative. They are simply explaining the rules to the student. Therefore the authority of the librarian to make this demand is clear. In the second sentence, we can see that what the librarian is doing appears much less authoritative and less confident. Throughout this book we will be looking at many such subtle ways in which the power and authority of social actors, or the lack thereof, can be communicated implicitly through language and where power can be attributed where there in fact is none.

The use of the quoting verb 'conceded' is also important here, as we can see in the following sentence:

> 'It was divisive and I'm sorry about that', he <u>conceded</u>.

Again, the verb 'explained' could have also have been used. But we can see the importance of this choice in the following sentences:

> The student conceded he had lost the library books.

> The student explained he had lost the library books.

In the first sentence, it appears that the student was attempting at some point, or at least had the intention of so doing, to deny losing the books. In the second sentence, the student appears much more honest. From these examples we can see how participants can be represented as untrustworthy simply through an accumulation of quoting verbs that after all are purely the interpretation of the author. All utterances can be accurately reported, as can sequences of events, but nevertheless the ideological mark of the author can be simply worked into the story.

In contrast to the quoting verbs used for the utterances of Blair, we can see that the Chair's utterance is represented with a neutral structuring verb 'tell'. Of course such a term is not neutral in itself, as all choices used by an author are motivated, but its use implies an utterance without emotion, which here serves to present the Chair as neutral. It is often the case in such reports that the officials are represented through neutral structuring verbs. Police representatives simply 'tell' or 'say' or use metapropositional assertives such as 'explain' and 'announce'. In a text it is always important to identify who is represented as neutral.

A range of prosodic descriptive verbs are used to describe the audience's negative reaction towards Blair. 'Heckled', 'cries', 'chimed', 'shouted', 'erupt and cry' and 'booed' are used to emphasise the considerable size and collective anger of the audience. Their loudness is further emphasised by noting the chairman 'had to tell' them to be quiet.

Overall, this text is clearly intended to suggest that Blair's actions were not going to be accepted or forgiven by the British public. Interestingly, in the news media at the same time, there was little concrete information about what the war meant, why it was fought and what the consequences were. All of these issues, as they did at the time of the invasion, remained largely absent from public debate. This story clearly is an attempt to use these events as one way to attack the former Prime Minister, rather than to explain in concrete terms what went wrong.

Case study 2: Quoting verbs and lack of agency

In this example we find the British Prime Minister at the time, New Labour leader Gordon Brown, represented as having little power, where quoting verbs are one strategy by which this is accomplished. Again, this text is from the newspaper *The Daily Mail* (11 November 2009). This is an item dealing with an event where Gordon Brown (or one of his advisers) had written to the mother of a soldier who was killed in Afghanistan, but misspelled his name. At the time this text appeared, many people were becoming concerned about the very purpose of the conflict. No clear aims and objectives had ever been offered by the government. In the news media a theme of supporting our brave troops had emerged, which displaced any actual debate about the reasons for the war. This text therefore shows that news media are often so focused on political figures and political administration that they lose sight of actual events and contexts (Bennett, 2005).

(Continued)

(Continued)

Gordon Brown: Under siege over letter to soldier's family, he speaks of his own grief

Figure 7   Gordon Brown vulnerable (*The Daily Mail*, 11 November 2009)

Gordon Brown <u>spoke</u> of his personal grief at losing a child as he responded to criticism of his handwritten letter of condolence to a dead soldier's mother.

The Prime Minister <u>suggested</u> the awful experience of his daughter Jennifer Jane dying at just ten days old meant he understood the pain of bereavement.

He had already <u>apologized</u> to the distraught mother of Grenadier Guard Jamie Janes, 20, after she berated him for apparently misspelling her son's name and other words in his note of sympathy

Yesterday he <u>reiterated</u> his sorrow for her loss and said: 'The last thing on my mind was to cause any offence.'

A shaken-looking Mr Brown was forced to <u>defend</u> his treatment of the war dead – and again <u>try to explain</u> the purpose of the Afghan mission – during his monthly press conference.

He <u>revealed</u> he had asked for a full investigation into the circumstances of Guardsman Janes's death. An inquest has not yet been held.

At the beginning of the article Brown is represented as simply having 'spoken' of his own experience of losing a child, which through a neutral structuring verb represents this as simply a transparent account. Following this we find that:

The Prime Minister <u>suggested</u> the awful experience of his daughter Jennifer Jane dying at just ten days old meant he understood the pain of bereavement.

Here we find 'suggested', a metapropositional expressive, which appears here either as a lack of conviction, confidence or a lack of forcefulness. He does not simply 'say', or 'explain' that this allows him to understand, but 'suggests' this might be so. Here we can ask if the author of the text wished to represent Brown as weak and powerless, a man who was on the defensive rather than in control and decisive, or as a man who was tentatively 'suggesting', rather than 'knowing' in order to sound respectful. In the next line we are told:

Yesterday he <u>reiterated</u> his sorrow for her loss and said: 'The last thing on my mind was to cause any offence.'

Here we find a discourse signalling quoting verb suggesting that he is repeating what he has said before. Subtly this gives a sense of a man who is trapped in an ongoing situation where people are not convinced. We can tease this meaning potential out with the following examples:

He reiterated to his girlfriend that he had not in fact kissed her best friend at the party.

He explained to his girlfriend that he had not in fact kissed her best friend at the party.

In the first case, the boyfriend seems to be stuck in a situation where he is not believed and where he is constantly justifying his behaviour. In the second, we get a sense that this is more of a one-off situation and that he may be more in control. As regards the representation of Brown as stuck in a situation, this would be one important part of the way the opposition might want to represent him as bedevilled with scandals and having generally lost his authority to govern the country.

In the next sentence we find:

Mr Brown was forced to defend his treatment of the war dead – and again try to explain the purpose of the Afghan mission.

Here he does not simply 'explain' his treatment of the war dead but has to 'defend' himself. Then he is represented as 'trying to explain' rather than simply 'explaining. Here the neutral structuring verb is changed to a metapropositional expressive through the use of 'try'. So it is implied either that he is not capable of explaining or that it is unlikely that he has an explanation.

Finally, Brown 'reveals' that there will be an investigation. The verb 'reveal' here could have been replaced, arguably, with the verb 'announce'. Officials who are represented as having agency often 'announce', as we saw above in the examples regarding workers and managers. But here the fact that he 'reveals' this information suggests less agency. Those who reveal may have something to hide in the first place. We can see this clearly in the following two sentences:

William revealed that he had a new girlfriend.

William announced that he had a new girlfriend.

(Continued)

(Continued)

In the second case, we can see some of the meaning potential of 'revealed', that it suggests that there had been some time when the fact was not announced, that it may have been a secret.

An important feature overall of the quoting verbs found in this text is that Brown is not actually initiating any of his speech himself. Rather he is having to 'respond', 'reiterate' and 'defend' himself from criticism he is facing. This is a politician on the back foot, no longer leading confidently.

In summary, we can see that the *Daily Mail* newspaper uses this story not to inform readers about the war, but simply as an opportunity to shape the reader's perception of Brown the politician.

Case study 3: Quoting verbs and emotional intensity

In 2005, the Danish newspaper *Jyllands-Posten* published a number of cartoons that were critical of Islamic extremism and the challenge to free speech. Some of these satirised the prophet Mohammed. After Muslim clerics from Denmark travelled abroad and communicated about these, there was much anger among certain Muslims who felt that it was blasphemous to represent Mohammed in this way. The Western news media reported on the angry protests by these people, many burning Danish flags and demanding the newspaper should be closed down. At this time in the Western news media the representation of Muslims had become largely dominated by negative coverage with links to various kinds of extremism (Poole and Richardson, 2006).

The following text is one such report from the British newspaper *The Daily Telegraph* (7 February 2006). We can clearly see that quoting verbs are used as one important tool in the way the events are represented.

How clerics spread hatred over cartoons

David Rennie

As world leaders <u>pleaded</u> for calm in the Mohammed cartoon row yesterday, the Danish Muslim leaders who set the crisis in motion <u>insisted</u> that they had been trying to promote a "dialogue of civilizations".

They also <u>angrily denied</u> allegations from moderate Muslims and European intelligence services that hidden "masterminds" triggered the sudden explosion of protests, a full four months after 12 cartoons of the Prophet were first published in the Jyllands-Posten newspaper.

Ahmed Abu Laban is the most prominent of a group of Danish imams and activists who toured the Middle East late last year, seeking to "internationalize" their campaign of protest at the cartoons, after deciding their complaints were falling on deaf ears back home.

Speaking from his office at the Waqfs mosque in Copenhagen, Mr Abu Laban said that the sudden explosion of anger at the end of last month was due to the rapid success of a "grass-roots" consumer boycott against Danish dairy goods and other exports.

Mr Abu Laban, a 60-year-old imam of Palestinian origin, also credited the hard-line "Salafist" television stations based in Saudi Arabia and the United Arab Emirates, such as al-Majd and Iqra, with a "big influence" in fomenting the trade boycott. […]

He denied claims from European intelligence and security sources that the Muslim Brotherhood, an Islamist opposition group banned in Egypt and other Arab nations, had worked hard to whip up Muslim anger over the Danish cartoons.

At the start of the item we find that world leaders 'pleaded' for calm. They do not simply 'ask' for calm, which would have suggested something much more moderate than 'plead'. This provides a sense that the situation must be out of control. It also suggests that the leaders are not themselves in control. If we plead with people, then they have become almost unable to be reasoned with.

In the next line we find that they, the Muslim leaders, 'insisted that they had been trying to promote a "dialogue of civilizations"'. Here we find the use of 'insist', which appears to throw some doubt on what they say. We can see the difference if we replaced this with the quoting verb 'said'. 'Insist' also gives a sense of emotional involvement. This appears to be important in the way that the events are being framed.

This emotional temperature is continued in the next sentence, where we find that the Muslim leaders 'angrily denied allegations from moderate Muslims and European intelligence services'. This could have been written 'they have "rejected" allegations'. 'Denial' here, as we have seen in previous examples, again can hint at the possibility of guilt, and the use of 'angry' adds to the lack of measure in tone.

We then find the neutral structuring verb 'said' for the next section, which communicates a sense of a more official and neutral role as regards Ahmed Abu Laban. We are told at the same time that he speaks from his office. It is important for news media reporting that sources appear to be official and legitimate, even if at the same time they are being represented as corrupt or extreme.

In the next line we find the use of the verb 'credited' to characterise the way he spoke of the influence of the television stations. This suggests that he feels that this is something positive. The wording might have been that 'Mr Abu Laban, a 60-year-old imam of Palestinian origin, also blamed the hardline "Salafist" television stations based in Saudi Arabia and the United Arab Emirates'.

In sum, we can see how quoting verbs are used to communicate not simply how a person relates to events, but their very character and the nature of events. Here leaders have to 'plead' for calm where the Muslim cleric 'insists', 'angrily denies' and 'credits' other sources with fomenting anger.

Representing speakers' attitude through visual semiotic resources

In texts where we find participants being cited, as in the examples above, we often find images of these persons. Sometimes we see them as if they have been captured in a moment of speaking, as in the case of the text about Tony Blair and Gordon Brown. These images too are managed to present a particular interpretation of the attitude, character and identity of the person and consequently is another semiotic resource by which events and comments can be evaluated implicitly. We might find, for example, that a particular text speaks of charges made against a politician. As well as using quoting verbs that connote lack of agency we might find a photograph of them which shows them speaking in a way that suggests lack of composure, as we find in the case of Gordon Brown.

It is usual for newspapers to have access to a collection of stock images for prominent social actors, which they can use depending on whether they wish to present them as confident, defeated, sensitive, etc. The photograph that we find accompanying a story may therefore not have been captured in a moment related to that story. However, even if it is the case that it has been, there is still the matter of the choice of this particular photograph. In this section, we look at some of the ways we can assess these representations and how they also encourage us to implicitly evaluate participants, to attribute particular kinds of meanings to their utterances. We look at the meaning of gaze and of poses in the image. We show that gaze in a photograph, where a person looks, and how they look, can be one important way of encouraging particular kinds of interpretations and of relationships between viewer and participant. We show that we appear to have a kind of dictionary of poses in our head that can be drawn upon as reliable signifiers of kinds of attitudes, moods and identity.

Gaze

An important part of poses is the gaze of the person(s) depicted, whether or not they look out at the viewer, or whether they look downwards or upwards. All these can be resources for guiding the viewer as to how they should evaluate the participant, even if this is not explicitly stated. In this section, we present a set of observations that provide tools for analysing gaze and the way it can signify meanings more systematically.

Kress and van Leeuwen (1996) were interested in the way that images can be thought of as fulfilling the speech acts as described for language by Halliday (1985). When we speak, Halliday argued, we can do one of four basic things: offer information; offer services or goods; demand information; demand goods and services. In each case there is an expected or alternative response possible. Kress and van Leeuwen (1996) thought images could fulfil two of these: 'offer' and 'demand'. So images can be seen by viewers as referencing actual acts of interaction in talk.

Both speech acts and image acts can be realised by 'mood systems'. For example, in speech, commands can realise the imperative mood, as in 'Don't do it!' We can state facts and make offers through the indicative mood, as in 'You will like this cake?' And we can indicate our attitude through other cues, such as tone of voice and posture. In images we can find both demands and offers realised visually along with the form of address.

In the case of the *Cosmopolitan* image found in the Introduction to this book, we can see that the woman looks at us. This has two functions. On the one hand, this creates a form of visual address – the viewer is acknowledged. On the other hand, it is used to do something to the viewer. This is what Kress and van Leeuwen (1996: 124) describe as a 'demand image'. It asks something of the viewer in an imaginary relationship, so they feel that their presence is acknowledged and, just as when someone addresses us in social interaction, some kind of response is required. The kind of demand, the mood of the address, is then influenced by other factors. There might be a slight frown that is unwelcoming and maintains a social distance. There might be a pout, as in the case of the *Cosmopolitan* woman. We might find gaze accompanied with postures that are welcoming, such as open arms or some kind of activity being undertaken in which we appear welcome. In this particular example, we find the woman looking at the viewer, thus acknowledging their presence and demanding some kind of reaction. She shows no clear emotion, but through this acknowledgement there is a sense that this world of glamour is more accessible to the viewer.

In real life we know how we should respond when someone smiles at us. We should smile back or else risk offending the other person. In the case of images, while we know that there will not be the same kind of consequences if we don't respond appropriately, we still recognise the demand.

In the previous chapter we looked at the example of the Heart of England Health Trust website. Its homepage shows members of the Trust apparently in places of work. What they are depicted as doing and which roles are represented are crucial here, and will be explored in later chapters. What we want to note here is that three of the participants look out at the viewer. We are not simply asked to watch hospital activities, but are being invited into a relationship. In the last chapter we showed how, through language choices, the Trust represented itself and its aims through abstractions: 'Cherishing', 'Excellence' 'Finding a Way', 'Innovation for Advancement', 'Working Together'. We considered the way that this was part of the empty corporate business language that has come to dominate public institutions, thereby backgrounding actual concrete matters of facilities, staffing and treatment. We can see that gaze is one semiotic resource that can be used to communicate interest and engagement with public needs, even though at the same time these may be farthest from the concerns of the Trust.

Where a person does not look out at the viewer there is a different kind of effect. There is no demand made on the viewer. No response is expected. This is what Kress and van Leeuwen (1996: 124) call an 'offer image'. The viewer is offered the image as information available for scrutiny and consideration. Had the *Cosmopolitan* women not looked out at us, we would have been invited to simply observe what she does without any required response. This can be seen in the photograph accompanying the *Marie Claire* text on page 45. In the case of the *Cosmopolitan* image on page 8 it appears that this is a demand image that invites us to be like her, after all she is making the effort to acknowledge our existence.

Looking off frame also has meaning potential. When we see a person in an image looking off frame rather than at an object in the image, we are invited to imagine what they are thinking.

Figure 8   David Cameron (*The Daily Mirror*, 16 April 2010)

The metaphorical association of 'up' and 'down' is also important in the meaning potential of gaze. Metaphorical association has been shown to be central to visual communication (Arnheim, 1969). For example, we might make a small distance between our thumb and forefinger to represent how close we were to verbally berating someone. In fact no physical proximity was involved in how close we felt at all, as it was simply a feeling of emotion. But the representation, the comparison, allows us to visualise this interaction. In Western culture 'up' and 'down' have strong metaphorical associations. We say 'I am feeling down' or that 'things are looking up'. We can say that a person 'has their head in the clouds', or is 'down to earth'. We have upper and lower classes and people with higher status are often seated higher than those with lower status. In images we often find politicians, when represented positively, looking off frame and slightly upwards. In images in women's magazines, in contrast, we often find women looking slightly downwards, alongside captions like 'Can you trust your boyfriend?' In the *Marie Claire* image earlier in the chapter, we can see that the woman looks slightly upwards too as she feels 'up' about the possibility of using the 'hot tips' in the article.

Politicians might be represented looking upwards to lofty ideals and to high status or downwards when they are worried, as in the photograph of David Cameron. Where people in images look directly outwards, this can communicate a sense of dealing with issues straight on, as can be seen in the photograph of Nick Clegg on page 76. These photographs all appeared in the British Press on the same day after a televised leadership debate. The press, eager for a more lively election, presented Clegg as new, direct and unfussy and Cameron as troubled and unnerved by the popularity of this new threat.

In the analysis of quoting verbs earlier in the chapter we looked at three texts that carried images. We can apply our toolkit for analysing gaze to these images in order to look at the way that gaze encourages viewers to evaluate events implicitly.

In the first case study, we found that Tony Blair is represented as being defensive through metapropositional quoting verbs such as 'refused to express', 'rejected', 'insisted' and 'conceded'. 'Heckled', 'cries', 'chimed', 'shouted', 'erupt and cry' and 'booed' were the quoting verbs used to emphasise the considerable collective anger of the audience. We found that these verbs are one of the main devices through which his speech is implicitly evaluated. We are not told explicitly that Blair was on the back foot, or that the crowd was impatient and angry. This work was done by the quoting verbs. The photograph of Blair also plays an important part in this more implicit evaluation.

The photograph shows Blair in an offer image. The viewer is invited to watch not in a way that encourages a personal relationship, as in the *Cosmopolitan* image, or that of Nick Clegg, but as an observer. We see Blair in a moment of what appears to be irritation as he regards someone side-on, waving his finger. Had he been represented with the same posture looking at the viewer this would have meant the viewer would have been required to produce a response. But this is not the point of this text, which appears to be to encourage the reader to see Blair as remote, struggling and as a failure. Again it is notable that news readers here are not informed about the details of the war. They are not provided with facts upon which conclusions about Blair's activities and decisions can be put in context. Both in terms of language and visual, the reader is only encouraged to evaluate the personality of the politician. We could imagine the different effect of the text were we shown an image of bodies of civilians mutilated in the streets of villages of Iraq.

We find an even more extreme use of a close-shot in the photograph accompanying the text about Gordon Brown's misspelling of a soldier's name. Here we are encouraged to focus closely on his suffering. We find him looking off frame, slightly downwards. Again the viewer is invited to look at the participant as an observer rather than being invited into an interaction. We see Brown in a slumped position touching his own face, thoughtful, where the downwards gaze here appears to suggest negative thoughts. This image objectifies Brown as a man who is not fit to be appointed as Prime Minister again at the upcoming general elections. What we can see from both of these stories is that powerful evaluation of participants can be accomplished not only overtly or through sensationalist headlines, but much more subtly through their representation in images.

Poses

A photographer, who specialised in taking publicity shots of musicians for record companies, interviewed by one of the authors said that postures of the artists must suggest something about them, whether they are approachable, independent or moody, whether they are to be thought of as a unit or as individuals. She said she would photograph a boy band being playful and cheeky. This would mean they would be moving, perhaps jumping around in order to convey energy and fun, be touching each other in order for them to appear sensual and affectionate and have open postures to appear approachable, and would smile to suggest friendliness, look romantic or even 'snarl' a little to show a very mild sense of unconformity. In contrast, she would show an indie band as not giving out energy, so they would not jump around but have more closed or self-contained body shapes. They would be disengaged from the viewer, certainly not touching and she said she would find a way to distinguish the members to emphasise that they were individuals, often through making them strike slightly different and 'odd' postures. We can see that these simple decisions about poses can be connotators of identities and broader ideas. The boy band is available for the romantic fantasies of the younger fans. The indie band must appear darker, troubled and non-mainstream, even if they rely on a rather familiar set of connotations to communicate this.

According to Barthes (1973), poses are one important realm of connotation in images that are able to signify broader values, ideas and identities. Image makers therefore can rely on these established meanings to shape how we will perceive the ideas, values and behaviours of those persons depicted.

In the case of the *Cosmopolitan* image in the Introduction of this book, what kinds of discourse does her posture connote? What broader ideas and values are communicated by the way the woman is standing? She is leaning towards the computer keyboard as if about to press a key yet is clearly doing nothing of the kind. Of course this leaning posture will be one reason the page editor has chosen this image to illustrate an item on exercising. She also has one hand on her hip and her torso appears curved rather than rigid and straight. We can bring out the meaning potential of these if we consider a man striking the same pose. Placing hands on hips is one way we can communicate that we are squaring up to a person. If we place our legs slightly apart and our hands on our hips we take up physical space. We can imagine a much less confident and shy posture where we might take up little space. Yet when this posture is combined with curvature, something feminine is suggested. The model in this image is taking up space and appears confident, yet at the same time feminine. Of course pose should in all cases be considered in relation to other iconographical features, such as objects, setting and clothing.

So we can ask whether a pose involves taking up space or not and whether the pose is an open or closed one. We can also ask whether a pose suggests either activity or stillness. In this case, the pose of the *Cosmopolitan* woman suggests activity. Often in women's lifestyle magazines we find photographs of women who are jumping in the air or waving their arms about. While it appears that they are doing nothing in concrete, this helps to bring a sense of fun and energy to the magazine. Again, this is important in connoting discourses of female identity that take women outside the mother/housewife role.

We can also ask if a pose suggests relative bodily control and discipline or the opposite. We find soldiers standing in controlled postures whereas we might find a group of teenagers standing in slumped or loose poses. This physical control and discipline metaphorically represents conformity and obedience whereas the physical lack of deliberate control and regimentation of the body in the case of the teenagers represents the opposite.

Recently, one of the authors was driving down a road in a very poor neighbourhood. Four youths of around 14 years of age walked out into the road so that he had to slow right down. They walked lazily and slouched with arms hanging, connoting lack of interest and lack of discipline, when in fact this manoeuvre of hassling drivers had been experienced on several occasions by the author and clearly required some dedication and organisation. We can imagine the difference had the youths walked out into the road, but stiffly and upright. This would not have communicated the same meanings.

In the text above we find Tony Blair appearing to be quite rigid. In this case, the control suggests tension and seriousness. Of course the firm gaze is also an important part of pose in this case. Below, in contrast, we find Nick Clegg in relaxed pose. This image was carried in the press prior to the general election in 2010, when he was being depicted as posing a real threat to the other party leaders, which in fact, as it turned out, he was not. Photographs tended to show him in relaxed, loose poses.

In the text above we showed how quoting verbs represented Blair as defensive, threatened and disapproved of by the audience. The image shows him not being composed and commanding, but being aggressive and cross, waving his finger. We could imagine the same text, but with an image of Blair in the fashion of the Clegg image. Because of the pose and gaze we would have been encouraged to feel much more sympathy and warmth towards him.

In the image accompanying the *Marie Claire* work item in the last chapter, pose is also an important connotator of broader meanings. While the text communicates a cynical self-interest, using trendy language and confident directives along with technical business terms, the image appears much softer, creative and pleasant. Importantly, her pose shows her sitting looking very relaxed, gazing out of the window, not blankly, which would suggest boredom. She also has a positive, contemplative smile.

When we analyse what is connoted by pose, we can ask a number of basic questions:

- To what extent does the person take up space or not?
- Do they perform for the viewer or are they self-contained?
- Is there an emphasis on relaxation or intensity?
- Does the pose suggest openness or closedness?

Figure 9 Nick Clegg relaxed (*The Guardian*, 16 April 2010)

- If there is more than one person, to what extent do they mirror each other or strike different postures?
- To what extent are they depicted as being intimate, in close proximity, or is there some indication of distance?

Conclusion

In Chapter 2 we dealt with more general lexical and visual content analysis. In this chapter we began to ask more specific questions of texts. We saw how very specific semiotic choices, through quoting verbs, gaze and poses, can be used to implicitly communicate kinds of identities and in turn evaluate the actions of participants. As we will continue to do throughout this book, we saw the value of systematically showing what kinds of semiotic choices character-ise representation of different participants. What is important is that these choices, which may not necessarily be attended to consciously by casual view-ers, are able to communicate broader discourses, values, ideas and sequences of activity that are not openly stated. It is these, the meanings that remain either implicit or only connoted in a text, that we must always observe to detect and make explicit. We must explain why a particular politician or other social actor is represented with particular quoting verbs, gaze and pose.

4

Representing People: Language and Identity

This chapter deals with the naming and visual representation of persons. As with any other kinds of use of linguistic or visual semiotic resources, the communicator has a range of choices available to them for deciding how they wish to represent individuals and groups of people who in CDA are often termed as 'social actors' or 'participants'. In CDA this realm of semiotic choices are referred to as 'representational strategies' (Fowler, 1991; Van Dijk, 1993; Fairclough, 2003: 145). These choices allow us to place people in the social world and to highlight certain aspects of identity we wish to draw attention to or omit. Like lexical and iconographical choices in general, they can have the effect of connoting sets of ideas, values and sequences of activity that are not necessarily overtly articulated. In this chapter we begin with linguistic resources for representing persons and then move on to visual communication.

Representational strategies in language

In any language there exists no neutral way to represent a person. And all choices will serve to draw attention to certain aspects of identity that will be associated with certain kinds of discourses. For example, consider the following sentence:

Muslim man arrested for fraudulently claiming benefits.

In fact there are many other possibilities that could have been used to characterise the man: an Asian man, a British man, a Midlands man, a local office worker, a Manchester United supporter, a father of two young daughters, a man named Mazar Hussein. Each of these can serve psychological, social and political purposes for the writer and reader (Reisigl and Wodak, 2001: 47). This is shown in the following sentence:

Father of two daughters arrested for fraudulently claiming benefits.

In this second case the meaning is different. In the first example the headline locates the story in a news frame emphasising his 'otherness', hence the man is part of something that is problematic. From 2005 in Britain, after bombings on the London transport system, Muslims often became represented through news frames that emphasised their threat to British society and resistance to cultural values (Richardson, 2007). Since the man was born in Britain, the headline could equally have stated that he was a British man. But this would have appeared odd and would have suggested 'one of us'. Crime reporting usually involves creating moral 'others', so that the perpetrator is not like 'us' (Wykes, 2001; Mayr and Machin, 2012). The second headline, which human-ises the man by referring to him as a 'father', has the opposite effect. Here he is 'one of us'. One possible effect on the reader may be that the fraud in this case was understandable, as the man was struggling to look after his children.

Van Dijk (1993) has shown that how the news aligns us alongside or against people can be thought of as what he calls 'ideological squaring'. He shows how texts often use referential choices to create opposites, to make events and issues appear simplified in order to control their meaning. Representational choices will always bring associations of values, ideas and activities, such as whether we describe a group of 18 year-olds as 'young people', 'youths', or 'students'. We can see this in the following sentences:

The students hung around outside the shop.

The youths hung around outside the shop.

An author might use the second of these to hint at anti-social behaviour or at disrespect. Teo (2000) carried out an analysis of the representation of drug dealers in sectors of the Australian press. He found evidence of overlexicalisa-tion of words emphasising that the protagonists were young:

'looks and sounds like is he is about 13', 'The 16 year old', 'five other youths', 'two young Asian gang members', 'some as young as 12', 'these kids', 'their leader at 13', 'had beaten two murder charges by 17', 'at least two of the accomplices were of the same age (i.e. 13 and 14)' (Teo, 2000: 21)

On the one hand, Teo suggests that such facts about age would be expected if this is part of the facts of the story. But on the other hand, why do we find this excessive use of terms related to youth? Of course emphasising youth in this way can be seen as one way to create sympathy for them. Youth, and specifically childhood, is often used in the press as a synonym for innocence and vulnerability. Teo, however, rejects that 'youth' is used as a mitigating fac-tor; rather it serves to add to the moral panic about drugs. 'The kids are out of control.' 'What is society coming to?' 'We need greater discipline, law and order in this society.' All these are common news themes that in fact serve to distract from actual concrete social processes and issues to do with drugs and drug dealing.

In the kind of news texts analysed by Teo, the participants are often evaluated not on the basis of what they do but through representational strategies. In this case, the young people may have been from deprived areas with many social problems. But the author/paper chooses to silence these aspects of who they are to foreground their youth, thereby signifying a specific discourse which suggests a threat to the moral order.

Van Dijk (1993) provides the example of different referential strategies in the reporting of sexual assaults in the press. Where a man is considered guilty, he will be referred to as a 'sex fiend', 'monster' or 'pervert'. In this case, he will *attack* innocent women who will be referred to as 'mother', 'daughter' or 'worker'. However, where the man is considered innocent, the referential strategy will be different. In this case, the woman will be referred to as a 'divorcee' or through physical features such as 'blonde' or 'busty'. In this case, she will have *provoked* an innocent man, referred to as 'hubby', 'father of four' or 'worker'. In this way, the referential strategy becomes part of the way we perceive people and their actions. A number of writers (e.g. Clark, 1992; Zeynep, 2007) have shown how such referential strategies in newspapers reveal some important ideological means through which women are represented in the press, demonstrating they are not considered as individuals but are judged against a Madonna–whore set of standards relating to appearances, motherhood and family. Crucially, these labels help to implicitly define the nature of the crime, victimhood, guilt and consequences for the reader.

Classification of social actors

To help us to be more systematic when describing referential choices, Van Leeuwen (1996) offers a comprehensive inventory of the ways that we can classify people and the ideological effects that these classifications may have. Later we will apply these to a series of examples in actual texts. But first we explain the kinds of observations they allow us to make.

Personalisation and impersonalisation

We can ask to what extent the participant is personalised or impersonalised. This can be observed in the following two sentences:

> Professor John Smith requires academic staff to give notification of strike action.

> The university requires academic staff to give notification of strike action.

In the second case, impersonalisation is used to give extra weight to a particular statement. It is not just a particular person but a whole institution that requires something. This conceals certain issues. We could argue that the staff, along with the students, *are* the university, so how could it be that the university can tell them what to do? But here this has been phrased in a way that giving notification may be in the interests of the university as a whole. We often come across the same process when politicians say 'Our nation believes...' or 'Britain will not be held responsible...'. This serves to conceal who actually believes what and who is responsible in each case. In the EMDA example in Chapter 2 (see p. 33) on lexis analysis, we read of 'the goals of the Regional Economic Strategy'. These goals, however, have their origins in a particular political organisation. The Strategy is not the holder of the goals, but is itself a set of goals established by particular interests.

Individualisation versus collectivisation

It is also useful to consider how participants are described as individuals or as part of a collectivity, as is shown in the following sentences:

> Two soldiers, privates John Smith, and Jim Jones, were killed today by a car bomb.

> Militants were killed today by a car bomb.

In the first case, by being named, these soldiers are individualised, bringing us closer to them. In the second case, the militants are simply a generic group. In the following example we can see how additional referential information individualises the participants in the first sentence even further:

> Two soldiers, privates John Smith, and Jim Jones, both fathers of two daughters, were killed today by a car bomb.

This information allows us to feel empathy with the soldiers. We can see the confusing effect of this in the following sentence, as we are not normally given personal details of participants classified as terror suspects because these details would humanise them:

> Terror suspects, both fathers of two daughters, were killed today by a car bomb.

It is useful to ask which kinds of participants are individualised and which are collectivised in texts, as we reveal which group is humanised.

Specification and genericisation

We can also look at whether participants are represented as specific individuals or as a generic type. In our earlier example, we saw that the person accused of benefits fraud could be either named or identified as a type. Consider the following two sentences:

A man, Mazar Hussein, challenged police today.

A Muslim man challenged police today.

In the second case, the man who challenged the police is represented as a type. The generic category 'Muslim' can place this story into a news frame where Muslims are a contemporary problem in Britain, either because of their extremism or their cultural and religious 'otherness'. However, this man may not even have been a practising Muslim. It could be like saying 'Christian John Smith challenged police today'. The use of such generic terms that can be used to give a newspaper story a 'racialised' slant, even though the newspaper itself may distance itself from a racist stance.

Nomination or functionalisation

Participants can be nominated in terms of who they are or functionalised by being depicted in terms of what they do. For example:

George Bush said that democracy would win.

The American president said that democracy would win.

This can have different effects. Use of functionalisation can sound more official, whereas nomination can sound more personal. Functionalisation can also reduce people to a role which may in fact be assigned by the writer or be generic, for example:

The demonstrator was injured outside the embassy.

The defendant was warned by Judge Peter Smithely-Smigely to be quiet.

In these cases the 'demonstrator' and 'the defendant' are partially dehumanised by referring to them with functionalisation, which highlights only their roles. Had both of these been named and been further personalised by referring to them, for example, as 'mothers', we would have evaluated them differently.

Functionalisation can also connote legitimacy. Machin and Mayr (2007), in their analysis of representations of multiculturalism in a British regional newspaper, showed that functionalisations, in the form of people's occupation, such as 'shop owner' and 'office workers', served to positively evaluate people as legitimate and 'decent' members of a local community. Those who were not so legitimate were represented in generic terms such as 'one local'.

Of course functionalisation can itself be an attempt to define what someone actually does. In a *Daily Mail* anti-immigration story, we find the following line:

> A teenage scribbler in a liberal Sunday newspaper, who normally seems to write reasonable sense, virtually accused me of being a neo-Nazi.

The author of the text does not name the journalist who has criticised him, but uses the pejorative functionalisation 'teenage scribbler'. The author also uses a technique pointed out by Van Dijk (1991) for the denial of racism, where he first states that he normally has no problem with this person, but in this case he does, pointing out that he is not normally biased. Denial of racism is often worded along the following lines:

> I normally I have no problems with ethnic minorities but in this case...

It is also worth pointing out that 'but' works as a presuppositional trigger (Levinson, 1983).

Use of honorifics

The way people are represented through what they do can also be achieved through the use of 'functional honorifics'. These are terms that suggest a degree of seniority or a role that requires a degree of respect. These will normally involve official roles, such as 'President', 'Lord', or 'Judge'. In short, these signal the importance of a social actor or specialisation. We might find that different ideological accounts of the same set of events will see honorifics ascribed or withheld. In the following two sentences, the level of importance of the statement changes.

> A government spokesperson said yesterday that there was no official involvement in the affair.

> The Minister of Foreign Affairs said yesterday that there was no official involvement in the affair.

In the second case, the use of the functional honorific makes the speaker appear more important and authoritative. A person's level of authority can be strategically diminished by removing honorifics and making them sound more generic, as is the case in the first sentence.

Objectivation

Here participants are represented through a feature:

'A ball of fun' for a baby

'A beauty' for a woman

This means that participants can be reduced to this feature. A tabloid news-paper might refer to a woman throughout an article as 'the Beauty' rather than naming or functionalising her. In this case, we might argue that she is reduced to her physical appearance and her 'womanness' becomes the key part of who she is. This can be found often in ideological squaring, where a female participant, whether she is involved in a legal or personal matter, is represented only through being a woman. In such cases we can ask what is backgrounded by this process. Van Dijk (1995) shows how this means that certain moral issues can be connoted by what is reasonable behaviour for a woman rather than for a man. For example, in crime reporting involving the abuse or neglect of children, journalists often attribute more horror where a woman is involved. A famous case in point is Myra Hindley, who was vilified by the press and public far more than her partner, Ian Brady, for the crimes they committed against children, despite the fact that Brady was the domi-nant force behind the crimes they committed together.

Anonymisation

Participants in texts can often be anonymised.

A source said today that the government would be focusing on environ-mental issues.

Some people believe that globalisation is a bad thing.

In the first case, it is common to see anonymised participants ('a source') in newspapers. On the one hand, we rely on journalists to have legitimate sources, but this conceals the way that certain social groups and organisa-tions may not have equal access to journalists. In the second example, we can see how politicians, in this case former British Prime Minister Tony Blair, can use such representations ('some people') to avoid specification and develop-ing a detailed and coherent argument. They allow us to conveniently summon arguments that are then easy to dismiss.

Aggregation

Aggregation means that participants are quantified and treated as 'statistics':

Many thousands of immigrants are arriving in...

Scores of Muslim inmates at a high security prison are set to launch a multi-million pound claim for compensation after they were offered ham sandwiches during the holy month of Ramadan. (*The Daily Mail*, 26 October 2007)

Van Dijk (1991) shows that this kind of statistics can be utilised to give the impression of objective research and scientific credibility, when in fact we are not given specific figures. Is 'many thousands' 3,000 or 100,000, for example? And what are 'scores'? In the news agency feed received by the IRN discussed in Chapter 2, we find the following line:

One of the few suspects to express remorse over his alleged involvement in last year's bombings on Indonesia's Bali island arrived at court on Thursday.

In this case, how many is 'the few'? Exactly how many have shown remorse and how many have not? What is the reason for not being informed? What becomes apparent from this particular text is the depoliticisation of the suspects' acts. We are not informed about the political aims of those who planted the bombs. They become generic terrorists and part of the news frame of the 'war on terror'. What kind of remorse they expressed is not clear either. Does this mean they now no longer believe in their political aims? So in cases of aggregation, where actual numbers are replaced by such abstractions, we can always ask what ideological work is being done.

Pronoun versus noun: the 'us' and 'them' division

Pronouns like 'us', 'we' and 'them' are used to align us alongside or against particular ideas. Text producers can evoke their own ideas as being our ideas and create a collective 'other' that is in opposition to these shared ideas (Oktar, 2001; Eriksson and Aronsson, 2005).

We live in a democracy of which we are proud.

They shall not be allowed to threaten our democracies and freedom.

We have to decide to be strong and fight this global terrorism to the end.

Fairclough (2000: 152) has pointed out that the concept of 'we' is slippery. This fact can be used by text producers and politicians to make vague statements and conceal power relations. 'We' can mean 'the political party', whereas in the next sentence it can mean 'the people of Britain', and further down an unspecified group of nations. In the first example above, does 'we' mean the people or a collection of superpowers?

We can see this vague use of 'we' in the *Daily Mail* anti-immigration story above. In this case, it is used to evoke a shared British culture although the exact composition of this 'we' is not overtly explained in the text. This can be illustrated as follows:

Britain has an indigenous culture.

We must fight the deluge of immigrants.

These two sentences imply what is said in the following without actually saying it:

We of the indigenous British culture must fight the deluge of immigrants.

Put in this way, the racist discourse becomes much more overt, whereas splitting the information into two sentences helps the writer to conceal this.

Suppression

What is missing from a text is just as important as what is in a text (Fairclough, 2003). Consider the following examples:

Globalisation is now affecting all national economies.

Market-based economies are establishing themselves in all areas of life.

In both these sentences the agent is missing. Globalisation is not something that has the power to change things, but is a theory which attempts to describe a perceived process or phenomenon that is caused by particular agents. It is driven by large corporations and world economic organisations such as the World Trade Organisation and World Bank. In the second sentence, market-based economies are not agents themselves but are a result of a particular political ideology. They have become established through specific political decisions and waves of privatisation that have followed. The result of these two sentences is that both globalisation and market-based economies appear natural and inevitable, something that must be responded to and adapted to rather than something that should be questioned.

Case study 1: Aggregation and suppression

The first case study is a text from *The Daily Mail* (26 October 2007).

Muslim prisoners sue for millions after they were offered ham sandwiches for Ramadan

(Continued)

(Continued)

Scores of Muslim inmates at a high security prison are set to launch a multi-million pound claim for compensation after they were offered ham sandwiches during the holy month of Ramadan.

They say their human rights were breached when they were given a special nightly menu – drawn up to recognise their specific dietary requirements – by officers at HMP Leeds last month.

More than 200 Muslim inmates at the jail are believed to have been offered the meat which is strictly forbidden by Islam.

The sandwich was one of three options on the menu card which was created to cover the religious festival during which Muslims are required to fast during daylight.

They later complained to prison officers on duty but say they were told that the menus had been printed in error.

Yet when they opened the sandwiches, having ordered cheese, some claim they were still filled with boiled ham.

They are now launching legal action, insisting that their human rights were breached and could each be entitled to up to £10,000 in compensation if they win their case at court.

One Muslim inmate, a 28-year-old who was serving a 16-week sentence for driving whilst disqualified, said: 'When I opened my meal that night I found I'd been given a ham sandwich. I'd asked for cheese.

'It was a breach of my human rights and I want compensation.'

He claimed that some inmates were so hungry they ended up eating the sandwiches.

The prison denied that any Muslim prisoners had been given ham sandwiches but admitted there had been a mistake when the menus were printed.

A spokesman for the Ministry of Justice said: 'An inappropriate menu card was printed during Ramadan. This mistake was rectified immediately.

'Appropriate menu options for the Iftaar evening meal were available throughout Ramadan.

'Prison Service guidelines state that prisoners must have a diet which meets the requirements of their religion.'

It comes as 16 Muslim inmates at Leeds Prison prepare to launch a separate legal case over claims of mistreatment, including being given food that is forbidden by their religion.

They are expected to claim at a hearing next year that they were given meat which was not halal.

Kate Maynard, from law firm Hickman and Rose Solicitors who is representing some of the men, said: 'One of the issues they are worried about is that they were being told food was halal when it wasn't.

'They are taking this to court to try to change conditions in the prison and make conditions better.'

Last year the Prison Service was forced to apologise to Muslim inmates at a category B jail after a kitchen worker was caught throwing ham into halal curries.

Prisoners at HMP Blakenhurst in Worcestershire each received a written apology.

The inmate behind the attack at the prison, which houses 1,070 offenders, was observed throwing tinned ham into curries destined for Muslim inmates and suspended from his job in the kitchen.

This text fuses two well-trodden news frames that are typical of this newspaper. One of these discourses is that prison inmates are treated far too well and that life inside a prison is like a holiday camp. Those who have visited prisons, as both authors have, will know about the depressing and soul-draining effect they can have on inmates. The other discourse is one which holds that foreigners who come to Britain are unwilling to adapt to its culture and values. In this discourse, the British themselves are represented as the victims. These discourses can both be seen in the following lines from the text:

One Muslim inmate, a 28-year-old who was serving a 16-week sentence for driving whilst disqualified, said: 'When I opened my meal that night I found I'd been given a ham sandwich. I'd asked for cheese.

'It was a breach of my human rights and I want compensation.'

Here we can see the implied outrage that such a person should dare to demand that British society should bend to their whims. But what we are interested in specifically in this chapter is the way that representational strategies, the way that some aspects of identity are foregrounded and others backgrounded, form an important part of the way the social world is mapped out for us. Other features of this text, which we will come back to in later chapters, are also very important.

In this text there are four categories of participants: those who are complaining about the prison food, other prison inmates, those who are part of the prison service and a lawyer. The first category is represented always through the word 'Muslim'. This term is overlexicalised in this text, being used nine times. Every time a prisoner is mentioned, whether collectivsed as 'Muslim prisoners' or 'Muslim inmates', or as

(Continued)

(Continued)

individuals, as in 'One Muslim inmate', the generic category 'Muslim' is used. In some of these cases, other representational choices could have been used, such as simply 'prisoner', 'inmate' or 'men'. To be fair, the Muslim prisoners are referred to as 'men' once: 'Kate Maynard, from law firm Hickman and Rose Solicitors who is representing some of the men, said...' On one occasion the nominal group is expanded to individualise a prisoner: in the case of 'a 28-year-old who was serving a 16-week sentence for driving whilst disqualified'. However, these details about his sentence might be said to further delegitimise his call to 'human rights'. Wherever there is such overlexicalisation we can assume that for some reason there is some kind of over-persuasion taking place which is normally evidence that something is problematic or of ideological contention.

Other prisoners are represented as 'an inmate', 'kitchen worker', 'the men'. Unlike the Muslim men, these prisoners are not represented in terms of their religion or through longer nominal groups describing their age and the offence for which they were imprisoned. They remain remote and impersonal. In another story about prisons a different set of representational strategies might have been used to position these men as 'others' in our society, such as 'offenders', 'monsters' or 'thugs'. In this case, it is clear that these participants are backgrounded and anonymised.

The people who work for the prison service are represented as 'officers', 'the prison', 'a spokesman for the Ministry of Justice'. Notable here is the use of functionalisation and honorifics. The prison system here is represented as anonymous and official. There is no personalisation of the prison itself by naming its officers.

We could imagine how the story could have been written differently, for example by personalising the Muslim prisoners much more. There is clearly nothing in this story to indicate that it might be the oppressive and unjust nature of the prison itself that might foster or instigate this situation. In fact, sociological and criminological research has revealed that prisons tend to be populated by the most vulnerable members of our society, the poor and ethnic groups who already find themselves at the hard end of the distribution of resources and opportunities (e.g. Scraton, 1997). Yet in this story the choice of representational strategies, along with other features we will mention later, serves to position the Muslim prisoners as 'other' in our society, while this is not the case for the other prisoners, who are simply 'inmates' and 'men' rather than 'offenders', 'lags' or 'hardened criminals', as they are often referred to in popular newspapers articles about prisons. The story could have been written as evidence of the way that all kinds of people in prison are treated poorly and their religious and cultural beliefs disrespected, or of financial cuts to the prison service which leave little room for such sensitivities. This could have been connected to the implications for retraining and rehabilitating the men in prison, the lack of which have been proven to result in much higher chances of reoffending.

What is most notable in this text, however, in terms of representational strategies, is the use of aggregation in 'more than 200 Muslim inmates', 'scores of Muslim inmates'. These vague aggregations are then followed by the sentences:

They later complained to prison officers on duty but say they were told that the menus had been printed in error.

Yet when they opened the sandwiches, having ordered cheese, some claim they were still filled with boiled ham.

They are now launching legal action, insisting that their human rights were breached and could each be entitled to up to £10,000 in compensation if they win their case at court.

Here we find the representational term of 'they' used where we have not yet been given a specific number. Are the 'scores' of Muslim inmates complaining and launching legal action, or a proportion of these? The text uses this ambiguity to create a sense of outrage and indicates a wider Muslim problem. Only towards the end of the article are we told that 'It comes as 16 Muslim inmates at Leeds Prison prepare to launch a separate legal case over claims of mistreatment, including being given food that is forbidden by their religion'. And even here the complaint appears to include those who have issues with other kinds of mistreatment.

In the text it is only the lawyer representing the inmates who is nominated. Her name sounds un-Muslim and her comments are presented in a way to make them appear much more measured than some of those she represents. Also, here it is the non-Muslim participant who therefore appears as reasonable and legitimate and as having agency.

The quoting verbs, which were dealt with in full in the previous chapter, are also important in this text. These are the verbs used to represent how someone expresses something. Here we can list some of those attributed to the prisoners.

Muslim prisoners complained to prison officers

Some claim they were still filled with boiled ham

Insisting that their human rights were breached

Where the prison officers speak we find:

Prison officers […] told that the menus had been printed in error

The quoting verbs chosen for the Muslim prisoners here are metapropositional expressives. In other words, they are often not simply 'saying' or 'reporting' that they had inappropriate food, but are rather forceful. Also the use of 'claim' lessens the

(Continued)

(Continued)

certainty of their argument. We can see the difference if we substitute the quoting verbs as in the following sentences.

Muslim prisoners <u>reported</u> to prison officers

Some <u>explained</u> they were still filled with boiled ham

<u>suggesting</u> that their human rights were breached

In the examples above the prisoners sound much more moderate and this reads as if it is a simple narrative of the events as opposed to the 'rantings' of prisoners who are, after all, offenders and therefore may find their claim to human rights somehow reduced.

We will be looking at more details in this text in subsequent chapters. Also important, for example, are the words that describe what people do as well as what they are. These too help to evaluate events implicitly.

Case study 2: Different discourse genres of participants

The following analysis of representational strategies is from the careers advice section of the women's lifestyle magazine *Marie Claire* (2010) that was analysed for simple lexical choices in Chapter 2. In this case we can think specifically about the work done through some of the participants being drawn from fictional domains. The text deals with the subject of how to maintain career opportunities in times of economic downturn when your company is making your colleagues redundant.

Ideologically, this text is very powerful, as it recommends not that employees should support each other or operate through trade unions in times of redundancies, but that the individual should work strategically to take advantage of the situation for their own gain. What we show here is that the fictional references help to soften this effect.

In this text, the social actors are: 'boss', 'manager', 'management', 'supervisor', 'Calandra', 'office hotshot', 'I', 'you', 'her', 'we', 'Pollyanna', 'cheerleader', 'co-workers', 'colleague', 'Tracy Flick', 'cubemate'. We can arrange these into four categories. The first are more formal work terms, the second more trendy language, the third fictional characters and, lastly, personal pronouns. Placing categories of social actors in a table can help to visualise them.

On the one hand, we have a set of participants that we might expect when dealing with the work environment as in 'boss', 'management', supervisor' and 'colleague', although markedly absent here is any reference to trade unions. In this text the

Table 4 Representational strategies in *Marie Claire* text

Boss	Office hotshot	Calandra	I
Manager	Cheerleader	Pollyanna	You
Management	Cubemate	Tracy Flick	Her
Supervisor			We
Co-workers			
Colleague			

woman who is addressed acts alone and strategically. She is not concerned about the possibility of further redundancies or how she and her colleagues might work together to prevent further job losses.

These work-type representational strategies place the events into a formal work environment, although we should note that there are no more specific functionalisations. We are not told what particular job is performed by these people, only that they are generic 'supervisors' etc. In Chapter 2 we considered the way that these lifestyle magazine articles do not document real workplaces and people, but symbolise them. The images we looked at showed glamorous women standing among a few props that connoted work. This was important to place the advice given not in real circumstances but almost as playful fantasies which nonetheless play an important role in signifying discourses where women are in control and have agency. This lack of specificity in details of work type and roles serves the same function. Van Leeuwen and Wodak (1999) suggest that wherever actual details are replaced by abstractions we can assume that some kind of ideological work is taking place. What is important to stress here is that just because these texts appear to be trivial and playful we must not underestimate their ideological power.

Other representational choices in this text help to lighten the topic. If representational strategies had relied only on formal work terms this may have made the text too dark. But this is changed, on the one hand, through the use of trendy language as in 'office hotshot', 'cubemate' and 'cheerleader'. We noted in our lexical analysis of this text in Chapter 2 that this trendy language, this use of the latest expressions, plays an important part in indicating that this is an up-to-date way of seeing the world. This is a crucial part of lifestyle discourse which is harnessed to the 'latest-thing' discourse of consumerism. So while this text, on the one hand, refers to actual functional categories, we also find further abstractions in the form of trendy language.

Central to the choices of representational strategies in this text are the fictionalised actors. 'Tracy Flick' is a fictional character portrayed by actress Reese Witherspoon in a comedy movie called *Election*. In this movie, Flick is largely unpopular as she is ambitious and self-focused but likeable, and is played by a very attractive Hollywood actress. Pollyanna is a girl from children's fiction who is 'naughty' and assertive but

(Continued)

(Continued)

in an endearing way. By drawing on these fictional characters the analysis offered by *Marie Claire* does not refer to real concrete issues of industrial dispute but is able to draw on connotations of assertiveness, likeability and individuality.

We can imagine the effect of this kind of representational strategy if it were used in an actual case of an industrial dispute. It would appear as bizarre if a news story of a strike at a manufacturing plant referred to workers as 'Pollyannas'. Yet in the world created by lifestyle magazines real-world terms and fiction blend seamlessly. The fictional references lighten the tone of the piece away from the ideological basis that we should all act only as individuals. In a time when the jobs of your colleagues are threatened, you consider this only in the light of how it might influence the way you negotiate your own career improvement. But what does it mean when, in the representation of industrial change, fiction and reality are ambiguously juxtaposed?

Finally, what is important in terms of representational choices in this text is the use of 'I' and 'you'. The use of personal pronouns is common in advertising and also in conversational language (Machin and van Leeuwen, 2007). This text claims to be neither but is drawing on both kinds of language. In advertising, these pronouns help to personalise products and producers and their relationship with the consumer. For example, an advertisement for mortgages might read: 'We agree with your wife. You can afford a new house.' The conversational style of speaking to 'you' also prevents this from reading as authoritative knowledge, but rather as the language of an expert who speaks closer to the level of the addressee. This language therefore aims to be trusted not on the basis of proscribed status, as is the case in the professions, but in terms of its claim to personal experience, which is communicated partly through being on your level through the use of personal pronouns and partly through the up-to-date language.

What is also interesting about the representational strategies found in these lifestyle texts is that while they generally contain personal address through the personal pronoun 'you', at the same time personal characteristics are suppressed. The text creates a world of generic types, the 'Tracy Flick', the 'Pollyanna', the 'office gossip', the generic 'boss'. Yet in reality how we experience our work lives depends on who we are, our dispositions, our appearance, our qualifications and also those of our boss. In these texts, as we often find in advertising, the world is reduced to a simple problem–solution formula. None of this envisages personal issues. In the problems and solutions offered, all persons can use them and they are universally applicable. Everything is displaced to a set of strategies.

Case study 3: Suppression of social actors

From a representational point of view, Fairclough (2003: 136) suggests that we can look at what elements of events are included in a text and what elements are excluded. Here we turn our attention to a text analysed by Kress (1985), where this process is particularly important. A revisit of this text at this moment is timely, given the way that established discourses on such topics have now changed.

Tropical savanna pastoral region

The environmental conditions of this region mean that it is poorly suited to most forms of agriculture. It receives most of its rainfall during the summer monsoons, and then experiences a winter drought. Furthermore, the natural savanna wood-lands vegetation and grasslands have few nutrients for intensive grazing, the soils are poor, the region is a long distance from markets, and transport facilities are poorly developed. Thus, the land is used for little else except extensive beef cattle grazing on farms which sometimes exceed 15,000 square kilometres in size. The large size of the farms is needed because of the land's poor carrying capacity, which may mean one beast needs 20 to 30 hectares to survive. Attempts were made to establish irrigation agriculture around the Ord River in the 1960s, but saline soils, high costs of long distance transport to markets, and the costs of dam and irriga-tion canal construction led to the virtual failure of the scheme in the early 1970s. It was intended to produce cotton, sugar cane and rice in the Ord River Scheme. Another land use, mining, is now of greater value than beef grazing. Important minerals include uranium (Rum Jungle, Ranger, Nabarlek), bauxite (Weipa, Michell Plateau), iron ore (Yampi Sound, Fraces Creek), managanese (Groote Eylandt), copper, lead, silver, zinc (all at Mount Isa) and gold (Tennant Creek). The largest towns in the region are Darwin and Mount Isa, each with just over 35,000 people.

(S.B. & D.M. Codrington (1982) *World of Contrasts: Case Studies in World Development for Secondary Geography*. Sydney: William Brooks, p. 193)

This text, intended for school children, contains some unspoken assumptions. The exploitation of land for resources and profit is taken for granted. Landscapes are to be assessed in terms of how much they can be used for a specific range of activities and not on their own terms; hence there are expressions such as 'poorly suited', 'soils are poor', 'long distance from market', 'land's poor carrying capacity'. This landscape could have been assessed by its own merit. Consider a statement such as 'the Amazon rainforest is poor for cattle grazing'. This is to see it only in terms of how it can be exploited for profit and not for its natural beauty. Capitalist motives, the importance of profit are not, however, expressed overtly.

This excerpt from a textbook for children published in the early 1980s clearly indicates a time before concerns about the environment and global warming became more widespread and more acceptable in Geography curricula.

We can investigate the language processes through which this takes place further by looking specifically at the participants. In fact, what is notable about this text is the suppression of social actors. All we find mentioned are '35,000 people'. Repeatedly, we find sentences that lack agents. For example:

(Continued)

(Continued)

Attempts were made to establish irrigation agriculture around the Ord River in the 1960s.

The land is used for little except extensive beef cattle grazing.

The large size of the farms is needed because of the land's poor carrying capacity.

It was intended to produce cotton, sugar cane and rice in the Ord River Scheme.

In the first sentence, who made the attempts to establish irrigation? In the second sentence, who is the land used by? In the third, who needs the farms to be large? In the fourth, who was intending to produce cotton? Why are the children not told who is behind these actions?

Where there is such a deletion of agents we must ask why this is the case. It appears that while it is regarded as important that children learn about the principles of capitalism, there may have been, during the 1980s, an emerging embarrassment about the exploitation of this area and the world in this fashion.

We can ask the same kind of questions about the East Midlands Development Agency mission statement also analysed for lexical choices in Chapter 2.

EMDA 'mission statement'

The vision is for the East Midlands to become a fast growing, dynamic economy based on innovative, knowledge based companies competing successfully in the global economy.

East Midlands Innovation launched its Regional Innovation Strategy and action plan in November 2006. This sets out how we will use the knowledge, skills and creativity of organisations and individuals to build an innovation led economy.

Our primary role to deliver our mission is to be the strategic driver of economic development in the East Midlands, working with partners to deliver the goals of the Regional Economic Strategy, which EMDA produces on behalf of the region.

I am committed to ensuring that these strategic priorities act as guiding principles for EMDA as we work with our partners in the region and beyond to achieve the region's ambition to be a Top 20 Region by 2010 and a flourishing region by 2020.

The participants in this text are: 'East Midlands Innovation', 'innovative, knowledge based companies', 'we', 'organisations', 'individuals', 'I', 'partners', 'the strategic driver of economic development'.

Fairclough (2003: 137) suggests that social events can be represented at different levels of abstraction or generalisation. At a low level of abstraction we would be able to see clearly what processes are being carried out with what kind of causality, by which social actors and in which times and places, if relevant. A high level of abstraction would be where these become obscured. In the Tropic Savanna text above, to a critical reader the processes of exploitation are fairly clear, although they are not described as such and although the participants involved in these are excluded. In the EMDA text, however, it is difficult to identify what exactly is to be done and how. There is also a high level of abstraction at the level of representational strategies.

To begin with, at the level of abstraction there is 'East Midlands Innovation', with connotations of 'ideas' and 'possibilities' through the use of the word 'Innovation'. But what this agent actually is and what they do is unclear. Is this a company, or simply a group of people? Later in the text we are told that the aim is to become 'the strategic driver of economic development'. But what does this mean exactly? Is this to happen through investment, through addressing government policy, through simply seeking to generate personal profits? Here we find that the text, rather than stating 'we will strategically drive economic development', turns the process 'to drive' into its identity. This strategy works to sidestep the act of making promises of actual change.

A further abstraction is the participant 'innovative, knowledge based companies'. Clearly all companies must have some kind of knowledge base, so in some way this is an odd kind of representational strategy. Also, the word 'innovation' is used, so we can assume that they will not be basing the economy on companies that wish to maintain established practices. We then find other generalisations, such as 'organisations' and 'individuals'. We are not told who these are specifically. They could therefore refer to anyone.

The use of the term 'partners' has the same effect. The discourse of 'partnership' was an important part of the rhetoric of the New Labour government's consensual style of politics, developed in Britain from the late 1990s (Newman, 2001). The term generally meant public and private agencies working together, although it also had the added meaning of the public being included in these partnerships, with all working together as 'stakeholders'. What is glossed over is the way that the interests between those parties may easily clash (Levitas, 2005).

In fact, the term 'stakeholders' glossed over the leading role often taken by private companies. Commentators (Newman, 2001; Levitas, 2005) have written on the effects of this attempt to deal with social issues – what became little more than an exercise in ticking the right policy and directive boxes and meeting the right targets. Hundreds of quasi-organisations become enmeshed with each other, adding layers of complexity with little practical outcome.

Texts like the one above are generally designed to avoid any kind of specificity. Occasionally the use of buzzwords can be seen to clash with reality, for example when abstraction meets with actual everyday issues. As part of the Plan to generate

(Continued)

(Continued)

growth, productivity and competitiveness, EMDA described the ideal workforce. Here the representational strategies are consistent with those found above:

EMDA 2010 Employment, learning and skills

A dynamic, flexible and skilled workforce helps businesses to thrive and individuals to maintain their employability. The East Midlands is characterised by a combination of high employment and a predominance of jobs demanding low skills and paying low wages.

What stands out in this short description is the fact that after stating the need for a 'dynamic, flexible and skilled workforce', the next sentence tells us that in the East Midlands there is 'a predominance of jobs demanding low skills and paying low wages'. Yet, clearly, if the EMDA had the aim of creating a workforce appropriate to the need for low skills and short-term contract work, this would not appear in line with the discourse of 'vision' and innovation. And what exactly does it mean to employees to be 'dynamic' and 'flexible'? These neo-capitalist buzzwords conceal unequal power relations. As Cameron (2001) has argued, the capitalist's flexibility is the worker's insecurity. Terrifyingly, these documents and policies do pass for legitimate and official stances on concrete issues in our society.

Representational strategies in visual communication

In the previous section on representational strategies in language we focused on one specific class of lexical choices, those used to represent people. We now carry out the same step of specialisation for visual communication. In Chapter 2 we looked at the way that the visual representation of objects and settings could be used to communicate more general ideas and discourses. We explored how images may seek to depict specific people and how these people can be used to connote general concepts, types of people, 'stereotypes', and abstract ideas.

When carrying out an analysis of the way that meanings are communicated through a combination of linguistic and visual representational strategies, it is important to identify how the different affordances of the two modes have been used to create different meanings. We can draw out the different affordances by asking how each carries meanings that could not be communicated through the other.

We begin by looking at some simple ways that image designers can represent participants in more or less personalised ways.

Positioning the viewer in relation to people inside the image

Distance

In pictures as in real life, distance signifies social relations. We 'keep our distance' from people we do not want to 'be in touch with' and 'get close to people' we see as part of our circle of friends or intimates. In images, distance translates as 'size of frame' (close, medium, or long shot). In Chapter 3 we looked at photographs of two politicians, Nick Clegg and David Cameron. Both of these are closer shots. Therefore the photographer, or page editor, as these may have been cropped to create this effect, has decided to take us close to these politicians to their inner states and feelings. In the case of Clegg, the photograph is perhaps meant to take us close to the 'real' Clegg, which is reflected in the discourse in the accompanying text, where he comes across as approachable and genuine. In the case of Cameron's photograph, the closer shot gives the impression of giving access to his worries, which again is supported by the language in the text.

Drawing on the analysis of gaze from the previous chapter, it is important to point out that Clegg looks right at the viewer, engaging with us. Combined with the close shot, these are important semiotic choices that help to show him as open and sincere. Cameron, however, looks away or 'off-frame', which tends to encourage us to observe participants more 'objectively' and consider what their thoughts are. We could imagine the difference in meaning had the two men been photographed in medium or long shot. The same image of Clegg, but in long shot, would not have connoted intimacy, but loneliness and isolation. At that point it was important for the news media to bring us close to the 'real' politicians as part of their attempt to dramatise the lead-up to the general election.

In the *Sun* article in Chapter 2, 'Our Boys Blitz Taliban Bash' on page 40 the accompanying photo depicts a soldier in medium shot. Here we are not meant to consider his thoughts on any personal or intimate level, but we are drawn to identify with his point of view more so than with that of the civilian, who is positioned in long shot. In many such news photographs, it is the civilians who appear in long shot unless the story is specifically about their suffering in wars or famines. The latter representations of civilians are normally the subject of special reports in Sunday newspaper supplements rather than in routine news reporting (see, for example, Machin, 2007b).

Coming back to the photographs from the women's lifestyle magazines we looked at in Chapter 2, women tend to be photographed in close or medium shot. Again, close-ups are used when we are meant to imagine the woman as the agent of the feelings expressed in the text, such as in relationship features like 'Can you trust you boyfriend?', where a young women may be found gazing off-frame looking thoughtfully. Medium shots are used where it is important that we see what the woman is wearing and to connote her acting in modernist settings, as in the image on page 45.

As for the Health Trust webpage of Trust workers that we analysed on page 54, we can see a montage of close shots. The doctor even overlaps the edge of the frame, bringing him further forward to suggest an increased degree of social intimacy. On the North Essex Trust homepage below, we can see two faces represented in close shot, symbolising patients of the Trust. Again, this serves to take us closer to their experiences and feelings. Important in foregrounding the experiences of these two 'patients' are other iconographical elements, as discussed in Chapter 2. The setting here is blurred with some green shading that connotes nature, although this was most likely a studio shot. Teeth here are particularly white and straight, and therefore connote health, attractiveness and 'vibrancy'. There is high key lighting with a bright background and highlights are visible on their faces, suggesting optimism as opposed to darker shadings that are often used to connote darker moods. Importantly, the effect of close proximity serves to bring the viewer into more intimate relations with the participants and therefore serves to personalise them. If we imagine the same image of these people positioned in the middle distance, this would have made them appear more as generic 'patients' rather than as individuals. It is clearly in the interest of the Trust to represent its users as highly personalised and special. Such techniques, as we have discussed previously, are one way by which matters of lack of quality of service actually offered is glossed over.

Linguistically, too, the North Essex homepage backgrounds matters of illness and treatment, and foregrounds actions like 'transforming lives'. They state that:

> Our services are for people of all ages and we involve local people in the planning and delivery of services. We are committed to treating everyone with dignity and respect.

In terms of representational strategies, we find not specific people who need specific treatment, but a sense of inclusion of 'people of all ages'. Would we expect the service to *exclude* people of certain ages? The 'local people' involved in planning and delivering services are generic people, which could of course conceal the fact that they are local business people. But the term 'local' connotes something familiar and safe. Participants are again individualised through nominating them: 'Sarah', 'Mrs Smith from Chelmsford'.

Angle

In pictures, as in real life, there are different ways we can engage with people. Becoming involved with people means, literally, 'confronting' them, coming 'face to face' with them. In certain interactions, of course, we may not come 'face to face' but merely observe others, for example, when two people are arguing. Here we will watch the action from side on. The side-on view is more detached, although combined with closeness, it can, depending on the

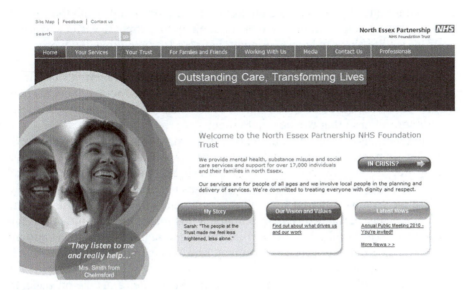

Figure 10   North Essex Partnership homepage

circumstances, index togetherness. So if we see a photograph of a person side-on but very close-up, this can connote a close alignment and a sharedness of position. This is sometimes communicated in side-on close-ups of British and American soldiers with their military equipment. We are encouraged to align with their thoughts and concerns. If we see them further away, there is a greater sense that we are a more remote observer of the scene.

On the North Essex Trust webpage above, we confront the two people, yet they look slightly to the side. Combined with the closeness, this appears intimate to a degree, yet they are represented as slightly to the side, so we are not directly involved – we are observing them.

In images we also see people from behind. In the image of the *Cosmopolitan* woman analysed in the Introduction, she is seen slightly from behind. Where we see people from behind, this can often serve to offer us their point of view, their perspective on the world. So if in an image we were to see the back of a person and then beyond them another person pointing a gun at them, we would take the perspective of the first person who faces the threat.

In the *Cosmopolitan* image we have something in between looking at a person as a voyeur and her engaging us. Since she is represented in medium shot this is not an intimate viewpoint. But since she looks back at us we are also acknowledged and therefore included in the image. In the work of Machin and van Leeuwen (2007) on the way such magazines work, it is noted that it is crucial that the reader is always addressed as part of a community of modern, attractive women. On the one hand this works linguistically through personal address 'you' and 'we', but also visually, through the address of gaze.

In photographs we may also engage with the participants from the vertical angle. You can either 'look down on' or 'look up to' people to various degrees. As in real life, this can have a number of effects. Often looking down on someone can give a sense of their vulnerability, looking up at them can give a sense of their power. For example, in the leaflets produced by children's charities, the children are often positioned in a way that we look down at them to show how vulnerable they are, whereas in lifestyle magazines, celebrities can be photographed so that we look up to them.

In the image of the North Essex Health Trust website above, we look up at the participants. We could say that this has the meaning potential to suggest that they are empowered. We also look up slightly to the soldier in Helmand province (see page 40 in Chapter 2), perhaps to connote that he has agency. Were we to look down at him, he might appear vulnerable in this terrain. Linguistically, in the text that accompanied this image, we found that the soldiers were represented as being professional and highly strategic, as opposed to the chaotic and unprofessional enemy. The image helps to reinforce what is expressed in the language.

We also look up at the woman from the *Marie Claire* article on page 46 in the same chapter, perhaps to suggest that she is somebody to emulate. However, in the image of Nick Clegg on page 76 we are positioned at the same height. This is one way to connote that he is 'an ordinary person'. On page 72 we also look slightly up at David Cameron. In this case, rather than giving him the appearance of agency, it combines with his downcast, thoughtful gaze to amplify a sense that we are being brought close to his more intimate thoughts. In the text that accompanied this image Cameron was presented as a man concerned about his performance in a televised leadership debate. The image communicates that we are being taken close up and intimate to a man who is worried.

Individualisation versus collectivisation

In the first section of this chapter we looked at some of the linguistic resources available for representing participants as individuals, groups or anonymous figures. We argued that all these could serve ideological ends in that they evaluate the participants positively or negatively and align the reader to events and actions in ways that are not necessarily stated overtly. There are also visual semiotic resources available for achieving these effects in images.

Individuals and groups

We already know that people can be depicted as individuals or as a group. If they are depicted as a group, they can be 'homogenised', that is they are made to look like and/or act or pose like each other to different degrees, creating a 'they are all the same' or 'you can't tell them apart' impression. Often we find images like these of immigrants or ethnic groups that accompany news stories about the negative consequences of 'mass immigration'. Such images serve to collectivise and generically represent people who may have many complex and different reasons for being there, and at least reasons that are highly compelling and personal. Yet they are represented as a homogenised whole.

In the images taken from *Cosmopolitan* (page 45) magazine and *Marie Claire* (page 7) we usually find women represented as individuals. This is common in these women's lifestyle magazines. It is very rare to find more than one woman represented. In the *Marie Claire* example, where the text tells us of tips on how to get ahead even when there are redundancies in your office, the image of the individual woman is one way to indicate that the agent in this situation acts alone; it is one way that the reader is invited to align with the events through this individual. Machin and van Leeuwen (2007) have shown how in such magazines the woman is depicted as always acting alone and strategically. In these magazines, there is no collective and no society. Machin and van Leeuwen conclude that this representational strategy is most suited to the requirements of the magazine to fit with the ideology of individualism that lies at the root of Western consumerism and corporate capitalism.

In the image of Helmand province we find only one soldier depicted. While he is not named, he is still individualised visually through being represented alone. Of course, it is unlikely that he would be out patrolling alone, and in the text, linguistically, a larger number of British soldiers are represented and for the most part they are collectivised. This visual depiction of the lone soldier calmly patrolling perhaps serves to make the British army's presence in the province seem less oppressive than it may seem to the civilians out there.

Generic and specific depictions

In images people can be depicted as individuals or specific people. They can be depicted as people who just happen to be black, Jewish or Muslim, or whatever, or they can be depicted as typical black people or Jews or Muslims. The latter is achieved through stereotypical representations of dress, hairstyle and grooming, and/or selected (and often exaggerated) physical features (particularly in cartoons). The effect is to make the individuality of people disappear behind the elements that categorise them. Cartoons in particular can stylise and exaggerate individual as well as stereotyped group character-istics (e.g. exaggerated facial features of certain ethnic groups). Clearly this is a matter of degree – a cline that runs from the most blatant stereotypes to a kind of selectivity that does not allow the actual variety of a group to be depicted. In a sense we cannot do without categories, and hence it could be argued we need stereotypes (Hall, 1997). However, if they carry negative con-notations, stereotypes can become derogatory and/or racist.

In the image of the soldier in Helmand province, the civilian in the background is included as a generic type. Commentaries on these kinds of representations of indigenous people from around the world in the media have shown how these often fulfil a number of expectations or stereotypes (Lutz and Collins, 1993). In images in some sectors of the British press at the time of writing, it was common to see newspaper items referring to Muslim people in Britain showing one woman or groups of women dressed in full burqa. The text itself does not claim that 'all Muslim women look like this', but such generic visual representations may serve to suggest or connote that they are.

Exclusion: Ways of (not) representing others

Certain categories of people are not represented in pictures of settings where they are in fact present, or in events in which they participate. In many of the images so far analysed we find important exclusions. Just as it is revealing to ask who is backgrounded or excluded linguistically from a text, so it is important to ask the same visually. In the image of the soldier in Helmand province, the rest of the soldiers and the victims of the attack described in the text are excluded. Of course, it is not so easy to visually represent a military attack through semiotic choices that communicate only strategy, professionalism and neutrality. Images of an actual military attack using artillery would have shown destruction with maimed and dead people. That this is not shown is ideologically significant. In photographs of the Vietnam war in the 1970s, images did show the horrors of war. War was represented for what it is: squalor, suffering, pain, cruelty and abuse. In the Helmand province article and in many other representation of the war in both Afghanistan and Iraq, the public is not to see war represented in this fashion. This change suggests the ideological requirement that authorities at this time do not wish the British public to contemplate the effects of the military presence in this way.

In the *Marie Claire* career text, while linguistically colleagues and bosses are represented, we do not see these visually. The people whom the woman works for or against for her own gains are not depicted. This is important. What if the text was accompanied by a photograph of a real office showing a woman surrounded by her colleagues? This would of course anchor the text in a real-life setting rather than the playful fantasy world couched in trendy language and with fictional characters. What is clear is that the ideology of individualism and rampant careerism communicated in this text is expressed through both linguistic and visual semiotic resources. The image here serves not to depict a particular woman at work, but to symbolise a generic attractive and fashionable woman shown in an intimate close-up, and in an abstracted setting. Linguistically she is trendy and confident, but also operates close to a fictional realm. Machin and Thornborrow (2003) suggest that these texts should be seen much like children's fairytales. They may take place in the realm of fantasy but nevertheless they carry very real messages about evaluations of identities, ideas, values and actions with possible social consequences.

Conclusion

This chapter has dealt with the naming and visual representation of persons. The communicator always has a range of semiotic choices available to them when they wish to represent a person. The choices they make will never be neutral but will be based on the way they wish to signpost what kind of person they are representing, or how they wish to represent them as social actors engaged in action. These choices allow us to place people in the social world and to highlight certain aspects of identity we wish to draw attention to or omit. Like lexical and iconographical choices in general, they can have the effect of connoting sets of ideas, values and sequences of activity that are not necessarily overtly articulated. And such choices, whether linguistic or visual, can serve to position those represented in relation to the viewer/reader. Such choices may serve to implicitly legitimise or delegitimise the actions of participants implicitly, since representational choices can connote broader associations of ideas, values and motives. In society at any one time different kinds of classifications tend to dominate and those who have power will seek to promote those classifications that best serve their interests, whether these are related to national or ethnic identity, or consumer lifestyle categories. In analysis, as we have shown in this chapter, we must carefully describe the different representational strategies for different participants and connect this to broader discourses. We must also carefully consider the relationship between linguistic and visual representation of social actors.

5

Representing Action: Transitivity and Verb Processes

In the previous chapter we looked at the way participants are represented, at how the words chosen to do this can signify discourses that shape the way that we perceive participants, events and circumstances. These choices are able to portray participants in ways that tend to align us alongside or against them without overtly stating that this should be the case. As such, they are able to align us likewise alongside the sequences of activity that these participants represent. In this chapter we see how the way we perceive people can be shaped not only by representational strategies but also by the representation of *transitivity* or of how they are represented as acting or not acting. Again, this can promote certain discourses and certain ideologies that are not overtly stated.

Transitivity is simply the study of what people are depicted as doing and refers, broadly, to who does what to whom, and how. This allows us to reveal who plays an important role in a particular clause and who receives the consequences of that action. A transitivity analysis of clause structure shows us who is mainly given a subject (agent/participant) or object (affected/patient) position. Based on the work of Halliday (1994), transitivity in this sense goes beyond traditional grammatical approaches which distinguish between verbs that take objects ('Mary opened the door') and verbs that do not ('John slept').

Halliday emphasises that the grammar of a language is a system of 'options' from which speakers and writers choose according to social circumstances, with transitivity playing a key role in 'meaning making' in language. This means that the choice of certain linguistic forms always has significance, some of which may be ideological. Language is always part of an intervention in the world, and we have stressed the importance of print media, in particular, in constructing our everyday world and our expectations of it through the patterns of its representation. For example, as we saw in Chapter 1 in the texts produced by the Regional Generation Agency EMDA, the responsibilities of authorities and of the government may be systematically backgrounded or omitted; agency and responsibility for actions may be left implicit. This makes transitivity analysis not only a powerful basis for analysing what is *in* texts, but also for what is *absent* from them. Van Dijk (1991: 215–16), for example, found that '...negative acts of in-group members, such as the authorities or the police, may be reduced in effect by placing them later in the sentence or by keeping the agency implicit, for instance in passive sentences'.

Van Dijk (2000) has demonstrated that ethnic minorities are mostly shown as active agents where they do something bad. Where things are done for or against them, they are represented in a passive role.

Muslims win a transfer out of too 'white' jail (*Daily Mail*, 21 March 2008)

Terrorism convicts granted move from 'white' jail (*Daily Telegraph*, 21 March 2008)

In the first headline, Muslims are the active participants in 'winning' a transfer from one prison to another, whereas in the second, they are the passive recipients of a privilege. Both headlines construct this as something negative, because prisoners should not be given privileges. The first headline 'others' the participants in terms of their ethnicity ('Muslims'), whereas the second does so in terms of their status as prisoners and terrorists ('terrorism convicts'). Both are negative expressions, although the second one is arguably more condemnatory.

When analysing agency (who does what to whom) and action (what gets done) we are interested in describing three aspects of meaning:

- participants (which includes both the 'doers' of the process as well as the 'done-tos' who are at the receiving end of action; participants may be people, things or abstract concepts)
- processes (represented by verbs and verbal groups)
- circumstances (these are adverbial groups or prepositional phrases, detailing where, when and how something has occurred). These aspects will be explained below. (Simpson and Mayr, 2010: 66)

For example, in the sentence:

Three soldiers attacked a civilian yesterday

the *actor* element is the 'three soldiers' who carry out the process of attacking. The *goal* is the 'civilian' who has been attacked, and the *circumstance* is 'yesterday' which locates the process in a temporal context. So in a transitivity analysis we have first to identify the participants in a clause and then the process types used. Halliday distinguishes six process types: *material, mental, behavioural, verbal, relational* and *existential*. We can use these to help us to think more carefully about what kinds of things are being done in a text.

Material processes

Material processes describe processes of *doing*. Usually, these are concrete actions that have a material result or consequence, such as 'The police arrested the burglar', although they may also represent abstract processes such as 'Prices have <u>fallen</u>' or metaphorical processes such as 'She <u>demolished</u> my argument'. The two key participants in material processes are the *actor* and the *goal*. The actor is the part which performs the action and the goal is the participant at whom the process is directed (the direct object in traditional grammar). Some material processes have one participant only, the actor, as in 'He <u>walked</u> away'. However, material processes can also involve processes that have no clear goal, as in 'He arrived' or 'The army advanced'. We can see the difference if we compare sentences with material processes where there is a clear goal: 'The army attacked the village'.

We also find material processes where the actor is 'lost'. This is done through passive clauses. Fairclough (2000: 163) has also argued that one important thing we must look for in texts is where who acts and who has responsibility has been obscured. For example:

The civilians were killed during a bombing raid.

The government found itself facing allegations of spin this week following the release of some confusing crime statistics.

In both of these sentences who carried out the action is missing. Who killed the civilians and who made the allegations? But passive verb structures can be used with agents such as:

The civilians were protected by the soldiers.

In an analysis of a text we can ask which kinds of participants are described in passive verb sentences and which are not. Van Dijk (2000) has shown, for example, that ethnic minorities are only shown as active agents where they do something bad. Where they are associated with anything positive, they are represented in a passive role, where things are done for or against them.

The Muslim community was attacked.

Muslim extremists demanded a change in the law.

Material processes can also have beneficiaries, as in 'He built the house for a customer'. Here the 'house' is the goal and the 'customer' the beneficiary. Material processes can further be linked to what is called 'range'. This is something that is unaffected by the process, such as in 'I am conducting research'. Here 'research' is connected to the process and is not a goal in itself.

What we can see from this account of material processes is that in a text we can ask whether participants are represented as actors, goals, or as beneficiaries of processes. By asking these questions we can get a clear sense of who is active and who is passive in a sentence or text.

Mental processes

Mental processes are processes of *sensing* and can be divided into three classes: 'cognition' (verbs of thinking, knowing or understanding), 'affection' (verbs of liking, disliking or fearing) and 'perception' (verbs of seeing, hearing or perceiving). Examples of the three classes of cognition, affection and perception are, respectively: 'I <u>understood</u> the story', 'Peter <u>liked</u> the film a lot' and 'We <u>saw</u> many interesting buildings'. Mental processes allow us to gain an insight into the feelings or states of mind of certain participants ('Women <u>worry</u> too much about their physical appearance').

It is often the case that participants who are made the subjects of mental processes are constructed as the 'focalisers' or 'reflectors' of action. These actors are allowed an internal view of themselves. This can be one device through which listeners and readers can be encouraged to have empathy with that person. For example:

> The mother had worried since her son's regiment had moved into the region.

Here the reader is encouraged to empathise with the mother by being informed of her worrying. In turn, this carries over to the soldier himself. Indirectly we are told that he has a mother who worries about him. The soldier is essentially an ordinary young man from an ordinary family. This serves to help humanise the occupying forces and can be seen as an important part of the humanitarian discourse of war. We might find that accounts of other participants in a text contain no corresponding details about their mental processes. So we learn nothing of the mental processes of the 'militants' or the concerns of their mothers.

Mental processes can also be one way of showing that these participants appear very busy, even though they participate in no material transactions. And if these mental verbs are mainly about sensing and reacting, this can also convey passivity. So, in the sentences above the mother is the only person allowed an internal view of herself. We might tend to align with her thoughts. But she still remains passive in the sense that she is not the agent of any actual physical actions. Were we given access to the fears and worries of the soldiers through sentences like:

> The soldier worried as he protected the civilians.

Here we might attribute more humanity to the soldier rather than seeing him simply as a member of an indifferent occupying force. During times where nation states have been involved in armed conflict, it has been common to see photographs of vulnerable-looking soldiers writing home to a loved one. In the same way we are invited to experience the feelings of that participant. Clearly, whether or not a soldier misses his family has no bearing on the actual political reasons for his presence in the occupied country nor on the violence it suffers.

One particular kind of mental processes can be characterised as 'reactions'. For example:

The marker was bewildered by the student's essay.

Here the mental process of the marker is a reaction to the work submitted by the student. We can also see this in the following sentence:

He had fears for the student's progress.

This is important as texts not only tell us what we should do, or what has happened, but also how people feel about things. Van Leeuwen (2008: 56) points out that social roles, as reinforced in texts, prescribe not only actions and identities, but also feelings.

In the *Marie Claire* text analysed in Chapter 2, where the woman is told how to compete with her workmates to get ahead even when they are losing their jobs, we find that we are given access to how she feels doing this:

I'm not looking to be promoted, but I also recognize no one wants chaos.

Throughout these feature items in many women's lifestyle magazines the reader is continually being told how she will feel or what the feelings associated with certain actions are. For example:

His reaction made me feel so powerful.

I feel good about being in charge in bed. It makes me feel confident about my sexuality.

When my best pal started playing games with me, I just didn't think the job was worth holding onto.

One reason for this use of mental processes, and specifically reactions, in such magazines is the fact that, as commentators have observed, women always act alone because they are oriented towards social interaction rather than creativity or intellectual skills. And for the most part they must get on in society through manipulating others and through the power that their body and sexuality affords them. In the *Marie Claire* article, and many others, behaviour that might be seen as selfish and coldly strategic is legitimised partly through reactions. Importantly, this can also be seen in this instance as the way that these lifestyle magazines are closely tuned to acts of consumption, where women are encouraged to align with both the brand of the magazine and the values and identities associated with this, and the products and services that appear in its pages.

In any text we can ask how many process terms describe actions and how many describe reactions. We might conclude that in particular areas of social practice reactions are more important than actions. So in a text about immigration, there may be a predominance of reactions attributed to those portrayed as 'us'. The immigrants meanwhile are the provokers of the reactions (Van Leeuwen, 2008). We might find in a text that one group is portrayed as producing actions, say terrorists, and the other group, the Americans, are producing reactions. These reactions might be moderate and reasonable, such as 'The soldiers feared for the civilians during the attack'.

It is important to note that rather than having goals or beneficiaries, mental processes relate to 'phenomena'. In the sentence 'I like you', 'you' is a phenomenon rather than a goal or beneficiary.

Another category of reactions are those that are not defined. Such as:

The policeman reacted.

The soldiers responded.

These can be used to conceal certain kinds of actions.

We can observe that different categories of participants are often given different types of reaction. In adverts, consumers tend to 'desire', 'need', 'want', whereas the advertiser tends to 'think', 'know' and 'understand'. Here it is the advertisers who position themselves to be able to fulfil our needs and wants through their knowing and understanding.

Behavioural processes

Behavioural processes, like *watch, taste, stare, dream, breathe, cough, smile* and *laugh* denote psychological or physical behaviour. They are semantically a cross between material and mental processes. For example, 'look at' and 'listen to' are classed as behavioural, whereas 'see' and 'hear' would be mental processes. Behavioural processes are also in part about action. Unlike material processes, however, the action has to be experienced by a single conscious being, i.e. a person. ('We heard loud music'). We can see that 'The man laughed' is an action, as is 'The soldier watched'. But neither of these suggests that the actor has a particularly strong agency, nor are we given any sense of a goal or a beneficiary.

Verbal processes

Verbal processes are expressed through the verb 'to say' and its many synonyms. A verbal process typically consists of three participants: sayer, receiver and verbiage. The *sayer* can be a human or human-like speaker, as in 'The teacher <u>explained</u> the theory', but it can also be an inanimate item, as in 'The paper <u>alleges</u> there was a lot of violence'. The *receiver* is the one at whom the verbal process is directed: 'They told <u>me</u> to leave at once', while the *verbiage* is a nominalised statement of the verbal process: 'The paper provided <u>a detailed account</u>' or 'He said <u>that this was the case</u>'. In any text we can ask which participants are represented as being associated more with verbal processes. On the one hand, those who are allowed to have a voice in the media may be those who have the most power. On the other hand, some may be seen to have too much to say, as we will see later in this chapter. But much can be revealed about agency when we analyse the extent to which some participants are represented as doers of material processes with goals, but others as thinkers and talkers.

Relational processes

These are processes that encode meanings about states of being, where things are stated to exist in relation to other things. They are expressed through the verb 'to be', which is the most frequent, but synonyms such as 'become', 'mean', 'define', 'symbolise', 'represent', 'stand for', 'refer to', 'mark' and 'exemplify' are also classed as relational processes. To 'have' in the sense of possessing something is another relational process, as in 'She <u>has</u> a car'. Relational processes allow us to present as 'facts' what could be classed as opinion, as in 'A lot of people <u>have</u> worries about immigration'.

Existential processes

Existential processes represent that something exists or happens, as in 'There has been an increase in enemy activity'. Existential processes typically use the verb 'to be' or synonyms such as 'exist', 'arise' or 'occur', and they only have one participant, as in 'There was <u>an attack</u>'. This participant, which is usually preceded by *there is* or *there are*, may be any kind of phenomenon and often denotes a nominalised action. In the above example, the verb 'to attack' has been turned into a nominalisation. This can have the effect of obscuring agency and responsibility, as we are not told who may be behind the attack.

When we look at these processes and participants out of context, as in the examples presented above, it is not clear what ideological function they have as such. However, things are very different when transitivity is embodied as discourse. For example, the relationship between actor and goal can be ideologically significant if agency is backgrounded through the use of the passive voice. In passives, the position of these elements is reversed, as in 'One civilian was killed by security forces', and it even allows the actor to be omitted completely: 'One civilian was killed'. Even more backgrounding is achieved through the use of a one-participant process such as 'One civilian died', where the action appears not to be caused by the police at all. As we will demonstrate, transitivity patterns, especially in the manipulation of agency at the grammatical level, can be significant in terms of language and power.

Another way of characterising transitivity is in terms of the way that participants in a clause, or social actors, can be *activated* or *passivated*. Activated, social actors are represented as 'the active, dynamic forces in an activity' (Van Leeuwen, 1996: 43–4), the ones who do things and make things happen. Being activated, in this view, is an important and generally positive aspect of representation. An activated actor's capacity for 'action, for making things happen, for controlling others and so forth, is accentuated' (Fairclough, 2003: 150). Action processes foreground agency, contributing to representations of power (2003: 113). Machin and Thornborrow (2006), for example, use this model to show how in women's magazines women are highly active but in terms of behavioural processes, mental processes and material processes which have no goal or outcome. So the women might be busy 'hoping', 'worrying', 'walking', 'watching', 'reading'. This is even though the magazine is branded as for the 'Fun, Fearless, Female', which would suggest a woman that indeed is 'out there' accomplishing things in the world. The same kinds of process patterns have been noted of the way that women behave in romantic fiction (Ryder, 1999):

She trailed through life in that red dressing-gown.

She moved languidly about.

She was so full of understanding.

She sat upright and quiet, with wide-open eyes.

The protagonists in these novels are not involved in material processes which bring about changes in the world or those which have beneficiaries. We can say, therefore, that they are 'passivated' rather than 'activated'. It is often the male hero who is activated.

Van Leeuwen (1996: 90) uses the same analytical framework to describe the way that children are represented textually in contrast to teachers. He analyses the texts for 'transitivity' – in other words, actions that have an outcome. The analysis reveals that children, in contrast to teachers, are rarely represented as having an effect on the world. He concludes that 'clearly the ability to "transit" requires a certain power, and the greater that power, the greater the range of "goals" that may be affected by the actors actions' (1996: 90).

There is a theoretical assumption here, therefore, that levels of an actor's agency are directly correlated to material process types and that individuals or groups not involved in such processes are represented as being weak agents. Teo (2000: 27), in his analysis of racism in two Australian newspapers, concludes that the agents or dominant subjects are those attributed with material or verbal processes. In contrast, those who are not may be 'ineffectual'.

As regards material processes, it is also important to think about the goals involved. Van Leeuwen (2008) explains that it is important to distinguish between transactions with things and with people. Those which affect people he calls *interactive* transactions, and those which affect things he calls *instrumental* transactions.

An example of an interactive goal would be:

I ushered Jenny into the room.

Instrumental transactions can also be applied to persons when they are treated as things. This is often found in bureaucratised discourse, for example:

Staff should be placed in clear skills categories.

We can illustrate the way that these different kinds of verb processes clearly point more subtly to the agency and lack of agency of different participants in a particular social practice even though this is not overtly stated. Such identities, signifying whole discourses of values, roles and sequences of activity have consequence in this case for actual professional practices.

Below are examples from medical journals relating to childbirth (from Scamell, 2011). There has been much discussion in such journals and in government policy about the way that women can be empowered to make their own choices for the kind of delivery they want, so that they can avoid unnecessary medical intervention. But this choice has never materialised and what is argued in the literature to be largely pointless medical procedures (Kitzinger, 2005) are carried out automatically. Central to this issue is that much government policy in Britain has emphasised that greater power should be given to midwives and less to obstetricians, whose very *raison d'être* is to carry our surgical procedures. In units run by midwives, for example, there are few caesarean sections, but these are usual in obstetrics-driven wards. If we examine recent journals, we find certain process types dominating the accounts of how the two groups behave.

The obstetricians:

common surgical procedures performed by obstetrician residents undertake perineal repair

obstetricians and gynaecologists formally instruct the repair

The midwives:

we have to really believe in our ability to give birth normally before we can convince others

We have to be able to talk about normal birth in a way that encourages people to want it

We have to really want normal birth before anyone will have any confidence in it postcards you can use to send to colleagues, exchange ideas or tell us how you feel

use stories to make a point

We can see similarities between the midwives and the women in Machin and Thornborrow's (2006) magazines and in Teo's (2000) description of the agency of immigrant groups. The obstetricians carry out material processes often with clear goals and beneficiaries. They 'undertake perineal repair', and 'surgical procedures' are 'performed' by them. Verbal processes of 'instructing' imply them to be authoritative. The midwives, in contrast, are engaged in mental processes where they 'believe' and 'want'. We can see clearly from these two cases which participants are most activated.

Adjuncts

The analysis of the medical journals on the subject of agency in childbirth revealed a further way that the midwives were de-agentalised through their grammatical positioning (Van Leeuwen, 1996). The lexical choice of adjuncts had a significant impact upon the actors' status as social agents. Adjuncts are simply lexical items that can be used to modify circumstances.

For example, in a key opening paragraph midwives are described as being:

routinely involved in assessing and recording the extent of perineal trauma ... and [being] responsible for initiating appropriate interventions and treatment.

From this we can see that midwives do not do the assessing, recording or intervention; rather, they are part of these processes or at best simply start them off rather than being their executors or managers. Thus, even when they are involved in an action profile with a material outcome, they are functionally decentred from their activity by the use of the adjuncts *involved* and *initiating*, both of which show that midwives are not really in charge of doing the action. Of the eight clauses within the text above representing the action processes of midwives, five are decentred through the use of adjuncts. This is not the case with the obstetricians.

The midwifery texts also reveal that there was a main social agent present, but that this agent was an unidentified third person. This presence was evoked through their business of *'expecting'*, *'accepting'* and *'recognising'* that midwives should or should not, must or must not, behave in a certain way.

For example:

midwives are expected to make assessments regarding management of perineal trauma that are vitally important to the long-term health of women.

it is common practice and a generally accepted rule within many maternity units'

Perineal repair is recognised as a role of the midwife

Who is doing the expecting and whose accepted rule it is remains unspecified. Clearly, those in control do not have such mysterious powers watching over them or defining their role and we found no such absentee actor included in the obstetrics text.

Grammatical positioning of actions

A further linguistic strategy for representing social action is within a circumstance, such as within a prepositional phrase or subordinate clause. These circumstances are useful for backgrounding certain acts and for foregrounding others.

Prepositional phrases begin with a preposition, such as 'for', 'at' or 'after'. In the sentence 'We bought it for them', there is the main clause 'We bought it' and the prepositional phrase 'for them'. A newspaper headline might use a main clause and a prepositional phrase as in 'Boy stabbed at school'.

A subordinate clause will begin with a conjunction such as 'because' or 'after' or a relative pronoun such as 'which' or 'whose'. So in the sentence 'I paid the shopkeeper when I left the shop', the last part, 'when I left the shop', is the subordinate clause.

Richardson (2007: 207) argues that prepositional phrases can be used to provide context for dominant clauses. In newspaper headlines, prepositional phrases are also often used to reduce responsibility for certain actions. The action may be in the dominant clause and the prepositional phrase may supply the details of the time, place and manner of action. In a headline provided by Richardson, 'Children killed in US assault' (*The Guardian*, 2 April 2003), the main emphasis is on 'Children killed'. Who is behind the killing, however, is de-emphasised through the prepositional phrase. Richardson suggests the editor could have written the same information as 'US kill children in assault'. Here 'US kill children' is the dominant clause, which makes it absolutely clear who is responsible for the action: the US are the actors in the material process 'kill' and the 'children' are the goal of the action, whereas the prepositional phrase 'in assault' just provides the details and context of how this was done.

Van Dijk (1991) has also discussed the way that actions can be played down when placed later in a sentence or embedded in a clause. He states that '[E] vents may be strategically played down by the syntactic structure of the sentences, for example, by referring to the event in a lower (later, less prominent) embedded clause, or conversely by putting it in the first position when the events need extra prominence' (1991: 216). For example:

The university management made severe staff cuts.

After extensive reductions in government funding, the university management made severe staff cuts.

In the second case, the information about the actions of the management has been given less emphasis by placing it in the subordinate position.

Actions that are represented in abstraction

This is where actions become generalised and non-specific. For example, in:

It is important for staff to interact with students at the event

the details of what is done are obscured. In such cases it may not be so important as to what is actually done but that staff *appear* to interact with the students. This may be one indication of the situation where students now paying higher fees need to be given the appearance that resources are being dedicated to them. We can see this in the EMDA text analysed for lexical content on page 33 in Chapter 2.

Our primary role to deliver our mission is to be the strategic driver of economic development.

In this sentence, the process 'deliver' is used to gloss over what is actually done by such organisations. We find it again in another line from the same EMDA text:

Working with partners to deliver the goals of the Regional Economic Strategy

Here we find 'deliver' again and also 'working', both of which are used to gloss over the micro-processes that might comprise these actions. In the Loughborough University mission statement also analysed in Chapter 2 (see page 34) we find:

Loughborough University is a dynamic, forward looking institution, committed to being a centre of excellence.

We can see here that processes like 'committed', a word that has become a staple of corporate branding language, is used to abstract what the university actually does in this respect. Do they mean they provide finance, a high number of teaching staff and high-tech equipment and training? 'Commitment' is not the same as actually 'doing', of course, but is a mental process. So when we find such abstractions at the level of social action we have to ask why and what is being concealed.

In Chapter 2 we looked at the way that a British National Health Trust homepage promoted itself in terms of this kind of corporate language. We considered this in the context of substantial cuts in state funding of health services and waves of privatisation, with companies choosing the most profitable parts of services (Pollock, 2006). Looking at some of the process types we find on this webpage, again there is a predominance of abstraction:

To improve the health of people by pursuing excellence in healthcare

Here the Trust says that it will 'pursue' excellence. There is a clear goal of 'excellence in healthcare', but the verb process 'pursue' is an abstraction as it tells us little about what they will actually do. Will they appoint many high-quality doctors and nurses? Will they be funding all the latest medicines and treatments? It is clear that wherever we find such abstraction, as Fairclough (1989) points out, there is an indication of some kind of ideological manipulation. By using the word 'pursue', the Trust can give the impression they are actually doing something without specifying what this is. Pursuing excellence, in fact, in this case appears to be accomplished by the micro-processes of staff and services cuts.

Case study 1: Overlexicalised Muslim prisoners

In this first case study we carry out a transitivity analysis on a text analysed in Chapter 4 which reported on the following:

Muslim prisoners sue for millions after they were offered ham sandwiches for Ramadan.

The story used representational strategies to overlexicalise the word 'Muslim' and used extensive aggregation, such as 'scores of Muslims'. In contrast, those representing the prison authorities were largely anonymised and functionalised to foreground their professional roles. Those complaining were therefore represented as a numerous 'other' and as outrageously imposing their religious views on British culture even though they were criminals. Meanwhile the authorities were represented as neutral and official. We considered how the story could have been written differently in terms of the nature of the prison system and the broader lack of sensitivities to human rights. Here we now look at the way that transitivity too can shape the story ideologically.

Scores of Muslim inmates at a high security prison are set to launch a multi-million pound claim for compensation after they were offered ham sandwiches during the holy month of Ramadan.

They say their human rights were breached when they were given a special nightly menu – drawn up to recognise their specific dietary requirements – by officers at HMP Leeds last month.

More than 200 Muslim inmates at the jail are believed to have been offered the meat which is strictly forbidden by Islam.

The sandwich was one of three options on the menu card which was created to cover the religious festival during which Muslims are required to fast during daylight.

They later complained to prison officers on duty but say they were told that the menus had been printed in error.

Yet when they opened the sandwiches, having ordered cheese, some claim they were still filled with boiled ham.

They are now launching legal action, insisting that their human rights were breached and could each be entitled to up to £10,000 in compensation if they win their case at court.

One Muslim inmate, a 28-year-old who was serving a 16-week sentence for driving whilst disqualified, said: 'When I opened my meal that night I found I'd been given a ham sandwich. I'd asked for cheese.

'It was a breach of my human rights and I want compensation.'

He claimed that some inmates were so hungry they ended up eating the sandwiches.

The prison denied that any Muslim prisoners had been given ham sandwiches but admitted there had been a mistake when the menus were printed.

A spokesman for the Ministry of Justice said: 'An inappropriate menu card was printed during Ramadan. This mistake was rectified immediately.

'Appropriate menu options for the Iftaar evening meal were available throughout Ramadan.

'Prison Service guidelines state that prisoners must have a diet which meets the requirements of their religion.'

It comes as 16 Muslim inmates at Leeds Prison prepare to launch a separate legal case over claims of mistreatment, including being given food that is forbidden by their religion.

They are expected to claim at a hearing next year that they were given meat which was not halal.

(Continued)

(Continued)

Kate Maynard, from law firm Hickman and Rose Solicitors who is representing some of the men, said: 'One of the issues they are worried about is that they were being told food was halal when it wasn't.

'They are taking this to court to try to change conditions in the prison and make conditions better.'

Last year the Prison Service was forced to apologise to Muslim inmates at a category B jail after a kitchen worker was caught throwing ham into halal curries.

Prisoners at HMP Blakenhurst in Worcestershire each received a written apology.

The inmate behind the attack at the prison, which houses 1,070 offenders, was observed throwing tinned ham into curries destined for Muslim inmates and suspended from his job in the kitchen.

Let us first deal with the transitivity patterns used to represent the Muslims who complained about the ham sandwiches they were served. Their actions are represented in terms of material processes:

Muslim inmates at a high security prison are set to launch a multi-million pound claim for compensation.

They are now launching legal action,

This gives the impression that the Muslim will do something dramatic. The verbs 'started' or 'initiate' could equally have been used but would seem more moderate. It is important in this text, along with the overlexicalisation of the representational category of 'Muslim' and the aggregation that describes 'scores of Muslims' to show the magnitude of this event.

We can think about 'launching' in this case as an example of abstraction. Exactly what does 'launching' mean here? At which stage of the legal process are they? News reports of a sensational nature often use abstractions in this way to simplify stories.

We find the Muslim inmates actions represented through other verb processes in:

could each be <u>entitled</u> to up to £10,000 in compensation

This relational verb 'be entitled' adds to the sense of outrage as to prisoners, who are clearly not integrated in British society and culture, nor respecters of its laws, are 'entitled' to compensation.

We also find extensive use of verbal processes:

<u>insisting</u> that their human rights were breached

They later <u>complained</u> to prison officers on duty

some <u>claim</u> they were still filled with boiled ham.

He <u>claimed</u> that some inmates were so hungry they ended up eating the sandwiches

In this sentence we are given a sense of the prisoners being highly vocal. In contrast, we find no verbal processes for the prison officers, for example. Again, this adds to the sense that scores of Muslims are making a lot of noise, insisting, and complaining and launching legal action, despite being the 'other' and criminals.

We find one mental process, where we are told that the inmate serving time for driving while disqualified 'wants' compensation:

It was a breach of my human rights and I <u>want</u> compensation.

Here we are given a glimpse inside this prisoner's mental world. He 'wants' compensation. This adds to the cumulative effect of the supposedly inappropriate way that these men are behaving and how they think, demanding what they perceive to be their rights. Being told here what he wants enhances the sense of audacity. Those who are being punished in prison should behave appropriately. The text also forms part of an anti-immigration/racist discourse that portrays foreigners or members of other cultural groups as being unwilling to adapt to British culture.

We also find the use of dominant clauses to foreground the identities of the prisoners, and prepositional phrases, as in:

Muslim prisoners sue for millions after they were offered...

In these cases, the nouns 'Muslim', 'scores of Muslims', 'more than 200 Muslims' are regularly foregrounded by being placed at the beginning of sentences with the details of what they are doing placed further back in prepositional phrases and subordinate clauses. We can see the effect of these sentences if we change the clause order. The sentence

Muslim prisoners sue for millions after they were offered ham sandwiches for Ramadan

could be rephrased as:

After they were offered ham sandwiches for Ramadan Muslim prisoners sue for millions

Here it is the fact that the Muslim prisoners were offered ham sandwiches for Ramadan that is foregrounded, which helps to make their response seem much more reasonable. The sentence is now about the offering of the sandwiches and not the fact that they are Muslims. This appears to be precisely what Van Dijk (1991: 215–16) had in mind when he argued that 'negative acts of in-group members ... may be reduced by placing them later in the sentence'. We can see the same effect when we change the following sentence:

(Continued)

(Continued)

> More than 200 Muslim inmates at the jail are believed to have been offered the meat which is strictly forbidden by Islam.

Which can be written alternatively as:

> Meat strictly forbidden by Islam is believed to have been offered to more than 200 Muslim inmates.

This is all evidence of the way that the identities of the prisoners and their actions are foregrounded over and above those of the prison service. The reversal of the last sentence really captures what this whole event is about, and offering ham to Muslim prisoners during Ramadan, while it may have been a mistake, does not speak well for a country which has claimed to welcome multiculturalism.

In contrast to the Muslim prisoners, the prison authorities are represented as having acted reasonably. What we find are material processes that emphasise agency, but also moderation. In the following sentences we find that the ham was only 'offered', mentioned twice, as opposed to 'given'. This gives a sense of the prisoners having a choice. And the word 'offer' suggests some degree of grace and generosity:

> ... after they were offered ham sandwiches during the holy month of Ramadan.

> ... to have been offered the meat

And the same sense of shifting responsibility through there being choice is expressed by the relational verb 'available' in the following sentence.

> Appropriate menu options for the Iftaar evening meal were available.

Importantly, in all of these three cases we find passivised verb processes. The sandwiches 'were offered' and the menu options 'were available'. So there is no agent in these processes, even though 'offering' is itself a transitive verb. If these sentences were written differently we can see the effect of these passive clauses. For example:

> The prison offered ham sandwiches during the holy month of Ramadan.

This sentence makes it very clear what happened.

Other verb processes are used to increase a sense of the prison authorities behaving considerately. We find that the prison authorities 'drew up a special menu', suggesting actions carried out specifically with the Muslim inmates in mind as a result of the mental process of 'recognition'. So whereas we are given access to the internal mental world of the prisoners only in terms of what one man 'wants', the mental world of the authorities is one which 'recognises'. Then we find the use of the material process of 'created to cover' to describe the production of the menu. This again reinforces the sense of the intentions of the authorities.

a special nightly menu – drawn up to recognise their specific dietary requirements
the menu card which was created to cover the religious festival during
Finally, we find a sequence of verbal processes that also point to the stance of the prison.

The prison denied that any Muslim prisoners had been given ham sandwiches
but admitted there had been a mistake when the menus were printed

The prison 'denies' that anyone had been given ham sandwiches, a verb process
that is often used by journalists to imply guilt, as we saw in Chapter 3 on quoting verbs.
But here this is quickly balanced with the verb 'admitted'. So the prison authorities are
decent enough to accept something went wrong. The case made by the language
appears to be that the Muslim prisoners were 'offered' the sandwiches, which were
therefore 'available' but not 'given' to them. Nevertheless we are told that:

the mistake was rectified immediately.

In sum, it appears that the prison authorities made a mistake by putting ham
sandwiches on the menu during Ramadan, which caused the inmates to complain.
The story has been written in terms of verb processes to foreground the actions of
the Muslims and their aggressive attitude. The actions of the prison meanwhile are
downplayed. The result, combined with the representational strategies, is a story that
draws on two typical news frames of the more right-wing press: those in prison are
treated too well and the criminal justice system is now more concerned with their
rights than those of their victims (see Mayr and Machin, 2012); and immigrants and
different cultural/ethnic groups are swamping British culture with their demands. But
by drawing out the verb processes here we have been able to show some of the
mechanisms through which what actually happened has been recontextualised.

Case study 2: The Helmand province story

In this second case study we analyse the verb processes in the news report analysed
on page 40 in Chapter 2 on lexical analysis.

BRITISH commandos launched a devastating blitz on the Taliban – as the evil
terrorists held a party to celebrate Benazir Bhutto's murder.

The dawn raid was staged after messages were intercepted about the sick
knees-up in Afghanistan's Helmand province.

Royal Marines crept into position as the fanatics partied the night away just hours
after Ms Bhutto was killed in Pakistan.

(Continued)

(Continued)

The bash was being held in ruined compounds a few hundred yards from Our Boys' remote base in Kajaki.

Ragtag Taliban sentries tried to hit back with machine gun fire – but stood no chance against the heroes of 40 Commando's Charlie Company.

Bloodthirsty

The terrorists were pounded with mortars, rockets and heavy machine guns.

Two bloodthirsty revellers trying to creep towards Our Boys in a trench were spotted by thermal-imaging equipment – and targeted with a Javelin heat-seeking missile.

The £65,000 rocket – designed to stop Soviet tanks – locked on to their body heat and tore more than a kilometer across the desert in seconds.

Troop Sergeant Dominic Conway, 32 – who directed mortar rounds – grinned: "It must have had quite a detrimental effect on their morale."

Sgt Conway, from Whitley Bay, Tyneside, said of the Taliban lair: "It used to be their backyard and now we've made it ours."

The story tells of a successful attack by British soldiers on a group of Taliban. It appears that the Taliban were attacked by surprise when the British soldiers identified them and fired a high-tech missile into their midst. In this chapter we looked at some of the representational strategies, particularly that the British soldiers, who were described in professional terms as 'British commandos', 'Troop Sergeant', 'Charlie Company' and through other positive naming strategies such as 'Our Boys' and 'Heroes', whereas the Taliban were described as 'fanatics', 'animals', 'Ragtag Taliban sentries' to delegitimise and dehumanise them. Below we have placed the verb processes attributed to them in a table.

To begin with, the British soldiers are represented as agents in the text. We find the following material processes:

Launched

Intercepted

Staged

Targeted

Used

All of these connote professional activities and represent the soldiers as agents. They connote precision, as in the material processes 'intercepted', 'targeted' and 'crept'. On the other hand, some of these are abstractions. 'Launched a devastating

Table 5 Transitivity in Helmand province text

British soldiers	Taliban
Launched a devastating blitz	Held a party
Intercepted messages	Tried to hit back
Crept into position	Trying to creep
Staged a dawn raid	Were targeted
Targeted	Partied
Used missiles that locked onto their body heat	Stood no chance
Grinned	Were pounded with mortars
Directed mortar rounds	
Made their back yard ours	

blitz' appears to conceal the precise actions that were performed by the soldiers. For the most part, it seems that they simply moved into position and fired mortars and a heat-sensitive missile, designed to destroy tanks, at the Taliban. But 'launching' conveys much more magnitude and drama and glosses over what is involved in concrete terms.

All these verb processes suggest a clear attempt at representing warfare as an adventure performed by precision-trained troops. Anyone who has read accounts of frontline combat by former frontline soldiers will know more of the chaos, desperation, horror and pure luck that defines the situation.

The soldiers are also represented by verbal processes as they joke about the effect the operation has on their morale:

Sgt Conway, from Whitley Bay, Tyneside, said of the Taliban lair: "It used to be their backyard and now we've made it ours."

We are given access to their mental state through the behavioural verb 'grinned'. This could be interpreted as simply indicating pride in their work through an understated and ironic account of the results of the missile attack having a 'detrimental effect on their morale'. Alternatively, it could be seen more cynically in the context of the deaths and mutilation of the enemy.

The Taliban are represented as passive. Verbs position them as receivers, as in where they were 'targeted' and 'pounded with mortars'. Where they do attempt manoeuvres they are characterised with adjuncts 'tried' to hit back and 'trying' to creep.

(Continued)

(Continued)

We can see the differences in verb processes for the two groups. One behaves strategically and professionally, the other is the receiver of actions performed by the British army and since they only 'try' to hit back and creep they are neither competent nor successful. But one important question we can answer here is what processes have been backgounded in this text. The effects of the missile are absent from the text. There are no verb processes, such as 'being dismembered', 'maimed', or horrifically wounded'.

Case study 3: A predominance of verbal processes

In this third case study we see how a high quantity of verb processes can create an impression of a threat where there is none. This news item is from *The Daily Mail* (12 January 2010)

Guilty? It's a badge of honour say Muslim hate mob (and because we're on benefits, the state will pay our costs)

A group of Muslim extremists who screamed 'rapists' and 'murderers' at British soldiers went unpunished yesterday – and called their conviction 'a badge of honour'. The five were given conditional discharges for shouting 'baby killers' and 'terrorists' and waving placards at hundreds of soldiers returning from Iraq. Outside court they were surrounded by a mob of supporters and boasted they would do the same again, saying they wanted to see sharia law in Britain. The men, all of whom are on benefits, were each ordered to pay £500 in costs towards the prosecution. Outside the court, they defiantly declared: 'The taxpayer paid for this court case. The taxpayer will pay for the fines too out of benefits'. Surrounded by other followers of Islam4UK – the group led by so-called preacher of hate Anjem Choudary – they said they would protest again. Their backers waved a banner saying: 'Islam will dominate the world. Freedom can go to hell'. Some of the group members were linked to an egg attack on Tory peer Baroness Warsi when she visited Luton two months ago. The peer – who was hit by at least one of the eggs – faced a group of shouting protesters telling her that she was not a proper Muslim. No one was charged. During their six-day trial, the men argued they were exercising their right to freedom of speech and had been telling the truth about the conduct of British forces in Iraq. They were part of a demonstration against the 2nd Battalion Royal Anglian Regiment, who were marching through Luton after returning from Iraq. The protest sparked a hostile stand-off with angry members of the public who had been cheering the soldiers. Yesterday at Luton Magistrates' Court, five of the group were found guilty of using threatening, abusive, insulting words and behaviour likely to cause harassment, alarm and distress to others. They were Sajjadar Choudhury, 31, Munin Abdul, 28, Jalal Ahmed, 21, Yousaf Bashir, 29, and Ziaur Rahman, 32, all from Luton. Two others were acquitted. Although the offence carries a maximum fine of £1,000, the five were merely given a conditional discharge for two years by District Judge Carolyn Mellanby, which means if they are found guilty of anything else this conviction will be taken into account. The protesters had refused to stand for the judge as she entered and left court. But she yesterday said she did not wish to 'set a precedent' by charging them with contempt of court because of this.

This text provides a report on the court case for a number of Muslim men who had, the text explains, shouted abuse at marching British soldiers who had just returned from Iraq. This story can be seen as part of the same trend in some sectors of the British press at the time, for example the text we dealt with above on the soldiers in Helmand province. That text, we argued, sought to get the public behind 'Our Boys', rather than to garner support for this war in terms of its aims. What is particularly interesting in this text is the foregrounding of verbal processes to represent the 'extremists'.

First, we can look at the representational strategies in this text. On the one hand, we have those used to represent the accused men:

Group of Muslim extremists; the five; mob of supporters; them; followers; group; preacher of hate; backers; shouting protesters; Muslim.

Then we find a list names:

Sajjadar Choudhury; Munin Abdul; Jalal Ahmed; Yousaf Bashir; Ziaur Rahman

What is important in this text is that the arguments made by the accused men are not considered. We are to evaluate them on how they are represented, which we can see from this list is in terms of being a 'mob', 'followers' (rather than supporters) and 'extremists'. These are for the most part collectivised and generic. We do find personalisation through the use of the list of names. It is a usual convention in court reporting for journalists to supply the names, but when listed along with their ages in this manner this has the effect of collectivising them as offenders.

Next we have a collection of representational terms that are used for the 'us':

Taxpayer (twice); British forces; soldiers; 2nd Battalion Royal Anglian Regiment; members of the Public; judge; Peer; Baroness Wasi; District Judge Carolyn Mellanby.

Here we find honorifics, such as 'peer' and 'Baroness', and naming, as in 'Carolyn Mellanby', which does serve to functionalise and individualise the social actors. We also have examples of functionalisation in 'soldiers', 'judge' and 'taxpayers'. For the

(Continued)

125

(Continued)

long nominal group that is used to represent the soldiers 'the 2nd Battalion Royal Anglian Regiment', we could have found something much more generic such as 'the military', 'the army'. But such news items often include honorifics (Royal) and provenance (Anglian Regiment) in order to enhance the army's heritage and sense of it being part of the fabric of British public life.

There is also the collective and highly abstract term 'members of the public'. We are to assume that the accused men are not part of this category. Newspapers often use terms such as 'the British public', 'residents' or 'families' in ways that implicitly exclude certain kinds of people, such as 'anti-social' youth (Mayr and Machin, 2012). In some ways, of course, many members of the British public may also have extreme views and might also be 'followers'. But here they are described through a single abstract category. Together, we have the British public, those who represent them, the Regiment which defends their interests and official institutional figures which are part of British society. Many of us, however, might feel that we do not align with a generalised 'British public' nor feel any connection to peers and Baronesses and the system of privilege that they represent. Nor might we feel represented by the military.

So on the one hand we have the British public and its cherished and ancient institutions, and on the other a 'mob' of religious fanatics and of 'followers'. We can now look at what these two sides are represented as doing.

What stands out in this text is that the accused are represented mainly through verbal processes:

<u>screamed</u> 'rapists' and 'murderers' at British soldiers

<u>shouting</u> 'baby killers' and 'terrorists'

defiantly <u>declared</u>: 'The taxpayer paid for this court case. The taxpayer will pay for the fines too out of benefits

<u>argued</u> they were exercising their right to freedom

<u>called</u> their conviction 'a badge of honour'

<u>boasted</u> they would do the same again,

<u>telling</u> her that she was not a proper Muslim

<u>said</u> they would protest again.

<u>saying</u> they wanted to see sharia law in Britain

Verbal processes fall somewhere between mental processes and behavioural processes, as noted by Van Leeuwen (2008). In this case, we can see that these processes give us a sense of having access to the mental worlds of the speakers. We have also seen the way that these verbs of saying can be used by authors to shape the way we perceive intentions and identities of social actors in Chapter 3.

What we see here is that many of these suggest confidence and aggression. They 'scream', 'shout', 'declare' and 'argue'. We also find a sense of arrogance as they 'boast' and show 'defiance' and mock the taxpayer. They have the arrogance to say that they want to see Sharia law in Britain. This is supported by the metapropositional verb 'refused' to stand for the judge as she entered and left court.

In contrast, there are few material and relational processes:

<u>waving</u> placards

<u>waved</u> a banner

(<u>are</u>) on benefits

One could argue that the fact that these men are on benefits is beside the point in the context of the story. However, being 'on benefits' is important for the overall agenda of the newspaper in that it contributes to a typical representation of foreigners in general who wish to come to Britain, live off its resources, but then demand that their own cultural practices are respected over those of the British public.

They are shown as being recipients of processes:

led by so-called preacher of hate Anjem Choudary

linked to an egg attack on Tory peer Baroness Warsi when she visited Luton two months ago

Surrounded by other followers of Islam4UK

went unpunished yesterday

were merely given a conditional discharge for two years

Again, we find little agency on behalf of the accused men. They are 'led' by a preacher, 'surrounded' by other followers. Some sectors of the print media are fond of presenting such groups not as driven by thought through ideas and concerns, but led and pushed by charismatic, fanatical and embittered leaders. They are also 'linked' to an egg attack, which is hardly 9/11 and 7/7 again, yet which gives a sense of their persistence.

Finally, we find evidence that British society is not dealing with these people, as they went unpunished and were merely given a conditional discharge. Again, this is part of a well-trodden discourse about the British courts not protecting ordinary British citizens and victims of crime (see Jewkes, 2011).

The other participants in this text, 'the soldiers', are represented as 'marching' and 'returning from Iraq'. There is no indication of the soldiers responding to the shouts of the extremists.

(Continued)

(Continued)

We do find one sentence where the actions of the soldiers against which the accused are demonstrating are represented through a verbal process, where they argue they are:

telling the truth about the conduct of British forces in Iraq

In fact, the actions of the soldiers have been represented here by a noun 'conduct', which is an abstraction. It tells us nothing about the details of the actions in which the soldiers have been participating. In this way the text backgrounds actions by the military who are represented with honorifics (Royal) and provenance (Anglian), through '2nd Battalion Royal Anglian Regiment', and foregrounds the verbal processes of the accused.

We could also see the non-response of the soldiers as relational processes. They are professional and focused in contrast to the wild fanaticism of the extremist mob. We also find the crowds are 'cheering' which positively represents the crowd's feelings through a verbal process.

In sum, this text is about a mob of religious fanatics who follow a fanatical leader and who hate our national institutions and abuse the hospitality we give them. They do not actually do anything but are aggressive, vocal and arrogant and wish to replace our own institutions with their own.

That same story was represented slightly differently in other British newspapers. *The Observer* (12 March 2009), for example, did present the voice of other Muslims who saw the demonstration as politicisation rather than extremism. If these people are shouting their feelings in the street, should this not be the kind of behaviour that is to be expected. It is only a problem when this becomes violent. *The Observer* cites a postgraduate student:

"These people are certainly not extremists. They're just impassioned. Unless they're part of a group which is engaged in a violent organisation like Al-Qaeda, then just standing on the street with placards does not make them extremists. Rather, this is an example of politicisation. Second and third generation Muslims especially have become very politicised in Britain. One reason for this is the foreign policy of the UK and US etc, but another is the demonisation of the Muslim community. They've been pushed into politicisation rather than stepped into it willingly."

What becomes clear is the way that *The Daily Mail* ideologically seeks to background the notion of their being reasons for anyone's anger. The military, public institutions and the British public appear to be one entity with one common goal according to the discourse offered by this newspaper.

Case study 4: Female passivity in women's novels

The following is an extract from Stephanie Meyer's novel *Twilight*. The extract begins with the male character Edward using his hands to stop a van that was about to run over Bella. What we see is that while Bella is attributed many verb processes and the story is about her, she is the protagonist, these processes are of a certain type.

> [His hand] was suddenly gripping the body of the van, and something [Edward] was dragging me, swinging my legs around like a rag doll's, till they hit the tire of the tan car.
>
> "Bella? Are you alright?"
>
> "I'm fine." My voice sounded strange. I tried to sit up, and realized he was holding me against the side of his body in an iron grasp.
>
> "Be careful," he warned as I struggled. "I think you've hit your head pretty hard."
>
> I became aware of a throbbing ache centred above my left ear.
>
> "Ow," I said, surprised.
>
> "That's what I thought." His voice, amazingly, sounded like he was suppressing laughter.
>
> "How in the…" I trailed off, trying to clear my head, get my bearings. "How did you get here so fast?"
>
> "I was standing right next to you, Bella," he said, his tone serious again.
>
> I turned to sit up, and this time he let me, releasing his hold around my waist and sliding as far from me as he could in the limited space. I looked at his concerned, innocent expression and was disorientated again by the force of his gold-colored eyes. What was I asking him?
>
> Stephanie Meyer, 2006. *Twilight.* London: Atom, pp. 48–9.

In this passage it is Edward who is the main agent by being represented through material processes:

gripping the body of the van

dragging me, swinging my legs around like a rag doll's

he was holding me against the side of his body in an iron grasp.

releasing his hold around my waist

It is he in the passage who has the capacity for agentive action, to affect another entity (Fowler, 1991: 71). We also find prepositional phrases, such as 'in an iron grasp' to stress the dynamic force of the doer. Meanwhile, Bella is the patient of these processes, which foregrounds her passivity. The verb 'let' in the line 'I turned to sit up, and this time he let me' makes her passivity overt.

(Continued)

(Continued)

Bella is attributed two mental processes:

trying to <u>clear</u> my head,

<u>get my bearings</u>

We also find the adjunct 'trying to clear my head', which further dilutes her level of agency through positioning her not as doer, but at best as actor attempting to do. To some extent these verbs also serve to give us access to Bella's internal mental world. This is also accomplished through mental verbs which Edward is not attributed:

<u>realized</u> he was holding me

<u>was disorientated</u> again

We also find Bella's actions represented through material and behavioural processes which do not convey agency:

as I <u>struggled</u>

tried to <u>sit up</u>

I <u>looked</u> at his concerned, innocent expression

and verbal processes:

<u>trailed off</u>

<u>said</u>

In some contexts 'struggle' could be seen as a verb of agency, as in 'We struggle to overthrow the oppressors', but here we are given no goal; we only find that she struggles. These verb processes represent her strongly as having a 'being' kind of agency.

And Bella's process 'struggled' is also backgrounded through its representation within a prepositional clause. The main processes of warning Bella is attributed to Edward in the dominant clause.

This extract is typical of a particular genre of women's fiction. Through an analysis of transitivity patterns rather than lexical items that would connote passivity more overtly, we find a world where women appear to need and depend on men. This discourse incorporates participants (powerful, dynamic men; weak, passive females), behaviours (men's actions bring about change in world; females submit to consequences while not acting consequentially themselves) and values around men protecting and acting on behalf of women.

In other kinds of women's fiction, as Machin and Thornborrow (2003) show, women are attributed material processes, but mainly in relation to their sexuality and acts of seduction. In the text in the Chapter 2 on lexical analysis, we saw that in a *Marie Claire* item on how to get a promotion, even where colleagues are being made redundant, the woman had agency to do things like:

Scale the corporate ladder

Negotiate a title bump

Mind your alliances

Be a relentless cheerleader for your company

Align yourself with the office hotshot

Commiserate with your axed colleague over cocktails

In the analysis of this text in this chapter and on social actors we found that there was a mixture of professional terms (such as 'colleague' and 'manager') and trendy language (such as 'canned', 'title bump', 'cubemate') and that participants also included fictional characters from movies and children's stories as reference points (such as 'Tracy Flick'). In terms of transitivity, we find a predominance of abstractions where the details of certain actions are not explained and where actual goals are never very clear. Being a 'relentless cheerleader', a relational process, is unspecific, as is 'commiserating with an axed colleague over cocktails'. What exactly would you say to a colleague who has just lost their job when it is clear you are not supporting them but looking to turn this into an opportunity for yourself?

The visual representation of transitivity

We can use the same set of verb categories offered by Halliday to think about the visual representation of social action. We can think about what, visually, participants are represented as doing, whether there has been deletion of agents and whether the image helps to bring in an abstracted sense of what is going on. This too can be one way we can ask who is represented as agents, who is passive and where we are offered access to internal mental worlds. So here we can modify Halliday's (1978) six processes to deal with visual representation.

What will be important when we analyse visual representation of transitivity is the extent to which this is the same as the linguistic representations of transitivity. Are these the same or different, and if so in what ways? We can ask how this helps to foreground and background certain meanings in different contexts.

Case study 1: *Marie Claire* woman on page 46 in Chapter 2

We considered the actions carried out by the woman in this text earlier in this chapter. Here we are interested in how she is represented visually in terms of transitivity. We can then return to the linguistic representation to consider the relationship between the two.

The woman in the image is engaged in the behavioural process of looking. It is this looking off-frame in such magazine images that encourages the viewer to imagine what the woman's thoughts are. In women's lifestyle magazines women look off-frame either upwards and optimistically or downwards and pessimistically as discussed in Chapter 3, although looking downwards can also be interpreted as looking wistfully as if remembering or recollecting. The viewer is then encouraged to imagine the depicted person as the agent or subject of the accompanying text. So in this case the woman is thinking positively about the possibilities of the actions described linguistically. As we discussed in terms of social actor analysis (page 91) and transitivity (page 131) these are essentially highly selfish acts. Her colleagues are facing job losses. She does not rally alongside them and there is no sense of collegial spirit or union representatives. The point is only how to turn this to one's own advantage.

Linguistically, the actual impact of this selfish act is toned down through the use of abstractions in terms of transitivity, as in 'Scale the corporate ladder' and 'Commiserate with your axed colleague over cocktails', which hide the actual micro-details of what is involved. It is made to appear fun through trendy language, as in 'office hotshot,' 'canned', 'title bump', 'cubemate', and also placed slightly outside naturalistic reality and into the realm of playful fiction by reference to the protagonists of comedy films and children's fiction. Visually, we see a woman who is dressed in casual clothing – not a sharp business suit that might have connoted ambition and ruthlessness – who also smiles pleasantly and softly. We do not see a woman engaged in the same activities depicted linguistically. We do not see her manipulating people or commiserating.

Visual representation appears to have an important role in the representation of discourses in women's lifestyle magazines. In stories about sex, a woman might report that she has had sex with a waiter in the restaurant toilets, while she was in fact out with her boyfriend. Such a story would be typical of female sexual transgression found in such magazines (see Caldas Coulthard, 1994), where women are portrayed as naughty and as challenging traditional female roles. Such stories are often accompanied by photographs, such as the image shown below, which depict gentler and sensual sexual acts and which take place with soft lighting and in abstracted settings. But what would happen if the story was accompanied by a naturalistic photograph of the woman in the toilet? This would immediately change the story.

These images, of the sensual kiss and of the woman in *Marie Claire*, are not naturalistic ways of representation, but something more sensory. Backgrounds are never clearly articulated. These images are generally of a particularly abstracted and sensual nature. These are abstract empty settings that evoke a deterritorialised

Figure 11 Sensual kiss from Marie Claire.

simplicity and modernist aesthetic. As Machin and Thornborrow (2003) point out, the events and actions depicted linguistically are therefore placed in an exciting and sensual fantasy world. As Fairclough (2003) explains, wherever abstractions replace actual places, actions and persons, we must beware that ideological work is being done. In these lifestyle magazines women are depicted in texts as being sexually transgressive and as getting ahead at work. Visually, they are represented in sensual moments and exciting modernist settings engaged mainly in mental, existential and, in the case of sex, behavioural processes. Much of the agency represented, or at least connoted, in the texts would not have the same nature or implications if carried out in the real world. But placing these into fantasy worlds helps to amplify the opportunities for representing social practices without their normal consequences. Hawkes (1996), in criticism of 'power feminists' such as Camille Paglia, who celebrated the use of seduction by pop stars such as Madonna as indicative of true female power, argued that in the world outside stage and video, such behaviour can be problematic for young women. Sexual explicitness and overt seduction are on the whole not viewed by most men as a political statement of women's power. The same argument could be made as regards these images in lifestyle magazines.

Case study 2: Soldiers in Helmand province

This is the story we have analysed in terms of lexical analysis (page 40) and above in this chapter in terms of transitivity. We found that the soldiers, represented as social actors in terms of professional and functional categories, were engaged in the following kinds of verb processes:

Launched a devastating blitz; crept into position; staged a dawn raid; used missiles that locked onto their body heat; grinned; directed mortar rounds.

These verb processes were both material and behavioural, emphasising precision and professionalism. We concluded above that these were often abstractions that concealed actual actions and that they backgrounded the real effects of war on people. We also found the process 'grinned', where a soldier apparently gloats at the effect of the attack. It is only at this point that professionalism appears to be diminished, although it is included in the text possibly as an indicator of the pleasant humour of 'Our Boys', therefore humanising them.

Visually, we find the soldier engaged in the material process of walking, seemingly without any clear aim, or perhaps 'patrolling'. A civilian is engaged in the behavioural process of 'watching'. We can see that while linguistically the chaos and squalor of war is backgrounded through a series of process terms that emphasise precision and professionalism, visually the processes are completely suppressed and replaced only by an image of a patrolling soldier. Civilians are represented as completely passive and therefore, we might argue, in need of protection. Different wars have been represented visually in different ways over time. It is only during the Vietnam war that actual ongoing combat and its effects on soldiers and civilians were shown to the public. In Afghanistan, at the time of writing, we mainly see images intended to gain support for the troops. Here we see not an army attacking or seeking to kill enemies, but single soldiers walking. Civilians are not shown as large groups that might become affected by the conflict, but as a lone civilian watching calmly or in need of protection.

Case study 3: Health Trust websites

In earlier chapters we considered the lexis and representation of social actors on two National Health Service Trust homepages. We considered these as part of the wave of changes to the Trusts in terms of privatisation, reduction of services, lack of equal access, etc., and other rafts of government cuts. Alongside these we found language that relied on abstraction and signifiers of action, such as 'innovative' 'excellence' and 'vision', with an emphasis on 'partnership' and 'cooperation'. All this was typical of the empty business language described by Chiapello and Fairclough (2002). Such language serves to give the impression of there being dynamic action where in fact there is little.

We can also ask what kinds of visual transitivity are represented on these homepages. On page 54 in Chapter 2 we find the Heart of England homepage. For the most part we see behavioural processes as three of the participants smile at the viewer. We might have expected to have found images of actual workers carrying out the material processes that are involved in health care. So we could have found a nurse bandaging an arm, a surgeon examining someone's head, a health support worker demonstrating how a piece of equipment worked. We do see two people who appear to be engaged in work. One of these has her back to the viewer and appears to be working at a computer and the other appears to be a switchboard operator, smiling and presumably directing a caller. So the work processes represented are related to communication and administration and not to actual health care processes. The practices of the health service are therefore backgounded, while communication and dealing with clients are foregrounded. The (linguistic) focus is on the attitudes and 'values' of the Trust. It is committed to cooperation. Visually, too, we find behavioural processes that signify the same cooperation, through smiling faces and though verbal processes showing the telephone operator and the administrator, who will be presumably also smiling as they log your appointment in two years' time. All of this conceals increases in temporary working contracts, job freezes, low staff morale and the reliance on agency staff.

The homepage for the North Essex Partnership Health Trust represents two people as engaged in the behavioural processes of looking and smiling. They are not depicted as the beneficiaries of the material processes carried out by the Health Trust. In line with the Heart of England Trust, the woman is cited as saying 'They listen to me and really help'. Government policy has emphasised the need for public bodies to offer choice and accountability (Levitas, 2005), while at the same time dismantling the possibilities for these bodies to offer high-quality services. The effectivity of such bodies becomes measured by arbitrarily contrived target criteria, many based around the concepts of choice, cooperation and partnership. Levitas points out how these may have little to do with the quality of actual received services and may end up being aims in themselves. What we can see from these homepages, by looking at the representation of action visually, is the level of abstraction and the centrality of behavioural processes as actual concrete activities are replaced by smiling care workers, the activities of those whose job it is to log and direct our calls and the reactions of former patients who respond not in terms of whether they are now well but whether they were 'listened to'.

Conclusion

What we have shown in this chapter is that it is fruitful to analyse texts for what participants are represented as doing both linguistically and visually. This is important since it is one more way that we can examine the details of texts to reveal the underlying discourses. We have provided a set of categories for analysing action that allow us to break down actions in ways that permit us to observe more precisely who has power and who does not, who is humanised and who is not, and a number of other issues that point to the ideology buried in a text. We also saw that there could be differences in linguistic and visual representations. Visually, a soldier might be represented as being thoughtful and watchful while a text represents them behaving aggressively. In such cases, we can ask how the two work together to communicate discourses – that the image can provide a humanitarian setting for the action in the written text. What we have shown is that one useful way to carry out this kind of analysis is to create tables that allow us to compare the kinds of actions attributed to different participants.

6

Concealing and Taking for Granted: Nominalisation and Presupposition

In this chapter we look at two linguistic strategies of concealment: nominalisation and presupposition. Nominalisation typically replaces verb processes with a noun construction, which can obscure agency and responsibility for an action, what exactly happened and when it took place. Presupposition is one skilful way by which authors are able to imply meanings without overtly stating them, or present things as taken for granted and stable when in fact they may be contestable and ideological. In this chapter, we first look at nominalisation, exploring how it can be identified, and then look at how it can be used as an ideological tool analysing a number of case studies. We then move on to presupposition and return to look at examples in the same set of case studies.

Nominalisation

In Chapter 5 on the representation of social action we were concerned with the way that agents can be concealed through the use of passive verbs. We can see this in the following example:

The civilians were killed during a bombing raid (by the American bombers).

In a passive sentence like this, those responsible for the action may be either backgrounded or left out completely. If we want to make explicit who is behind the action, we have to turn the sentence into an active sentence. An active verb form would reveal the agent, as in:

The American bombers killed the civilians during the raid.

Here 'Americans' are the actors, represented through the active material process 'killed', with 'the civilians' being the goals of that action.

As we just have seen, the passive verb form is useful for backgrounding who performed the action represented by the verbal process. So we might hear:

Student fees have been increased by four hundred per cent.

Those who are behind 'increasing' the fees may prefer to use such a verb form to avoid having to say:

We have increased fees by four hundred per cent.

However, active agent deletion can be moved a stage further into nominalisation. This is where a verb process is transformed into a noun construction, creating further ambiguity, which can be intentional. For example, the previous sentences regarding the American bombers and the killing of civilians would be written as:

The killing of civilians during the bombing raid

In this case, all sense of agency is removed as the act of killing is represented as a nominalisation. Where we include the agent, we are told that the American bombers did the killing. When the passive verb form is used we either know that the civilians were killed by the Americans, but then this information is backgrounded, or it can be left out completely. The nominalisation obscures those responsible for the killing even further and also distances the event from any moment in time.

The following two examples illustrate the important difference between passive verbs and nouns:

The global economy was changed

The changed global economy

Here too we can see here that there is an important difference between simple removal of the agent and nominalisation. While the first of these two sentences uses a passivised verb to conceal the agent of the change in the economy, the second presents it as a noun, as a thing. There is no question of it being changed by an agent; it simply has changed. In fact 'globalisation' is often used as a nominalisation when it is actually a process. This itself can make it appear a simple fact rather than the result of political decisions. Fairclough (2000: 26) points out that in such constructions there is:

no specification of who or what is changing, a backgrounding of the processes of change themselves and a foregrounding of their effects. In backgrounding the processes themselves, nominalization also backgrounds questions of agency and causality, of who or what causes change.

This is an important observation, as what might be a process that we can challenge or do something about, is presented as simply a thing that is. Often politicians speak of 'the changed global economy' being a reason for the fact that life is now different in many ways. Yet by presenting it as a fact they hide that they have contributed to this state of affairs and have made decisions that have been unpopular with many people.

In the following example, a management consulting group gives advice for businesses:

> [the talk] looks at the longer-term picture and examines which countries will emerge in better shape and what should be done to respond to the changed global economy.

There is no sense that any agents have been changing the global economy. The global economy is basically a result of free trade unhampered by national governments and trade tariffs. After the Second World War, the USA pushed for the loosening of trade restrictions to sell its products around the world, using its military and economic power to motivate governments to do this, in the latter case using the International Monetary Fund (IMF) and World Bank to provide loans and foster development. Much of this went to support projects run by Western corporations. The World Trade Organisation, formerly known as GATT, gradually opened up world trade to manufacturing and, later, to service industries, allowing Western and other large international corporations to establish themselves around the planet. The changed global economy has been, and still is, the result of a deliberate project promoted by specific agents for their own purposes. The nominal group 'the changed global economy' simplifies what this actually means, which is a world economy where large corporations are able to move into increasingly newer markets to take advantage of cheaper labour and resources and take advantage of their existing economies of scale.

It should be now clear that nominalisations can be important ideologically. In a text, we may find that one set of participants are responsible for actions, meaning that they are responsible for the circumstances, whereas another group is unable to act. Or by representing processes as things, the necessity of having to deal with them can be omitted. As well as the effects of nominalisation we have just considered, there are a number we can look for in texts. What follows is a list of these effects.

Effects of nominalisation

In summary, changing a verb or process into a nominalisation can have eight important effects:

1 People are removed and therefore responsibility for the action has also been removed. This makes it seem as though events just happen

We can see how this process works in the following example:

The student lost his course work and was rather upset.

The student was upset about the loss of his course work.

In the second case, the fact that the student was the person who lost the coursework is concealed by turning the process 'to lose' into 'the loss'. This removal of responsibility can be seen equally in the next example:

I am sorry I have failed to return my library book on time.

I am sorry about the failure to return my library book on time.

Here the student appears able to gloss over the fact that she personally has not returned the library book, simply by representing it as a 'failure'. By using such constructions the student can suggest that the failure may have been due to other reasons than she forgot or did not bother.

In the following case we can see that this can also make the process appear as neutral and more objective once presented as a fact:

We analysed (process) the data. This revealed a number of trends.

The analysis (nominalisation) of the data revealed a number of trends.

We can imagine the different impressions these two sentences would create about the validity of a piece of research, say on crime trends, offered by a political party or local council:

Analysis of statistics has been shown to reveal no relation between crime and poverty.

As compared to:

We analysed the statistics which revealed there is no relation between crime and poverty.

In the first case, the use of the nominalisation 'analysis' implies that there may have been some independent research carried out, whereas in the second there could be some personal interest involved. Often in advertisements for products or services we find that 'analysis' and 'research' are cited, although we are not told who did the analysing and researching. We can see the use of the same technique in a statement made on behalf of a nuclear power plant reported by the BBC on 1 March 2010. The headline was 'Gulls contaminated with radiation culled at Sellafield'. We will just look at one sentence here:

> Monitoring and analysis has shown that the contamination is at such a low level that it poses no threat to health.

Here we can see that the first two nominalisations conceal who has carried out the monitoring and analysis. The third nominalisation is used to conceal the agent of the contamination. Was there a leak somewhere or was safety compromised and by whom?

2 Nominalisation can clearly hide both the agent and the affected since our vision has been channelled and narrowed

> Fighting has affected the supply of services to rural areas.

This is a general and not specific act and is used here to gloss over who is the initiator and who is affected. This is a hypothetical example, but what is concealed is whether one set of forces blew up roads, bridges and infrastructure, say through carpet bombing, or was there a more equal level of combat. This can be one way in which taking responsibility for affecting civilian lives can be sidestepped.

We can also see this process of obscuring who exactly did what in the following:

> A demonstration against increased tuition fees took place in front of the main building caused disruption to classes.

This could have been written:

> Students demonstrating against increased tuition fees in front of the main building caused disruption to classes.

In the first place, there is simply 'a demonstration'. When we include the agents, the students themselves, we change the nature of the disruption, as it is the very people that benefit from the classes who have decided to demonstrate rather that attend. One of the authors can recall being infuriated many years ago when a radio news item reported on a strike he was participating in in the following way:

> The strike has now prevented workers from entering the plant for over a week.

In this case, it may have been that the picket line consisted of workers and it was only members of the management who were inside the plant. But the nominalisation of 'the workers who are striking' into the noun 'the strike' obscures this. This kind of language use helps to represent strikes as enemies of the ordinary people and the ordinary worker and as mere disruption to the smooth running of services.

3   Nominaliation can remove any sense of time

We can see this in the following example:

> The Prime Minister rejected a <u>call</u> to carry out an inquiry into <u>allegations of corruption</u>. He announced that the <u>tightening of sanctions</u> was a decision that had been made through all the legal channels.

Here nominalisations are not marked for tense so they are outside time. This has the effect of avoiding when and how likely something is, which is necessary with verbs. When did someone call for an inquiry? When were the allegations made or the sanctions tightened? When was the decision made through legal channels? We can see here that as well as agent deletion, all sense of time is omitted. Yet we are given a sense of receiving information that is filled with actions and events.

Whenever there is deletion of actors, processes or circumstances, we must ask why this is the case. In the above statement, had the times and identities been included, the simple announcement made by the Prime Minister may have seemed less conclusive.

4   Since actions become a thing, it can be counted, described, classified and qualified through the resources of the nominal group, but this means that causality is now of secondary concern

We can see this in the following sentence:

> There were two precision strikes on the installation.

By turning an action (to strike) into a thing (a strike), a sense of the action is retained, but as a nominalisation, we can now point to it, describe its physical qualities, classify it and qualify it. So we can say it is a *precision* strike. We can see the same in the following regarding the failure to return the library books:

> The <u>regretful</u> failure to return my library books on time.

Here the student can express an apology, yet still sidestep actually taking responsibility. The same process can be used to 'dress up' other kinds of actions that have been nominalised:

> <u>Decisive and precise strikes</u> on enemy positions have been successful.

This addition of words that evaluate the noun or nominalisation creates nominal groups. The nominal group is a noun (called the 'head') surrounded by other words that characterise or evaluate that noun. Within any clause this nominal group works as though it were a single noun. So, 'decisive and precise strikes' functions as a single noun. These can then themselves become units used for the basis of discussion. So the complex process of performing an attack, performed by a particular agent with a particular subject, becomes something remote and formal in subsequent uses. Newspapers begin to refer to 'decisive and precision strikes'.

5   Nominalisations can function as new participants in new constructions

We can see this in the following sentence:

> The Vice Chancellor said that the <u>demonstration</u> regrettably caused <u>disruption</u> to the <u>education</u> of students.

In this example, 'the demonstration' has become an actor in itself rather than a process. This further increases the opacity of the other nominalisations. And in such cases other student action can be simply merged with the first one. So a later demonstration against increasing class sizes can then be spoken of as follows by the Vice Chancellor:

> Demonstrations over the past month have caused extensive disruption to learning and teaching.

Both of these times (where students expressed unhappiness with university life) are lumped together as factors that are disrupting 'learning and teaching'. Of course it could be argued that massive increases in tuition fees and increases in class sizes are the biggest disruption to learning and teaching.

6   Nominalisations can themselves become stable entities that will enter common usage

This can be seen in the following example:

> Globalisation should be seen as an opportunity for all of us.

People commonly refer to globalisation as a noun, so that it has for the most part been forgotten that it is a process and one that has been a result of specific kinds of political and economic decisions.

In the following example we can see that 'precision strikes' themselves become the thing that is referred to rather that the micro-actions that comprised the original process that was replaced by the nominalisation:

> The President said that <u>precision strikes</u> had not been responsible for civilian deaths in the region.

7   The process is still in the sentence, so the text accumulates a sense of action but avoids agents, times and specificity through simplification

We can get a sense of this in the following sentence, which is a headline from a newspaper describing the capture of Saddam Hussein by US forces:

Instant blitz on his lair

Rather than explaining the details of what the US forces did, we find the entity 'a blitz', which has also been classified as 'instant', connoting decisiveness on the part of the US forces. What this also shows is that the use of nominalisation in headlines is perfect for creating a sense of action through punchy, pacy language.

8   The text is becoming more dense or compressed. Details of events are reduced.

Fighting has affected the supply of services to rural areas.

We can see in this sentence that the nominalisations 'fighting' and 'supply' allow the omission of who is fighting and who is doing the supplying and what processes this involves. We observed the same above in the text from which this extract is taken:

The Prime Minister rejected a call to carry out an inquiry into allegations of corruption.

By deleting times and agents, this text becomes very compressed as we are not told who made the 'call', who should carry out the inquiry, who made the allegations, or when any of this took place. Compression of events in this way can make simple solutions appear more reasonable and feasible. In the example above regarding the student demonstrations, we can see that it is much simpler to say

Demonstrations must no longer be allowed to disrupt teaching and learning

than it is to make the same kind of statement where all details about actors and processes are included, as in

Students demonstrating against increased fees and excessive classroom sizes must no longer be allowed to do so as this disrupts teaching and learning.

Making nominalised sentences

Learning how to make nominalised sentences yourself is one good way to get used to identifying them in other texts. This process can be illustrated with the following example:

The staff constructed the course with the aim of generating maximum income.

Here it is clear who constructed the course. In the following sentence we delete the agent to create a passive verb:

The course was constructed with the aim of generating maximum income.

Then to create the nominalisation we do the following:

1   Identify the active verb in the clause
2   Change the verb into the nominalised form.

Active verb: 'constructed'
↓
Nominalisation
↓
'Construction'

The resulting sentence is:

The construction of the course aimed at generating maximum income.

For reasons covered above on the effects of nominalisation, this sentence might be preferred by those describing how the course came about. On the one hand, it is shorter and more concise. In addition, 'the construction' appears to be more objective and conceals who did the constructing. In universities it is not uncommon for instructions on new courses and the kinds of assessment criteria to be adopted to come directly from management, rather than being generated by academics or practitioners who believe them to be necessary for purposes of skills or knowledge transferral. This may be understandable where management have the responsibility to run the university in times where there are extensive budget cuts.

The nominal group and relative clauses

We can expand, modify or describe the information contained in a nominalisation through the addition of a clause containing further nominal groups.

A type of clause common to nominal groups is a relative clause. These are dependent clauses, meaning that they cannot stand alone without the main or independent clause. They are linked to the main clause by relative pronouns such as 'which' or 'who', or by relative adverbs such as 'where', 'when' and 'why'. For example:

> It was the demonstration taking place in front of the building which was found threatening by many staff and students.

Here the actions of the students have been replaced by the nominalisation 'the demonstration', which, as we saw above, conceals that it was the students actually demonstrating and backgrounds the need to provide their motivations to do so. In addition, the use of the nominalisation means that it can then be further qualified, namely that it was found threatening and linked to consequences. The use of the nominalisation rather than the process facilitates the addition of this information.

Case study 1: Tony Blair

In the Introduction to this book we considered the way that former British Prime Minister Tony Blair used language to create a sense that he was presenting a solution to certain global conflicts, particularly in the Middle East, without actually saying anything concrete. Nominalisations were one key part of his linguistic strategy, the result being that the identity of the agent, when they carry out the process and its effects are all sidestepped:

'Religious understanding is key to defeating hostilities threatening the world'.

'Understanding religion and people of faith is an essential part of understanding our increasingly globalized world.'

Throughout this particular speech, Tony Blair talks about 'understanding' and 'knowledge' as nominalisations and nouns rather than processes. By taking this step he is able to background what exactly it is that we need to understand or know. Following on from this, he states: 'What needs to be globalized is knowledge and understanding. ... It is knowledge that gives us foresight and help people realize what they have in common.'

The key here is that Blair avoids having to state any facts at all. He avoids any concrete explanation by treating 'understanding' and 'knowledge' as *things* rather than *processes*. Rather than saying 'We need to understand....' or 'We need to know...', we simply need the *things*: 'knowledge' and 'understanding'.

We emphasise that the problems to which Blair refers involve fundamental differences in world-view. If one group believes that global capitalism should be allowed to dominate all aspects of life and the other group that global capitalism is fundamentally wrong and immoral, what level of understanding are we referring to here? And many world conflicts such as that between of Israel and Palestine involve complex and brutal histories, military occupation and wider political and economic interests. In both these cases, will what we need to 'know' and 'understand' about each other prevent such hostilities? In his speech Blair never says what he means by 'knowledge' and 'understanding'. Nevertheless, by avoiding saying what we need to know and understand he is able to give a stirring and humane speech filled with hope and certainty since these two terms connote compassion and a humane liberal attitude.

Case study 2: The EMDA mission statement

Coming back to the EMDA mission statement, we also see the way that nominalisation can be used:

EMDA 'mission statement'

1   The <u>vision</u> is for the East Midlands to become a <u>fast growing, dynamic</u>

2   <u>economy</u> based on innovative, knowledge-based companies competing

3   successfully in the <u>global economy</u>.

4   East Midlands Innovation launched its Regional Innovation Strategy and

5   action plan in November 2006. This sets out how we will use the <u>knowledge</u>,

6   <u>skills</u> and <u>creativity</u> of organizations and individuals to build an <u>innovation</u>

7   <u>led economy</u>,

8   <u>Our primary role</u> to deliver our mission is to be the <u>strategic driver</u> of

9   <u>economic development</u> in the East Midlands, working with partners to

10 deliver the goals of the Regional Economic Strategy, which EMDA

11 produces on behalf of the region.

This text is full of nouns and nominalisations. Since they are nominalised, their connotative powers can be used without the inconvenience of having so be specific about agents, times and outcomes.

(Continued)

(Continued)

In line 1 we find

The vision is for the East Midlands to become…

Here 'the vision' appears to replace the process of 'seeing' or 'predicting'.

We predict/see that the East Midlands will become…

Of course 'vision' connotes something that is not simply seeing, but has almost religious associations. And in this sense it appears less as a firm prediction or promise. But 'vision' here can also be thought of as concealing agency, time and causality. 'The vision' as a nominalised process allows for much more generalisation than 'seeing' or 'predicting'.

In lines 1 and 2 we find:

… the East Midlands to become a fast growing, dynamic economy

Leaving out the noun 'economy', this could be written as

the East Midlands will grow fast and become dynamic

The problem is, as in the case of the use of 'vision' rather than 'seeing', this sounds too specific and implies a sense of time through which 'it will grow fast'. Organisations that make this kind of promise are much more likely to be held accountable than those who have 'visions' that regions will become 'fast growing dynamic economies'.

In line 2 we find:

based on innovative, knowledge-based companies

In the fashion of Tony Blair's comments above regarding understanding other cultures, the nominalisation 'knowledge' replaces the process of 'knowing'. By taking this step, the author can avoid stating what they 'know'. Of course all companies must have some kind of knowledge; they must know something. Here the text may refer to companies that provide information. But again, who do they inform and about what? Stating this in the nominalised form retains the connotative powers of these terms without the requirement to specify.

We see other uses of nominalisations that can then be referred to as fixed entities in the following use of 'innovation':

East Midlands Innovation

Regional Innovation Strategy

an innovation led economy.

Here, the act of innovating, where agents and other details must be provided, has been replaced simply by the nominalisation 'innovation'. It is this switch from actual concrete processes that involve bringing about the new, change and knowing, to nominalisations that are then referred to consistently as entities that has become the stuff of corporate and government language (Chiapello and Fairclough, 2002). This linguistic stepping away from processes of what is predicted, known and innovated towards abstracted entities is one clue to the way that these official bodies seek to conceal from us who is doing what to whom, who provides what kinds of services and takes what kind of responsibility. At the same time this is carried out in a culture of accountability characterised by league tables and appraisal criteria, which many argue carry information equally as abstracted and divorced from everyday practices, procedures and attainments.

On page 34 of Chapter 2 we considered the corporate language of the Loughborough University website, which stated:

> Loughborough University is a dynamic, forward looking institution, committed to being a centre of excellence in teaching, learning and enterprise.

Rather than Loughborough University stating that it 'looks forward', it is nominalised as a 'forward looking institution'. Presented in this way, what is being looked forward to is backgrounded. And as we considered in Chapter 2, 'forward' here carries connotations of something good, whereas backwards or 'looking at where we are' presumably is bad. In Chapter 7 we will consider the way that we tend to think about our experiences metaphorically. Here we find the metaphor of a journey, where there is a need to look ahead to where we are going rather than back to where we have come from, but metaphors, while foregrounding some aspects of an experience, can background others, just like other forms of language. Perhaps important institutions in our society should mostly be looking backwards, considering historically what has produced the best teaching and learning, rather than being distracted by the next obstacle on the journey.

Case study 3: The *Marie Claire* article and Muslim prisoners story

In earlier chapters we have analysed an article from *Marie Claire*, which offered advice on how women can still get promotion while people around them are losing their jobs. While the article promotes a highly cynical act of individualism rather that collective action, it does so through certain kinds of choices of representation of social actors and of social action that make this appear as slightly abstracted fun, with one foot in a fictional domain. Nominalisation, too, is used in the article to background processes, agents and those affected, and is another strategy by which the advice offered by the magazine is legitimised. We find this in the first lines:

(Continued)

(Continued)

> Yes, it is still possible to scale the corporate ladder in spite of layoffs. Here, Bob Calandra, co-author of *How to Keep Your Job in a Tough Competitive Market*, offers advice for gingerly negotiating a title bump.

We find two important noun constructions. The first is the nominalisation 'layoffs' in line 1. It could have been written using the verb process 'laid off' to explain that 'colleagues are being laid off', but here the use of nominalisation helps to background the fact that there are people suffering, which might compel a different kind of more collective action.

The second noun construction is found in the last line in 'title bump'. By turning the process of 'seeking promotion' into a noun, it distances its connection to actions, and also allows the use of the trendy language. Along with the other linguistic devices in the text, already discussed, this aids abstraction and fosters a sense that this process is a simple one and with few moral implications.

In the next line we find:

> Be a relentless cheerleader for the company, even if it means irking co-workers. Your manager is bound to pick up on your positive outlook and use you as a model.

Again, there is the use of trendy language in the nominalisation of 'cheerleading'. Of course this is also a complete abstraction as it is not specified what 'being a cheerleader' in the context of a company entails. Nonetheless, the use of nominalisation allows it to become an entity that can be discussed as a thing rather than a process linked into a cause/effect chain.

In the following example of the news text about Muslim prisoners analysed in Chapters 3 and 5, we can see how nominalisation can be used to increase the pace of a story. In this text we found that there was an overlexicalisation of the word 'Muslim' along with non-specific aggregation of their number as 'scores'. They were also represented through mainly aggressive verbal processes, where they were 'complaining' and 'demanding', and the actual causes of their grievances were often placed in subordinate clauses to background them:

> Scores of Muslim inmates at a high security prison are set to launch a multi-million pound claim for compensation <u>after they were offered ham sandwiches during the holy month of Ramadan.</u> (*The Daily Mail*, 26 October 2007)

Here the noun 'claim', replacing the verb process 'to claim', allows the creation of the nominal group 'multi-million pound claim'. This is how the sentences would have read had the verb process 'to claim' been used:

> Scores of Muslim inmates at a high security prison are to claim millions of pounds in compensation.

Here, by using the verb 'to claim', we lose the dramatic verb 'set to launch'. The nominal group 'multi-million pound claim' here can be used to increase drama, but also to increase abstraction and causal links, because details become naturally compressed. We will look at this process in news texts in the following example.

Case study 4: 'Blitz on Lair' story

In the following newspaper item from *The Sun* (20 March 2003) about the Iraq war, we find extensive use of nominalisation to compress information and to give the story added pace, which is particularly in the tradition of tabloid newspapers. There are many linguistic features we could analyse in this story, such as the lexical euphemisms used to represent acts by the American army, as in 'soften up' and 'isolated strikes', and the overlexicalisation of terms that point to advanced technology, which is used to background the actual violence and destruction that results (such as 'satellite-guided bombs', 'F117 Nighthawk stealth fighters', 'Unmanned spy drones'). Here, however, we restrict our attention to the nouns and nominalisations found in this text. We will return later to the role of presupposition.

INSTANT BLITZ ON HIS LAIR

Saddam home blast

AMERICAN cruise missiles struck Baghdad early today in a surprise decapitation strike.

Three explosions were heard as the US launched an attack on what they called 'a target of opportunity'.

Forty-three missiles fired from warships in the Gulf and satellite-guided bombs dropped by Stealth jets hit a house in southern Baghdad.

Saddam and his two sons were thought to be staying there.

US military chiefs decided on the isolated strike after intelligence reports had pinned down Saddam's whereabouts yesterday afternoon.

US F15 strike Eagles and F117 Nighthawk stealth fighters were diverted from a mission to soften up targets in the southern no-fly zone.

They were sent north to Baghdad after intelligence reports were shown to US Commander-in-Chief General Tommy Franks giving him a shot at hitting Saddam and his top henchmen.

(Continued)

151

(Continued)

Unmanned spy drones were filming live pictures of movements above Baghdad and beaming them back to US Central Command in Qatar.

A Pentagon source said: 'It was a selective air strike – a strike of opportunity'.

The text begins with two nouns, both of which conceal the actual details of the operation and which serve, tabloid-style, to provide punchy, exciting language:

Instant blitz on his lair

Saddam home blast

Here 'blitz' and 'blast' conceal agents and what actually took place in concrete terms. What actually constituted a 'blitz' and 'blast' in this case? Of what magnitude was this explosion? How many houses were destroyed and how many people killed? The Blitz after all is a term used to refer to the prolonged bombing raids on London during the Second World War. This is a common way that news media such as *The Sun* abstract the actual processes involved in warfare. Through their abstract nature they background actual intentionality and levels of violence and destruction (Van Dijk, 2008: 823). Were many people injured and maimed after the 43 missiles and the bombs dropped from the planes exploded? This is not discussed. Instead the noun 'blitz' is used, which connotes 'energy' and 'action', but also communicate 'precision' and 'intelligence'.

This text is further evidence of the way that nominalisations become stable entities. We find the nominal groups 'surprise decapitation strike' in lines 2–3 and 'the isolated strike' in line 8. Both 'surprise' and 'isolated' here imply precise, contained and minimal collateral damage. Later in the article, in line 18, we are told 'It was a selective air strike – a strike of opportunity'. Again, the actual details of the attack have become a stable entity that can now be talked about in different ways using different modifiers. In fact, firing 43 cruise missiles and an unspecified number of bombs being dropped from aircraft suggests that the impact may have been slightly more than isolated, selective and instant.

It is also worth mentioning how the nominalisations in this text help to transform the outcome of the attack into circumstances, as in:

American cruise missiles struck Baghdad early today <u>in a surprise decapitation strike</u>.

The preposition 'in' positions the nominalised 'surprise decapitation strike' as circumstance or *context* of the material process 'struck', rather than as the *result* of missiles striking. And of course in this sentence it is the cruise missiles who are the agents that do the striking, rather than the Americans. The sentence could have been written:

> Americans fired 43 cruise missiles and dropped bombs on Baghdad earlier today in a surprise decapitation strike.

Here, the active material processes 'fired' and 'dropped' make the Americans responsible for the action, although this sentence still gives a sense that the firing was in the circumstance of the surprise decapitation strike rather than the strike being the same thing as the firing.

In line 4, we find a typical news language nominalisation of an attack:

> The US launched an attack on what they called 'a target of opportunity

We can only speculate why the journalist did not simply say 'the US attacked', but here the use of the nominalisation 'attack' allows the use of 'launched', which connotes additional drama.

Presupposition

Presupposition is to do with what kinds of meanings are assumed as given in a text, what Fairclough calls the 'pre-constructed elements' (1995a: 107). In fact, all language use is filled with presupposition. Even the sentence 'The bag is heavy' involves the assumption that you know what 'a bag' is and what 'heavy' is. But it is productive to look at texts or spoken language for the meanings that are present as given, yet which are highly contestable.

Much of how we process texts is of course subconscious. We are not continually monitoring what people mean, although in some contexts we may come to be aware that someone is using a slightly different meaning from the one we would normally use for something. Normally, people have to rely on shared presuppositions. We cannot say 'I will put this in my bag... what I mean by a bag is...'. People would give up talking, although sometimes we are called upon to be more precise about what we mean.

In many cases, particularly those we analyse in this book, what is presented as given, as not requiring definition, is deeply ideological. And we have shown so far that language is continually used to foreground certain things and silence others. Therefore looking what is assumed in a text can be revealing. What is a text setting out as 'the known'? We can see this in a sentence such as:

British culture is under threat by immigration.

This assumes that there is such a thing as 'British culture'. Studies in Social Anthropology and Cultural Studies have shown that this idea of monolithic or 'essentialised' cultures is mostly an illusion. Concepts like 'British culture' hide massive variation, differences and change within that culture. Yet such concepts can be used to advance particular interests and ideologies. Often, the concept 'British culture' is found in the more right-wing national press to create a contrast to 'immigrants' who threaten to dilute this culture.

We see the same use of presupposition in the following sentence:

> In a Christian society such as Britain is there place for single faith schools based on Islam?

Here the presupposition is that Britain is a Christian society. What this means, at what level, is not articulated. One of the authors grew up in Britain and experienced Christianity only at school in the form of what he perceived as oppressive moralising during morning assemblies, which seemed difficult to believe in at a time of economic upheaval and strikes, where authorities appeared largely as enemies of people. Therefore, Britain might be a Christian society only in the sense of an official religion rather than as the basic cosmology of the majority of inhabitants. Some writers even argue that places like Britain have never been true Christian societies (e.g. Duerr, 1985), arguing that more recent histories gloss over the central role of Paganism even into the twentieth century.

Presupposition can be used in order to build a basis for what sounds like a logical argument, as above. There is such a thing as 'British culture' and therefore immigration must be seen as a threat. If Britain is a Christian society, why should other religions be allowed to set up their own schools? These two examples serve to illustrate how text producers can establish what is to be known and shared.

Fairclough (1995a) discusses the way that language can reconstitute the social world. If the fact that there is a global economy becomes accepted as a given, as it has for the most part in the Western news media, then we sideline the fact that it is open for contestation, that it is part of political decisions and choices that are being made right now. If we can make everyone accept that there is a British culture, then people can be more easily persuaded that it is something that must be protected, and that things and people that are not part of this culture can be identified and dealt with. The same goes for the sentence:

> The British people are a generous lot, but their patience is being tried on the subject of immigration....

Here the presupposition is that there is a 'British people' who would identify themselves as such. The inclination to align with this group is made more attractive by the evaluation of them as generous. But this serves the same role as accepting that there is a 'British culture', although it is harder to argue that there is not a 'British people', as this can mean people who were born in the country and/or who closely associate with that country. For van Dijk (1991), this is a classic move of racist rhetoric. We can see how these kinds of presuppositions work in the following newspaper text, from *The Daily Express* (23 February 2010).

LABOUR SAY WE ARE ALL RACISTS

1 LABOUR dismissed the British public's widespread opposition to mass

2 immigration as 'racism', a Government document revealed yesterday. Officials

3 made it clear that public opinion was strongly against relaxing border controls. But

4 ministers were urged to ignore voters' 'racist' views and press ahead with a secret

5 policy to encourage migrants to flood into Britain. Whitehall experts even

6 proposed a major propaganda campaign to soften up voters in preparation for the

7 mass influx of newcomers. The details were laid bare in the original draft of a

8 policy document released for the first time under the Freedom of Information Act.

9 Last night critics accused the Government of snubbing the concerns of British

10 citizens in their deliberate pursuit of a multicultural society.

In line 1 we can see that it is presupposed that there is an entity called the 'British public', and that its views on immigration are widespread and not of a minority. Such a presupposition conceals the complexity of viewpoints and the different kinds of people that comprise a society like Britain.

In lines 1 and 2 it is presupposed that there is indeed mass immigration. No figures are presented to substantiate this claim. It is simply presented as a given.

In line 3, the presupposition is that there is a thing called 'public opinion', which again backgrounds the possibility of differing viewpoints held among tens of millions of people in a society that has experienced many generations of immigration.

In line 7 we are told details were laid bare in the original draft. So it is presupposed that there have been others, presumably those that have concealed the original plans. This is not explicitly stated, however.

In line 7 we are told there will be a 'mass influx of newcomers'. The way immigration is presented here presupposes that that there is such a thing as 'old comers', in other words an identifiable, authentic, real British people. The term 'mass' also presupposes that the intake of large numbers of people will not be gradual but sudden.

Lines 9 and 10 presuppose that a large number of British people have the same 'concerns'. Together, all of these presuppositions create a sense of a coherent British citizenry who have a shared heritage and shared opinion and who are accused of being racist by the Labour government simply for believing it wrong to accept the mass new comers.

We can see the way that presupposition is used below in a local Council policy document. This is an extract from the East Midlands Development Agency mission statement analysed for lexical content and nominalisation previously. What we see here is that the presuppositions are identities and entities that have become common currency in government-speak drawn from corporate business language. Such is the layering of these presuppositions, as taken-for-granted concepts, that it becomes impossible to grasp what is actually going on:

> The vision is for the East Midlands to become a fast growing, dynamic economy based on innovative, knowledge based companies competing successfully in the global economy.

> East Midlands Innovation launched its Regional Innovation Strategy and action plan in November 2006. This sets out how we will use the knowledge, skills and creativity of organisations and individuals to build an innovation led economy

This presupposes that there is indeed a global economy which is taken for granted and identifiable, despite the fact that many analysts see global economic processes as far from equal around the planet and being characterised by particular relations of power and driven by certain interests, particularly those of large multinational corporations and banks (Fairclough, 2003: 163). We can also ask what exactly is a 'dynamic economy'? 'Dynamic' suggests something moving. Therefore is it presupposed here that things that are stable are bad? And what is an 'innovative, knowledge based company'. Are there indeed such companies? 'Innovation' here has become a corporate buzzword with entirely positive connotations. What it implicitly implies is that change and adaptation are good things as opposed to stability and established practices. If this was expressed overtly rather than through presupposition, it might sound a much less attractive proposal in that there is a lack of respect for and value of existing industry and more traditional skills.

Of course this language of change and adaptation very much fits in with the economic patterns of global processes where we do indeed appear to have shifted away from times of relative stability to those of relative instability. What texts like this do, however, through presupposition, is help to conceal that such things might be choices as regards how we run our societies rather than facts to which we must inevitably adapt.

In the following sentences we can see how useful presupposition can be for allowing speakers to strategically avoid being explicit about what they mean, while allowing them to create the basis of what they can then go on to say.

These are all common in political speeches, news texts and can also be found in any case of language use where people engage in more strategic debates, such as in web blogs:

This new model of organisation...

This presupposes that there was an old model of organisation. And in current thinking it appears that 'new' is generally accepted as good and the 'old' as bad.

Militants launched a new wave of attacks today...

This suggests that there was an old wave distinctive from this one. The 'militants' themselves might see themselves as simply involved in an ongoing struggle against their oppressors. But presenting their activities as 'a new wave' can suggest that the danger is increasing or be a call to respond by the authorities or military.

The real issue is...

This presupposes that there are other issues, but that they are not so important. A politician faced with a set of social problems relating to teenagers that are clearly linked poverty and unemployment, related matters of marginalisation and lack of self-esteem might say: 'The real issue here is parental responsibility'. They avoid saying that the other factors are at play as well, but allow themselves to define the terrain and to sidestep responsibility for actual structural issues that cause the problem in the first place. A similar kind of presupposition would be:

We need to discuss the underlying issues...

Here the suggestion is that what we have already discussed is just the surface and that what is to be said will be more crucial and fundamental. Of course what are presented as 'the underlying issues' may be purely opinion and ideology. We can see Tony Blair's use of this idea of there being real and underlying issues in a speech given to the British House of Commons in 2003 in a debate on the war in Iraq and the link between terror and weapons of mass destruction (WMD). He uses expressions like 'real issue' and 'underlying issue' to legitimise his own agenda and to sideline others.

1   But, of course, in a sense, any fair observer does not really dispute that Iraq is in

2   breach and that 1441 implies action in such circumstances. The real problem is that,

3   underneath, people dispute that Iraq is a threat; dispute the link between terrorism

4   and WMD; dispute the whole basis of our assertion that the two
    together constitute

5   a fundamental assault on our way of life.

(www.guardian.co.uk/politics/2003/mar/18/foreignpolicy.iraq1)

In this extract, we see the first use of presupposition in line 1 to delegitimise
opposing views with the words 'any fair observer does not really dispute'.
This presupposes that anyone who does dispute this is therefore not a fair
observer. The second use is in the line 2: 'The real problem is that'. So there
may be other issues but this is the really important one that we should be
talking about. This is given emphasis in line 3 with the words 'underneath
people dispute'. This presupposes that there may be more superficial and
surface arguments made that are in fact simply concealing the real denial of
the fact that Iran is a threat and that there is a link between terrorism and
WMD. Blair here positions himself as therefore revealing what lies underneath. Finally, in line 5 we find the presupposition 'assault on our way of life',
presuming that there is a 'way of life' that we all share. What aspect of this he
means is not made clear; it is simply presupposed that this is self-evident. In
fact during the period where leaders such as Blair and Bush were referring
to the 'Axis of Evil' and WMD, they often characterised what was under threat
as being not political and economic power or access to global resources such
as oil, but 'our way of life'. What happens is that such presuppositions enter
into common usage in the media in a broader sense and increasingly come to
appear as self-evident and then background their original ideological usage.
We find Blair using the same term in September 2006:

> This terrorism isn't our fault. We didn't cause it. It's not the consequence
> of foreign policy. It is an attack on our way of life. It is global. It has an
> ideology.

Other typical uses of such presuppositions by politicians are:

> We should take this opportunity...

This can be used to portray something as an opportunity when others might
not see it this way. It could be one rhetorical strategy to give a positive spin on
something that might otherwise be seen as negative. We find this in a speech
given by George Bush in 2001 at the height of the 'War on Terror' rhetoric,
when Bush sought to promote the idea of abandoning a weapons treaty in
order to establish a new generation of missile defences:

> To maintain peace, to protect our own citizens and our own allies and
> friends, we must seek security based on more than the grim premise
> that we can destroy those who seek to destroy us. This is an important
> opportunity for the world to rethink the unthinkable and to find new
> ways to keep the peace.

Rather than present this situation as a difficult one, he represents it as an opportunity for the world to move on and find new ways to keep the peace.

We see the same use of presupposition in a speech given by David Cameron before the British general election in 2010.

1 It is time for change. And if we do not take this opportunity, grasp this hour, to set

2 a new direction for Britain then I tell you in all frankness it will be too late. It will

3 be too late in five years' time to say we should have got rid of them, too late to

4 reverse the decline, the debt will be too big, the bureaucracy too bloated, the small

5 businesses too stifled, the slope Britain is sliding down will be too steep,'

6 So to every voter listening to us now we say solemnly, if not now it will be too

7 late. It is time, time to say we can rescue our country, time to refuse to get poorer

8 and more indebted, time to say Britain is not doomed to decline, time to let the

9 Labour party fight its squabbles out of power where it can do no harm, time to

10 invite the forces of hell to get the hell out of Downing Street.

In line 1 we find 'if we do not take this opportunity', which assumes that this is in fact an opportunity, so presenting this in a positive light. In this extract we also find repeated use of 'Britain' represented through personification as an entity in itself that has coherent experiences. Cameron therefore sidesteps the complex nature of the electorate and the very different experiences of those who comprise it.

In line 2 we find the expression 'set a new direction for Britain', which assumes that Britain as a whole is moving in one coherent direction and that the old direction was not successful.

In line 7 we find 'time to refuse to get poorer and more indebted', which presupposes that we are aware of the country's and our personal financial situation and debt; it also suggests that we previously accepted the situation and agreed to become poor and indebted and that Cameron's suggestions need to be put into practice immediately as now is the time.

Every time you... (you are repeatedly doing something)

A politician might announce: 'Every time I hear an objection to the possibilities offered by the introduction of private finance into the health services....' This gives a sense of routine, that the politician is used to such objections, and even bored by them. David Cameron can be seen here using this strategy in a different speech when referring to the persistent undemocratic actions of the Iranian state without, of course, having to say specifically how many times this has happened.

> Every time the Iranian state has tried to choke the flow of information to dampen down the protests, people have turned to technology to share and access information.

We can see that Cameron is able to use 'every time' to create a sense of Iran being a constant and persistent problem.
A further example is:

> Let me address your concerns…

When a politician uses this presupposition they can make the assumption that citizens do actually have concerns and that the speaker/politician is claiming to know what they are. Politicians often use this presupposition to control what concerns you are permitted to have. A speech might begin: 'We are all shocked and appalled about the recent losses of life of our boys fighting for our country overseas. Let me today address your concerns…' They can use this to go on to lay out what kind of concerns people have, shaping these to fit their own aims and interests. In the case of 'our boys' overseas, they might go on to thoroughly address concerns regarding quality of equipment and support for those who get injured and killed and simply not mention matters of political reasons for the conflict.

In the speech extract below, New Labour leader Ed Milliband spoke of 'your concerns' after Labour's defeat in the 2010 general election in order to be able to list the kinds of issues that he would deal with.

> You wanted your concerns about the impact of immigration on communities to be heard, and I understand your frustration that we didn't seem to be on your side.

One set of common presuppositions used by speakers are the following:

> Every reasonable person knows that…

Politicians and people in general can use this kind of statement to suggest that what follows is universally reasonable according to some widely accepted and common sense standards of truth. Of course what they are saying is that if you are not in agreement then you are not reasonable. A very similar presupposition is:

Nobody in their right mind would think that...

Here the speaker is implicitly saying that anyone who disagrees with their point of view is insane. We have already seen something very similar used by Tony Blair in the extract from his speech above. Below we see how this is used as a typical rhetorical strategy found in discussion on a web blog about a war against Iran. We can see how successive replies also begin with presuppositions:

> As every reasonable person knows, the only side which benefits from a war with Iran & Iranians, is only and I mean really ONLY the dictatorship of the mullahs in Iran.

> Let's be realistic and see the situation in Iran without any pre-judgements. (One thing I must say here that I hope I am not discussing something with someone who is by any chance supporting the mullahs or the shah's dictatorship.)

> While not getting into a specific discussion regarding the sanctions, I felt it necessary to clarify the truth. Too many people make assumptions on what the sanctions are without spending the time to learn the truth. Thanks!

> (www.huffingtonpost.com/social/koroush1336/listen-to-iranian-voices _b_742416_62218194.html)

In the first line, the writer implies that if you do not agree with the statement, then you are simply not reasonable. The first reply, by beginning with 'Let's be realistic', implies that what has been said is not realistic but what they are saying is. The third speaker uses a typical rhetorical move used by politicians where they state that 'without getting into the specific details of the situation' they will clarify the situation. This implies that they do indeed know all the specific details of the situation and that these details do in fact support the argument they are about to make.

What is your reaction to that? Or What action will you take?

These sentences presuppose that you do or should have a reaction and that you should have some kind of plan of action. In either case to say you have no reaction or no plan of action might seem inappropriate. A journalist might ask a politician:

> What action are you going to take against the Afghan dictatorship after they have thwarted trade agreements?

Here it is assumed that action must be taken and that the politician should be able to simply say what this is in easy terms, when of course responses may require careful consideration and strategies at a diplomatic level. Some writers have argued that part of the success of American presidents, such as the two George Bushes over those like Jimmy Carter, is that they were better able to present easy decisive solutions to the public, even if in the longer term these decisions would have less favourable outcomes (McConnell, 2001; McClintock, 2002).

Conclusion

In this chapter we looked at ways by which, in the first place, identities, responsibilities and contexts can be concealed in language and, in the second place, where the contestable is presented as taken for granted and, finally, where meanings are implied but remain unstated. Nominalisation and presupposition are important tools where authors wish to persuade without stating ideologies overtly. Nominalisation is specifically important when authors seek to represent processes and events through abstractions rather than through the micro-details of who did what to whom. In our analysis, we can list the kinds of participants and actions that are abstracted and those that are not. We can also look, as we did above, at the ways that authors seek to promote certain kinds of concepts as taken for granted and ask what are the consequences of so doing.

7

Persuading with Abstraction: Rhetoric and Metaphor

There is a widely shared assumption that metaphor is about flowery language, that it is something associated with poetry and creative writing. But linguists have shown that metaphor is fundamental to human thought and that metaphorical thinking underlies all of our statements about the world (Lakoff and Johnson, 1980; Chilton, 1996; Hart, 2008; Semino, 2008). The study of metaphor and other rhetorical tropes has been closely aligned to the study of political rhetoric. Since the time of Aristotle, there has been an interest in how to persuade people in the context of public speaking. It was possible during his time to train in rhetorical skills that would include hyperbole, metaphor, metonymy and puns, all of which we will consider in this chapter. What we show in this chapter is that it is not so much that metaphor is opposed to truth, but rather that it is a fundamental part of human cognitive processes. We continually think of things by reference to others in order to understand them. But what is most important is that this process can influence the way we understand that thing or concept. For example, we can find in children's textbooks:

> The heart is the mechanism that pumps oxygen around the body to feed the important organs of the body.

Of course, the heart is not a mechanism. It is not literally made up of components. This view of the body as a machine can be traced to the industrial revolution, when the machine and engineering became popular models for thinking about society and the natural world. On the one hand, this metaphor can help us grasp that the heart can be seen as performing one role fitting in with other 'components' in the body. On the other hand, we might argue that this misrepresents the heart as it is not a mechanism.

Cameron (2003) notes that such metaphors are useful for pedagogical purposes as they appeal to kinds of knowledge the reader may already have. We might understand that when the heart fails, it is because part of the mechanism, one of its components, has a fault. An operation can then be performed to repair that part.

In other views of medicine and the human body, however, such as in Chinese and holistic medicine, this view of the heart as a machine would be problematic as it encourages a view of the body as being comprised of separate, distinct elements. This fragmented view of the body, some would argue, tends to shift attention away from more holistic pre-emptive healthcare practices that view the body as a whole. One of the authors has seen an acupuncturist turn a breached baby prior to labour by putting needles in various parts of the woman's body, but not in her stomach and not in the baby. Which part of the machine, which mechanism, is the acupuncturist adjusting or fixing?

What is important here is to grasp that metaphor is an everyday part of language and an important way of how we grasp reality. But metaphors can be of ideological significance. Which metaphors become accepted can have implications not only for how we think about and understand the world, but also for how we act, the institutions we build and how we organise our societies.

Fairclough (1995a: 94) points out that metaphors have hidden ideological loadings due to the way that they can conceal and shape understandings, while at the same time giving the impression that they reveal them. They are, therefore, one linguistic way of hiding underlying power relations. Metaphor and other rhetorical tropes provide excellent linguistics resources for those who wish to replace actual concrete processes, identities and settings with abstractions. This chapter will provide a set of tools and case studies that allow us to think more precisely about how this can be done.

Arnheim (1969) has shown the important role of metaphor in visual communication. For example, we might make a small space between our thumb and forefinger and say 'I was this far away from hitting him'. Yet there was no spatial issue at the time, rather one of mood. We might say of a person that 'they have their feet on the ground' to express that they are a sensible person, as opposed to 'having their head in the clouds'. Yet being sensible has no natural relation to height, to the ground or to clouds. Such metaphors become so widely used that they come to appear natural and commonsensical.

We can see how invisible metaphors can be by looking at the instance of 'happy' as 'up' and 'sad' as 'down'. Why is this accepted? Why should happy be up? We can say 'Things are looking up' and 'The house price market is sinking', but why should reduced prices be down? Our language is filled with such references. We can say 'We have run-away inflation', but is inflation a self-propelled being?

For Lakoff and Johnson (1980) and for Arnheim (1969), metaphor is one fundamental way in which humans organise their experiences. We understand and experience the world through a network of culturally established metaphors. Speakers can tap into some of these metaphors in order to make arguments seem more plausible or to delegitimise others, as we will be showing throughout this chapter. This is because when we use metaphors we can highlight one aspect of experience, while at the same time concealing others. For example, the heart-as-mechanism metaphor draws our attention to the idea that the heart carries out a role like the part of a machine, but conceals the fact that the body might be better thought of as a whole. Hospital patients who have health problems that fall between or overlap two specialist departments often experience great difficulties in accessing the appropriate treatment. One woman known to the authors had a degenerative bone condition and recurring non-malignant skin cancers. She was treated for each by separate departments who were not used to communicating with each other. It was only after much effort on her part over many years that she was finally granted a visit to a specialist geneticist who identified that her condition may have been one single problem caused by a genetic defect when she was an embryo.

Semino (2008) comments on the widely held view that science is objective and descriptive. She notes examples that are often discussed in science, such as 'the greenhouse effect', 'genetic codes', 'electrical waves and particles', which contain metaphors. Since scientists deal with highly complex concepts that are often poorly understood and difficult to perceive, the use of metaphors allows them to explain these in simplified terms and to persuade us that their explanations are valid. Of course we must ask, as in the case of the metaphor of the heart as a mechanism, what the effects of these metaphors are and in what ways they shape thinking, practice and even the way we organise our institutions. As Semino (2008: 33) points out, when metaphors become the dominant way of thinking about a phenomenon it may become very difficult to challenge the metaphors used to describe it, since these become the commonsense or naturalised way of understanding the world.

Metaphor domains

In Latin, *metaphora* denotes something that is carried somewhere else. So in communication, we transport processes of understanding from one realm or conceptual domain to another (Lakoff, 1993; Lakoff and Nunez, 1997). Here we use the term 'conceptual domain' as it expresses the fact that metaphor is not simply about language or visual communication, but about thought itself and the embodiment of human experience. That is why we understand personality differences sometimes in terms of colliding objects. This can help us feel that we understand them better and can more easily deal with them.

Lakoff and Johnson (1980) characterise this process of metaphorical construction in terms of 'source domain' and 'target domain'. These can be explained as follows:

Target domain: the topic or concept that we want to describe through the metaphor.

Source domain: the concept that we draw upon in order to create the metaphor.

A common conceptual metaphor in English is an 'idea is food', which can be found in expressions such as 'Your argument is half-baked' or 'I have to digest his nasty comments'. In this metaphor, the target domain (i.e. the entity being talked about) is 'idea', whereas the source domain (i.e. the concept for metaphor construction) is 'food'.

Cameron (2007) has shown that when we talk about certain subjects they might be dominated by reference to one particular source domain. For example, when we talk about relationships, this is often done in terms of a journey:

> They are just at the start of their journey together.
>
> After four years he wants to take a different path.
>
> It has been a bumpy road for the two of them.
>
> Look how far we have come.
>
> We'll just have to go our separate ways.
>
> We can't turn back now.
>
> This relationship isn't going anywhere.
>
> We've gone off the track.

Reconciliation draws on the same conceptual domain:

> There is another mountain to climb now.
>
> One step at a time
>
> The feelings that were there at the beginning
>
> I just have to keep looking forward.

Of course, relationships have no natural comparison to a journey, but this has become an established way of talking about them. In such cases we can ask how metaphors shape our experiences and perceptions of the world and how they serve to define solutions. Let us consider the following metaphors:

> Society is an organism
>
> Society is a market

If we accept the first of the two, then we have to work to make sure all parts of it are healthy and work together. If we accept the second, then society is a place where everyone has their abilities on offer for trade. In this case, it is those who have more to offer or who offer 'better value' who will get ahead. While the organism metaphor emphasises cooperation, the market metaphor emphasises competition.

If one of these metaphors becomes accepted as how we think of society, or is the model used by government, this will affect the way we organise that society. It will affect the kinds of institutions we build and the kinds of people who are given authority to run it. The ideas governing education will change as we think of children needing 'marketable' skills to compete with each other rather than abilities and skills that will ensure that our society is a just and compassionate community. This might exclude the arts, philosophy and literature, unless of course money can be made out of them. Such a society may not have a well-developed welfare state as this might be considered to be against the ideology of a society where people must compete.

Rhetorical tropes

In the rest of this chapter we will look at a number of different kinds of rhetorical tropes. We list these giving illustrations and then apply them to a number of case studies.

Metaphor

As we have seen above, a metaphor is basically the means by which we understand one concept in terms of another. For example:

> Banks have said that we must not let the economy stagnate.

> The housing market bubble has burst.

> The situation in Afghanistan has overheated.

Here we find the state of the economy described through reference to water that has remained still for too long. The housing market being compared to a bubble suggests that it was always fragile, and 'overheating' draws on the metaphor of cooking. In each case, the use of the metaphor obscures what has actually happened and can dramatically simplify processes. Such metaphors can also make the economic situation and war sound much more positive or negative.

In the EMDA example, we find the organisation will:

> work with our partners in the region and beyond to achieve the region's ambition to be a Top 20 Region by 2010 and a flourishing region by 2020.

This sentence uses a plant metaphor ('flourishing') to describe its aims. As we have stated in Chapter 2, problems, solutions and outcomes in this text are all concealed in rhetoric. What exactly will be done is not specified, so no one can in fact be held accountable. Another popular metaphor in documents like these as well as in political discourse is where we collectively 'build' our future. We 'lay foundations', 'cement' parts together, 'lay cornerstones'. The building metaphor allows the author to avoid specifying just what they will do while at the same time summoning up a sense of progress and collaboration (Charteris-Black, 2004).

We can see the use of yet another metaphor in the following statement:

The minister will have to prepare for the political fallout.

This is a nuclear war-based metaphor, which suggests that there has been a big problem that has exploded and therefore had an impact, and that there will be consequences that could be long-term and complex to deal with.

This tidal wave of generosity will help them rebuild their flattened homes and shattered lives.

A sentence like this one is typical of journalistic clichés during a disasters. Here the use of the tidal wave metaphor suggests overwhelming generosity, so is used in a positive sense. Very often, however, the tidal flood metaphor is used negatively in tabloid newspapers to refer to immigration (e.g. Baker et al., 2008).

Media storm

Storm of controversy

This suggests something relentless that may last for a while and cause damage. We can say that the media storm has passed, but of course storms are neither rational nor purposeful.

Metaphors can be quite deliberately persuasive, particularly when used in political discourse. For example, Lu and Ahrens (2008) quote examples from Taiwanese political speeches to show how politicians use metaphor to give a sense of their commitment, plans and how they create unity through abstraction rather than concrete details:

Ever since the beginning of the country, [our countrymen in the past] have been trying to construct a country of the people, by the people, for the people.

We will complete the sacred mission both of constructing the base for our comeback and of glorifying China.

Every achievement we have come from the cornerstones which were laid down by the sacrifice and perseverance of innumerable forebears.

The national father directed the revolution... The new groundwork of the ROC was laid down at that moment.

Taiwan is striding across invisible thresholds ... and it will finally go through the gate of hope to democracy and prosperity.

We can see in these examples that the source domain is buildings and construction. The history of the country consisted of laying down the groundwork, constructing the base, laying down the cornerstones. This is portrayed as a collective act that obscures how this was actually achieved. Cornerstones sound strong and solid, a basis for the structure that follows, but to what do these actually refer? Building metaphors are commonly found in political speeches (Charteris-Black, 2004). They convey a sense of progress, of building something together, without actually stating what this might be. In the above case, many people in Taiwan would not have wanted to be part of mainland China. The 'cornerstones' may have been seen rather as agencies of oppression and control and certainly not of the order that might lead to moving through a gate of hope to democracy.

In the following example, Charteris-Black (2006) shows the use of source domains that reference natural disasters in different media representations of immigration in Britain.

> Britain is facing a nightly tidal wave of asylum seekers from Cherbourg, France's biggest port. (*The Daily Telegraph*, 25 August 2002, in Charteris-Black, 2006: 570)

> We will also clamp down on the flood of 'asylum seekers', the vast majority of whom are either bogus or can find refuge much nearer their home countries. (British National Party Manifesto, 2005, in Charteris-Black, 2006: 570)

> Since the trickle of applicants has become a flood and Parliament has been called upon to pass six substantial Acts in eleven years, trying to cope with the increasing numbers and progressively tighten up procedures at the application and appeal stages... (Asylum and Immigration Act, 2004, in Charteris-Black, 2006: 571)

In these examples, asylum seekers are described in terms of a 'flood'. No actual flood is involved, but this metaphor brings with it connotations of a natural disaster rather than a social matter, from which terrified people are seeking refuge. Foreigners overwhelming a country like a flood removes any sense of the needs of these people or the possibility of compassion on our behalf. Unless careful measures are put into place, this flood will be difficult to contain.

In the following metaphor in a speech given by former British Home Secretary Michael Howard on asylum and immigration on 22 September 2004, Charteris-Black points to something more subtle:

> Take housing, for example. The majority of immigrants settle in London and the South East, where pressures on housing are most pronounced. By contrast, many disadvantaged communities will perceive that newcomers are in competition for scarce resources and public services, such as housing and school places. The pressure on resources in those areas is often intense and local services.

> (http://news.bbc.co.uk/1/hi/uk_politics/3679618.stm)

Here Howard uses the metaphor of 'pressure' to describe the effects on housing. However, there is no actual 'pressure', which describes a physical force. So we are given a sense that this pressure amounts to physical force. We also know that when the pressure in containers becomes too great they explode.

These kinds of metaphor are so familiar with us that they often go unnoticed. Nevertheless they bring with them different kinds of qualities, foregrounding some things and concealing others. For example, immigrants are constructed in certain sectors of the press mostly as a problem, whereas the benefits they bring to a country remain relatively under-discussed. In the last example above, the term 'pressure' means that the problems are caused by the newcomers rather than by those whose responsibility it is to provide an adequate supply of housing.

Hyperbole

This is where there is exaggeration, such as:

I felt ten feet tall

We all died laughing

I've told you a million times not to call me a liar

We also might find it in news texts, for example in the following sentence:

The demonstration was a mob rampage

or

The frenzied bloody attack

When representing 'our side' in the conflict, a journalist might want to describe this last example rather as:

A strategic frontal assault.

In the fashion of Van Dijk's ideological squaring (1995), we could imagine that enemies carry out 'frenzied bloody attacks', whereas our own side carries out 'strategic operations'. A favoured demonstration may be described as a 'human tide', whereas an unfavoured one may be a 'mob rampage'. We can always look for the use of hyperbole in texts and think about what they conceal and how they evaluate persons, places and events.

Personification/objectification

Personification means that human qualities or abilities are assigned to abstractions or inanimate objects. Again, this can obscure actual agents and processes. For example:

Democracy will not stand by while this happens.

Democracy is not an agent but a political model. Yet politicians often speak of it in this way to mean that they, their party, or their government, along with a selection of other allied national governments, will not stand by. By personifying democracy as an agent, they are able to conceal who the actors are. They are also able to hide behind a concept that is generally highly valued by many. If democracy indeed has a problem with something, then it must be an enemy of freedom and fairness.

We can also see this process of concealment in the following line:

The credit crunch has made all of us rethink.

Again, the 'credit crunch' is not an agent that can make us think. It is a term that has come to be used to characterise a complex set of economic circumstances caused by banks speculating wildly in the property market through offering unsecured mortgages. But using the term 'credit crunch' allows the actual causes and agents behind the economic crisis to be suppressed.

Metonymy

This is the substitution of one thing for another with which it is closely associated. For example, instead of saying 'I am making progress with the writing and editing of the book' we might say 'the book is coming along'. Or it can be a trope that substitutes an associated word for another word. So instead of 'senior police officers', we might say 'top brass'.

The suits in the office upstairs (officials)

Downing Street/The Kremlin said today (the British/Russian government)

The Redtops all carried the story (the tabloid newspapers)

Metonymy can be yet another strategy to conceal the actual people behind an organisation/institution and their actions. We might say 'The top brass want this done', meaning in fact our line manager, in order to make our task sound more important.

Synecdoche

This is where the part represents the whole. This also has the important function of allowing the speaker to avoid being specific. Here are some examples:

We need a few bodies to fill the room (a few people)

There are a few good heads in the department (good people)

I want a new set of wheels (a new car)

Want a few jars tonight? (come and drink a few beers)

We need some new blood here (some new people)

There are few new faces here

The country won't stand for it (the government and its citizens)

When British Prime Minister Tony Blair was once asked about the solution to poverty, he replied that it was mainly a matter of 'banging a few heads together'. Here these heads represent those placed in positions to implement policy. But through this utterance he avoids saying exactly who he means and what processes he will implement to make sure the right policies are introduced. In fact, Blair's party was often credited with having good ideas, but regarded as rather weak at actually realising these.

Metaphor signalling

There may be linguistic devices in texts that draw attention to the use of metaphors. Goatly (1997) refers to these as signalling devices. This is where a speaker might say 'metaphorically speaking', 'so to speak', 'as it were', or 'literally':

My head was literally ready to explode towards the end of that lecture.

In this case, it appears that the signalling device points to how appropriate the metaphor is in this instance.

I was ready to murder them all, so to speak.

In this case, 'so to speak' has the effect of hedging the use of the metaphor. It signals a more self-conscious use.

We now move on to look at a number of case studies where we find all of the above rhetorical tropes used for potentially ideological purposes.

Case study 1: George Bush Speech

First of all, we can look at a classic use of rhetorical tropes in a speech by George Bush just after the events of September 11, 2001. As is typical of times of conflict, we find objectification and personification of the nation and the cause. And we find metaphors used to abstract the reasons and nature of the conflict which therefore simplify the nature of the response.

President Bush's address to a joint session of Congress on Thursday night, September 20, 2001

After all that has just passed, all the lives taken and all the possibilities and hopes that died with them, it is natural to wonder if America's future is one of fear.

Some speak of an age of terror. I know there are struggles ahead and dangers to face. But this country will define our times, not be defined by them.

As long as the United States of America is determined and strong, this will not be an age of terror. This will be an age of liberty here and across the world.

Great harm has been done to us. We have suffered great loss. And in our grief and anger we have found our mission and our moment.

Freedom and fear are at war. The advance of human freedom, the great achievement of our time and the great hope of every time, now depends on us.

Our nation, this generation, will lift the dark threat of violence from our people and our future. We will rally the world to this cause by our efforts, by our courage. We will not tire, we will not falter and we will not fail.

We find objectification and personification in the following:

this country will define our times

We can see that here the country becomes the agent. This kind of personification sidesteps who exactly will be doing the defining, connoting the 'country' as a coherent single voice rather than consisting of people with differing views and competing ideologies. We can see this in the following:

As long as the United States of America is determined and strong

Our nation, this generation, will lift the dark threat of violence

(Continued)

(Continued)

Politicians have traditionally evoked the nation as agent in order to rally people to their own intentions. This personification can be used to gloss over the differences between people and between the views held by different people and those held by the politician. The following examples help to draw this out:

The university requires prior notification of any individual strike action by staff.

Here it is not the 'university' as a whole that requires this information. The university can be thought of in the first place of comprising lecturers, researchers, students, library staff, administrators, etc. It is in fact in this case only the university management who would require notification. However, phrasing it in this way, using personification, glosses over different interests and points of view that may exist across the university. The staff may well be striking for reasons of resource cuts that they feel will affect students' quality of learning and teaching in the longer term. In the same way, we can see that Bush attempts to convey a sense of common response and common interest. Both authors knew American colleagues who at the time were highly concerned about US foreign policy. Yet the power of such objectification in these kinds of speeches and other media representations at the time served to position the voices of these academics therefore outside 'our country', 'our nation'. This allows the speaker to conceal exactly whose interests and actions are being referred to and also creates the impression of a shared interest.

We also find personification in the line

Freedom and fear are at war.

So it is not so much that America and other interests are in conflict, but that it is the concepts themselves that are in dispute. The actual nature of the problem is therefore abstracted. It also provides one step towards the nature of the solution.

We also find objectification in the following:

all the lives taken and all the possibilities and hopes that died with them

Here the possibilities and hopes become entities that have lives which can be ended. Here this is both objectification and synecdoche as the hopes and possibilities come to represent the future lives of the people. But turning these into real tangible things, and then speaking of their death, makes them appear more tragic.

Other metaphors are where Bush refers to acts of terrorism as a 'dark threat'. The possible effect of this is that Bush is able to construct an image of the threat as concrete, as terrorists constituting an evil to be feared, and one which equally positions the future as a 'thing' in need of protection. Thus, where the act of 'lifting the dark threat' is not literal, Bush uses this metaphor to instigate fear, incite activism, and to legitimate the fight against terror.

We find synecdoche in the line

We will rally the world to this cause by our efforts, by our courage

It is not in fact the world, but the people who live in it. This creates an impression of magnitude and importance and of the 'rightness' of what must be done since the whole world will be rallied behind a common cause. And does this mean the whole world population or those people or specifically those Western governments who have certain shared interests with the USA? The verb to 'rally' is an abstraction. It conveys motivation and persuasion, although this can gloss over a wide range of micro-processes. Does this involve and include military and economic pressures put on countries that are believed to harbour terrorists, for example?

Also of note in this extract is Bush's metaphorical construction of time. For example:

this country will define our times, not be defined by them

Here, time is given a commodity status, a sense of being a concrete entity which can be physically shaped and which embodies human experience. Time therefore becomes something that can be shared, protected and defined. This is also found in the idea of an 'age of terror', in which personification is used to construct 'age' as an entity in itself that can commit acts of terror against America. Again, this abstracts the nature of these threats, their causes and consequences. We also find time represented as a thing in the line

we have found ... our moment

Here, time becomes an object or entity that can be discovered. 'Moment' represents purpose, or the time to act. The kind of representation suggests that such moments are out there waiting to be found. As such, this use of metaphor represents this as a kind of opportunity and therefore a chance to do the 'right' thing.

We also find a metaphor of journey in the lines:

The advance of human freedom

After all that has just passed

Events are metaphorically constructed as scenes on a journey. Alongside the personification of nation and concepts such as freedom, journeys are also often used as one important source domain in political speeches. These are useful as they can give a sense of travelling together, of being on the right or wrong path, of moving in the right direction.

Other metaphors include:

all the lives taken

will lift the dark threat of violence from our people and our future

(Continued)

(Continued)

In the first case, lives are constructed as commodities. People are not just killed but are described as 'taken', implying something unjust and premature, which America as a collective must fight. The second sentence uses the metaphor of 'lifting' to represent the acts that must follow that will rectify the situation. What shall be done is not specified, but there is a sense of lifting and removing the dark threat, which is therefore represented as an object that can be physically removed.

In sum, we can see that there is little concrete description of events, victims, agents, and causality in Bush's speech. Rather, America is personified as a physical entity with intentions. Time is a commodity and also an agent that can be acted upon and have an identity. Who will side with America is abstracted through synecdoche as 'the world'. The events in question are part of a bigger journey of freedom, and actions involve 'finding our moment' and 'lifting dark threats'. Such speeches are clearly engineered to conceal differences of opinion behind a personified nation that is positioned on a greater journey which involves a greater cause where actual threats and subsequent actions are abstracted to avoid complexity and difficulty.

Graham et al. (2004) speak of a number of key features of calls to war by politicians over the past thousand years. These include the creation of an evil enemy, an appeal to a greater cause, an appeal to the history of the nation, an appeal to unity behind a greater power source. We can see these above in Bush's speech and the important role of metaphor in their construction. The enemy is a 'dark threat', the greater cause is one of the 'advancement of human freedom', the history of the nation is represented by the 'great achievement of our time', presumably with America as leader. The greater power source in this case appears to be the 'mission' which is bound up with freedom itself.

Case study 2: David Cameron Speech

In this second case study, we look at an extract from a speech by David Cameron, at the time leader of the opposition. In previous chapters we have considered Fairclough's (2003) suggestion that the more actual, concrete details about persons, events and processes are abstracted, the more we will find ideological work being done. In the following, we find that metaphor is one key part of the way that Cameron remains entirely in the realm of abstraction:

David Cameron: Let's mend our broken society

Rt Hon David Cameron, Tuesday, April 27 2010

Something is broken. Society is broken.

The broken society is not one thing alone. It is not just the crime. It is a whole stew of violence, anti-social behaviour, debt, addiction, family breakdown, educational failure, poverty and despair.

This is life – or the backdrop of life – for millions of people in this country. So how should we respond? The first response – the human response – is to feel unutterably sad at so much waste. Wasted hopes. Wasted potential. Wasted lives.

But sadness and anger aren't going to change anything on their own. Mending the broken society needs head as well as heart. It requires us to have an understanding of what has gone wrong as well as a clear approach to putting things right.

And my argument today is this. We have arrived at this point in our society for a number of reasons, many completely divorced from politics and what government does. But I am certain that government is a big part of the problem – its size has now reached a point where it is actually making our social problems worse. That's because by trying to do too much, it has drained the lifeblood of a strong society – personal and social responsibility. And the biggest victims are those at the bottom, who suffer most when crime rises and educational standards fall. They are the victims of state failure. They are the victims of big government. There is, I believe, only one way out of this national crisis – and that is what I have called the Big Society. A society where we see social responsibility, not state control, as the principal driving force for social progress. A society where we come together, and work together, to solve problems.

In order to draw out the level of abstraction here and the role played by metaphor, we analyse this extract in terms of the problems identified, those effected by them, and in terms of the solutions proposed.

The problem

In this speech, the problem is represented through two metaphors. First, that 'society is broken' and that it is in need of 'mending'.

Let's mend our broken society

Something is broken. Society is broken.

Here, society is represented as an object or thing rather than as a concept or idea. And this object or thing is broken. The source domain here would be objects, such as plates, toys, windows or machines that break. In speeches it is often the case that we hear society spoken of, as we mentioned above, through a metaphor of it being either

(Continued)

177

(Continued)

an organism or a market. Of course in this case it could not be broken, although in the first it could be ill or diseased. What matters here is that if something is broken, the question is can it be mended? And here Cameron urges that this is what we must do. Given the nature of the source domain of the metaphor, society must either be put back together or repaired in some way. What is implied through this metaphor is that society should be put back into its prior state where it was not broken. It is not that it should be changed, rethought, but only returned to how it was before it was broken. What exactly this means remains implied, appealing to a nostalgic view of 'when things were better'. At precisely what point in the past society was broken is not specified. We are not told how things were before they were broken or how they can simply be mended, when the world as a whole has changed and is constantly changing.

The second metaphor used to describe the nature of the problem draws on a cooking metaphor:

It is a stew of violence, anti-social behaviour, debt, addiction, family breakdown, educational failure, poverty and despair.

If we think about this literally, it is an odd juxtaposition of metaphors.

Society is broken – it is a stew.

On the one hand, it has been observed that this mixing of metaphors has traditionally been thought of as bad language use (Semino, 2008), even though it is something we frequently find in language. However, in this instance, the second, 'stew' metaphor is so well-trodden that is virtually invisible. And it may be a clue to the high level of abstraction in the text that such mixing does not appear to be obvious or incongruent.

Nevertheless the 'stew' metaphor has an important role to play here. We are not told if 'violence', 'anti-social behaviour', 'debt', 'addiction', 'family breakdown', 'educational failure', 'poverty' and 'despair' are part of one common problem, or if they might be interrelated. They are simply a stew, which is a kind of meal that bubbles away on the heat while a collection of non-specific ingredients merge into its mass, often becoming slightly indistinct. But crucially, the elements of a stew have no causal connection; they simply float around in the stew and merge. In contrast, the list of phenomena offered by Cameron has causal links. Educational failure has been linked to poverty which in turn may lead to anti-social behaviour, violence, debt and family breakdown.

The fact that we are not told how these different 'ingredients' in the stew are connected means that the complexity of the solution can in itself be more abstracted. Had the causal sequence and relations been made explicit, this would not have fitted with the solution Cameron has to offer. Is it that poverty is caused by poor distribution of wealth, high unemployment by jobs shifting abroad in the global economy, and has debt led to despair and family beakdown? It has been shown (e.g. Levitas, 2005) that many of the changes now faced in British society are due to economic policies in favour of global capitalism. This has led to a gradual removal of Britain from manufacturing-related trade, which provided jobs across the country. Accompanying free market policies and the privatisation of public services has resulted in other dramatic changes in quality of life for many people. What is concealed from this list of features, therefore, through the use of the metaphor, is causality.

What is also of interest in the list of things in the stew provided by Cameron is that the causes are placed towards the end of the sentence, such as 'poverty' and 'educational failure', and the consequences such as 'anti-social behaviour' and 'debt' are placed at the top to raise their salience. In fact, the order of causality is reversed in the sentence. As Van Dijk (1991) points out, this is one device by which identities and events can be made more or less salient. Here we also see the way that natural sequences of events are inverted (Van Leeuwen, 2008).

Those who are affected

We are told that the victims in this 'broken society' are:

And the biggest victims are those at the bottom, who suffer most when crime rises and educational standards fall.

In the first place, those who are affected are represented as 'victims'. The term 'victim' is usually associated with crime, where there is a perpetrator or criminal. And we are not told who these victims are in any concrete terms, yet a metaphor of 'those at the bottom' is used. Of course, a society can have no physical top or bottom, but up and down/top and bottom are accepted metaphors used to represent social order. Here Cameron is seeking to appeal to those who might have traditionally been Labour voters or even more right-wing voters, who may not see themselves as being at the 'top' of society. Cameron could have used an expression such as 'those who are socially excluded', 'those at the margins of society' or 'poorer people'. Research has shown the extent of poverty and social exclusion in Britain (Levitas, 2005). Cameron, however, glosses over why there are people 'at the bottom' and what this really means.

We also find a deletion of agents and causality in the following sentence:

when crime rises and educational standards fall

Here, the verb constructions conceal who causes crime to rise and educational standards to fall. One part of Cameron's new policies after winning the general election has been the introduction of far-reaching cuts in education.

Overall, Cameron's speech appears to be an excellent example of how to obfuscate causes in a way that allows more abstracted solutions to carry weight, as we shall see below.

(Continued)

(Continued)

The cause of the problem

Causes lie not in clear economic policy, but in abstractions:

They are the victims of state failure.

government is a big part of the problem

it has drained the lifeblood of a strong society

Exactly what the government has done or not done is not specified. Again, we find the use of the word 'victims', which obscures who exactly these people are, what their structural position in society is and how they have been affected. Government is a 'big part' of the problem, where the problem is an object that can be divided up into parts, rather than a complex history of decisions and factors. And what the government has done has 'drained the lifeblood of a strong society'. Again, this is a metaphor that is used so often in English that it appears neutral. But it is an abstraction. Here society is not an object that can be broken, but an organism from which the blood has been drained to make it weak.

So far we have seen that the nature and causes of the problem have been presented as abstractions. Where actual concrete social phenomena have been mentioned, these have been presented in ways that silences their relations and reverses causality. It is in this context that Cameron then offers his solution.

The solution

The solution too remains firmly in the realm of abstraction:

There is, I believe, only one way out of this national crisis – and that is what I have called the Big Society. A society where we see social responsibility, not state control, as the principal driving force for social progress. A society where we come together, and work together, to solve problems.

First, we find the spatial metaphor of 'only one way out'. The crisis is therefore a kind container where Cameron is the politician who can lead us to the exit. This is a typical move in political rhetoric, where Cameron positions himself as the one to show us this exit, which will then take us outside the container. Presumably, the container is the one which contains the heady mixture previously characterised as a stew.

Next, we find the metaphor of the 'Big Society'. Cameron does not specify that the previous situation is a 'Small Society'. But 'Big' suggests that society can be thought of as a physical entity where 'Big' is a good thing. In other contexts a 'Big Society' could be taken as something oppressive and controlling. And this large physical entity is one where the state has less control but where we instead take responsibility. Exactly what kind of change will be produced is not specified, but represented through a sense of movement, of society moving forward, again in terms of the metaphor 'driving force' and the journey of 'social progress'.

In this society, Cameron continues, we 'come together and work together' to solve problems. Who exactly the 'we' is remains unspecified as does what 'coming together' means. Cameron's discourse of a 'Big Society' and image of state control alludes to a familiar Conservative Party discourse of laissez-faire politics, where the state plays a minimal role and supports a free market. His metaphors of a 'broken society, of the 'stew' of problems and his 'Big Society' are all new metaphors that communicate a familiar discourse. But what exactly the problems are, and how they are to be dealt with, is communicated only at the level of abstraction. We can imagine how his solution would have appeared had he been specific about the problems. Had he explained the changes in the global economy and its consequences for British society, or the likely effects of increased privatisation, and had he looked at increasing unemployment and temporary contract work and its relation to poverty, crime and other social problems and then offered his solution, it would have seemed absurd.

What in fact is communicated here is very little at all apart from a repetition of older Conservative free market ideology. Yet exactly how this will mend the broken society is not specified. This kind of speech was typical of those made by Cameron leading up to the general election which he won in 2010.

Case study 3: Housing Crisis Report in *Times* Newspaper

The following text from the Business section of the British *Times* newspaper (9 November 2008) deals with economic decline in Detroit, of which the housing market is one part. At the time in the press, particularly in the UK, price changes in the housing market after several years of increases had begun to fall. While there was some more accurate and measured debate about what was actually happening, much of it was characterised by hyperbole and metaphor. We find one such example in the text below. What is interesting here is that this text is from the Business section of what presents itself as a serious newspaper. Yet there is very little concrete information present in this item, in which hyperbole, metaphor and personification conceal causality and actual processes.

America's Darkest Fear: To end up like Detroit

The $1 house has become symbolic of one city's nightmare decline, writes Tony Allen-Mills in Detroit.

(Continued)

(Continued)

On a quiet, tree-lined road near Detroit's city airport, sits a house that was briefly the most famous in America.

When the three-bedroom home at 8111 Traverse Street found a buyer last summer, the purchase price made headlines around the world – the house sold for one dollar, then worth about 50p.

The unnamed buyer was a local woman who bought the house as an investment.

Yet two months later, America's spiraling financial crisis is wreaking so much new havoc in decaying property markets like Detroit's that even a $1 house cannot be resold for a profit. As the home of America's once-omnipotent automobile industry, the city of Detroit is scarcely a stranger to adversity.

'Blight is creeping like a fungus through many of Detroit's proud neighborhoods,' an article in Time magazine noted in 1961.

It has since become America's poorest city, the Motown that lost its mojo. Last week the city's big-three motoring manufacturers, Ford, General Motors and Chrysler, announced their worst monthly results for car sales since 1993.

The house on Traverse Street tells part of the story of a decline so dizzying that other cities around America have begun to talk fearfully of 'Detroitification', a seemingly irreversible condition of urban despair that slowly takes grip of once-flourishing communities and strips them of value and life.

For much of the world it might seem unthinkable that a house in a large American city could be sold for a single dollar, but the shocking reality of Detroit's urban implosion is that there are tens of thousands such homes in varying states of calamitous disrepair, with no hope of finding buyers.

Officials still debate the varying causes of the city's ruin, but race riots in the 1960s, competition from foreign carmakers, a galloping murder rate and a flourishing drug culture all took a heavy toll.

In the past 40 years, Detroit has lost half its population, which is now estimated at 850,000 – more than 80% of them African-American.

The credit crisis of the past year has exacerbated the city's woes. Downtown have been frozen for lack of funding.

Last week the city tore up a project to build new blocks of up market flats along the Detroit river…

As neighborhoods wilted in a blitz of foreclosures, prices sank like stones…

The kind of decay that was primarily restricted to poor black neighborhoods is spreading to much grander homes.

This news story uses a mixture of metaphors and is an example of just how diverse the source domains can be even in one text. What they have in common is a sense of motion that is out of control and of organic decay and putrefaction.

In the first place, the fact that this is far from a measured assessment of the situation is signposted by the use of hyperbole:

nightmare decline

spiraling financial crisis

galloping murder rate

a blitz of foreclosures

the city tore up a project to build new blocks

All of these add to the magnitude and pace of the story. What they also do is draw on a number of source domains to convey a sense of fast pace and uncontrollability to the unfolding events. The murder rate draws on the movement of horses, the financial crisis is represented as an object moving in widening circles, the housing project has not been cancelled but 'torn up'. We find other metaphors of the same nature:

decline so dizzying

Detroit's urban implosion

prices sank like stones

'Dizzying' here suggests rapid, fast-spinning motion, 'implosion' suggests an uncontrollable force and 'sinking like stones' is at the same time fast, relentless and inevitable.

We also find a number of metaphors drawn from the source domain of fungal diseases:

decaying property markets

Blight is creeping like a fungus through many of Detroit's proud neighborhoods

flourishing drug culture

neighborhoods wilted

The kind of decay that was primarily restricted to poor black neighborhoods is spreading to much grander homes

Here, the problem of house prices and economic decline is represented in terms of a fungal attack that creates decay, blight, a disease caused by fungi, and which creeps across the city, spreading to new areas. Other phenomena are then described through the language of fungal disease, such as the way the drug culture is flourishing.

(Continued)

(Continued)

All this is leading to neighbourhoods simply wilting. These language constructions completely remove agents and causality. Fungal attacks spread without intention or reason; it is simply what they do. But economic decline in cities has concrete causes and agents. What and who is causing these problems and how can they be solved?

We also find extensive personification in the text, which can also have the effect of removing agents and causality:

America's spiraling financial crisis is wreaking so much new havoc

Here the financial crisis itself is represented as having agency when at the time it appeared to be clear that it was decisions made by banks that were the actual drivers of these problems.

urban despair that slowly takes grip

'Urban despair' cannot literally take grip of anything, but it is given this human quality as it makes for greater drama, and again as it removes agency. The despair, which is the result of the situation, is made the agent. But what are the processes that have causes this result?

There are a number of examples of personification that refer to the city of Detroit itself as having feelings and as the agent of verb processes:

It continues to lose residents

exacerbated the city's woes

the city tore up a project to build new blocks of up market flats

These personifications allow the writer to state that this problem affects the whole of the city, rather than certain sections of the population. One of the authors knew a colleague who was living in Detroit at that time, who, when asked, was not aware of the situation, of the fungal-like spread of decline and dizzying problems. This rhetorical move allows the author of the newspaper article to then state:

other cities around America have begun to talk fearfully of 'Detroitification'

Cities themselves do not talk, and stating it like this avoids having to cite who exactly it is that is talking fearfully.

These personifications demonstrate how causality can be concealed. Who was it who actually made the decision to not build the flats? Was it property investors?

In sum, this article uses metaphors of energy and movement – 'spiraling', 'galloping', 'blitz', 'sank like stones' – to create drama, along with metaphors of fungal-like disease. It also uses personification, so that the whole city and individual areas are experiencing problems rather than specific people who have specific problems. The background of the banking crisis – banks who speculated on housing, and the governments who bailed them – out is excluded. What exactly needs to be done is not dealt with. In sum, we have a text filled with abstraction which is low on actual agents, processes and causality. Yet it is found in the Business section of a major British newspaper. Ideologically, it appears to serve to distract from the actual concrete situation.

Conclusion

In this chapter we have shown that metaphor is not simply about flowery and poetic language. Metaphor is fundamental to human thought. And it can be used as a tool to help us to make sense of things. But it can also be used strategically as a tool for abstracting processes and agents in order to recontextualise practices and to foreground and background. We have seen that the broader normalisation of a metaphor can have consequences for the way we might organise our societies, as in the case where we view society as a market where we all compete to offer our services. This has implications for how we run our schools and how we take care of and support each other. We have seen that rhetorical tropes are excellent tools for abstraction, for glossing over micro-details, but we have also seen how powerfully compelling they can be as they drive our understanding of one thing by another that can be much more emotive or simplistic. So the tendency of the mass media to draw on highly sexualised images to advertise commodities can become a kind of 'pollution' that our 'children' are breathing. In our analyses we must identify these rhetorical tropes but then also point out the wider discourses that these communicate, identifying what is abstracted, glossed over, and what kinds of sequences of activity are promoted as a result.

8

Committing and Evading: Truth, Modality and Hedging

In this chapter, we discuss a characteristic of language that tells us about people's commitment to what they say. In language, people might want to appear to be firmly aligned to an idea or thing but at the same time wish to limit how much this is represented in terms of a firm promise or command. This system is called 'modality' (Hodge and Kress, 1979/1993). According to Fairclough (1992, 2003), modality includes any unit of language that expresses the speaker's or writer's personal opinion of or commitment to what they say, such as hedging (I believe/think/suppose), modal verbs, modal adjectives and their adverbial equivalents. There is 'high modality' and 'low modality'. We use these language structures all the time when we speak and write. These indicate our judgement of probabilities and obligations, signal factuality, certainty and doubt.

As well as being able to convey and obtain information, language also provides resources for being able to communicate and assess how we and others feel about that information, how certain we are about it. Since language is about concealing as well as revealing, to deceive as well as inform, there are components of grammar that will help to facilitate this without being too obvious. Hodge and Kress (1979) identify modals as one important tool for accomplishing this.

In visual communication, Kress and van Leeuwen (1996) have suggested, too, there are features and qualities that can be usefully thought of as carrying out the same role as modals in language. They identify visual qualities, such as the level of articulation of detail in objects and settings, degrees of naturalistic lighting and colour, and the way that these create distance from how things appear in the real world. As with modals in language, these 'visual modals' can be used to conceal and 'dress up' levels of truth and commitment to reality.

In this chapter, we will look at both linguistic modality and visual modality. As we look at linguistic modality, we will also consider the phenomenon of 'hedging'. This is a term used to describe the way that in language we often use terms or grammar to soften the impact of what we have to say, or to mitigate something.

Modality in language

We can see how modals communicate our levels of certainty in the following example:

I will have a beer tonight.

I may have a beer tonight.

In the first sentence, the speaker indicates much more commitment than in the second sentence. This is only a trivial example. But it shows the way that modals are used in everyday language to express levels of commitment to what we do or do not do.

Modality has been categorised in many ways, but here we distinguish three:

Epistemic modality: This is to do with the speaker's/author's judgement of the truth of any proposition. So if I say 'I may have a beer tonight', I am expressing uncertainty about the proposition 'I am having a beer tonight'. Slightly more certainty is expressed in the proposition 'I will probably have a beer tonight'. In other words, epistemic modals show how certain you are something will happen, or is the case.

Deontic modality: This is to do with influencing people and events. So if I say 'Students must do the essay', I am expressing greater influence than if I say 'Students may do the essay'. Deontic modals are therefore about how we compel and instruct others.

Dynamic modality: This is related to possibility and ability, but is not subjective in the manner of the first two modalities. For example, if we say 'I can do this essay' or 'Tomorrow I will go to the dentist' or 'You can eat your lunch in this room', I am not so much expressing my judgement nor attempting to influence others, but indicating an ability to complete an action or the likelihood of events.

Modality can also be associated with hedging terms, such as 'I think', 'kind of/sort of', 'seems' or 'often'. This becomes clear in the difference between:

This is the correct procedure.

I think this might be the correct procedure.

This seems to be the correct procedure.

The second sentence is an example of epistemic modality, where we find evidence of the speaker's judgement of the level of truth of the proposition 'This is the correct procedure'. The third sentence is an example of dynamic modality, where the speaker offers a sense of possibility. An example of deontic modality here would be:

You have to carry out this procedure.

Modals expressing high degrees of certainty might be used in order to convince people. We can see this in an excerpt from a text on multiculturalism by British Conservative leader David Cameron (*The Observer*, 29 January 2007):

We must not fall for the illusion that the problems of community cohesion can be solved simply through top-down, quick-fix state action. State action is certainly necessary today, but it is not sufficient. But it must also be the right kind of action, expressed in a calm, thoughtful and reasonable way.

Here Cameron uses the modal 'must' frequently, asserting his certainty and confidence. Imagine if he said in the last sentence: 'It should be the right kind of action' or 'It might be the right kind of action'. Where we find texts filled with uncertainty and lack of commitment, we are dealing with an author who feels much less confident. Later in Cameron's speech we do find lower commitment:

But I don't believe this should mean any abandonment of the fundamental principle of one people under one law. Religious freedom is a cardinal principle of the British liberal tradition. But liberalism also means this: that there is a limit to the role of religion in public life.

Here while there is certainty about religious freedom being a cardinal principle, Cameron slightly reduces his commitment to the idea of the abandonment of the fundamental principle of one people under one law by using 'I believe' and 'should' in the first line. He could have said:

This cannot mean any abandonment of the fundamental principle of one people under one law.

or

This will not mean any abandonment of the fundamental principle of one people under one law.

But the lowered modality here allows him to appear sincere. By saying 'I believe' rather than 'it is the case', he is able to communicate a sense of his moral stance, giving access to his internal world. Politicians must strike a balance between being perceived as certain and decisive and being approachable and humane.

Finally, we can see how Cameron attributes less certainty and commitment to others:

> Some say the risk is inflation. Others say it's recession. So some think there should be more intervention by the Government in the financial markets. Some say there should be less.

He does not specify who the 'some' are, anonymising them, but they are not described as 'knowing' or even 'believing' that there should be more intervention by government, but only 'think' it. This is a technique often used to detract from what others hold to be the case. But importantly, the use of modality here allows Cameron to tell us, through the way he indicates levels of commitments and sincerity and the doubts of others, something about his own identity as a sincere and committed man, yet one who is thoughtful and certainly not authoritarian. Fairclough (2003: 166) points to the way that modality plays an important role in the 'texturing of identities'. What you commit yourself to, what you show caution about, is one way that we communicate about the kind of person we are. Language must not only be able to convey information, but must also allow us to gauge how speakers relate to this information.

Murray (2002) offers an excellent example of talk that shows a lack in confidence through the use of modals. This is a statement by a nurse:

> Yeah. I think it, sort of, provided very holistic care for the elderly lady coming through the unit, who actually gained more benefits than simply having a wound dressed on 'er leg. Erm, I think that had it, had she 'a' been seen in an ordinary unit without nurse practitioner cover, the chances are that the, er, medical staff there would've dealt with 'er leg.
>
> (2002, www.peter-murray.net/msc/dissch6.htm)

We find extensive use of 'I think', rather than simply a description of facts. We also find other devices for lowering modality, as 'sort of' and 'actually', 'the chances are'. In the first line, even the word 'very' lowers the nurse's commitment to exactly how holistic the care was. The first line could have been worded in this way:

> It provided holistic care for the elderly lady coming through the unit,

Such use of modals would probably not be found, for example, in the speech of a doctor, even though the doctor may have no more knowledge than the nurse. Again, here we find that modals are a strong indication of identity. Murray suggests that here the nurse indicates her lack of sense of power over knowledge.

Modals and authority

The use of modals tells us something about the author's identity and crucially, therefore, how much power they have over others and over knowledge. If we read a document from our employers saying the employee 'will' do something rather than they 'should' or that the employer 'thinks we should do it', these will give us a very different sense of the power that they believe they have over us.

> Staff will notify the University about any strike action.
>
> Staff should notify the University about any strike action.
>
> We think that staff should notify the University about any strike action.

Clearly, here there is a descending order of authority. In the last case in particular, it is unlikely any staff will feel compelled to submit a notification.

This order of authority is made more explicit in the following. Again, we see the descending order of power by the speaker:

> You will come with me.
>
> You must come with me.
>
> The authorities order you must come with me.

In the first sentence, the speaker has the power to state what *will* happen. In the second, also, using deontic modality, they appeal to some unmentioned power using 'must'. In the last sentence, their own power is so weak that they have to name the authority. We often hear children use this last one, when they say to a sibling 'You've got to come – No, I won't – Mummy says you've got to'.

We often find that pop psychologists and style gurus on TV and in lifestyle magazines use modals like 'will' and high modality verbs such as 'is' to create a sense of their own authority over knowledge.

> People who are successful in life are those who can adapt quickly. I call these 'adaptors'. The next category are those that worry...

Pop psychologists are therefore able to provide authority for their opinions not by the citation of research or other established professionals in psychology or sociology, but through use of modals such as 'can' and 'are'.

The case of the pop psychologist brings us on to our next point. Certain modals also have a function in concealing power relations. 'She may talk' can either express permission or suggest a possibility. Again, a speaker can use this to build up a sense of power while at the same time being able to deny it. This means that coercion can be masked in surface forms of rationality. In some cases there is no ambiguity, but this is rare. This suggests that the ambiguity is highly functional and is an important part of the quality of language, rather than a problem (Hodge and Kress, 1979: 122). We can see this ambiguity in the following:

You cannot swim here.

You may do any of the essay questions.

The first example might refer to the fact that you cannot swim for legal or safety reasons. Or it could have been placed there by an annoyed neighbour. The second suggests both a sense of having an option but also that you are being *allowed* to do so. We can see the same ambiguity in a political speech:

We must take globalisation as an opportunity.

This ambiguity can be captured in two separate sentences, which indicate the two possible meanings of the sentences:

The evidence compels us to take globalisation as an opportunity.

I am telling you to take globalisation as an opportunity.

We find the same ambiguity in the following:

We cannot avoid the fact that we are now part of a global economic order.

Does 'cannot' here mean that since national economies are now subordinate to the World Trade Organisation and the World Bank that there are legal reasons why we cannot avoid the fact? Or does it mean that it would not be reasonable to think otherwise?

Importantly, modal verbs are also ambiguous about temporality.

We must adapt to changes in global markets through building a knowledge-based economy that is dynamic and versatile.

Here, the modal 'must' is ambiguous about the time frame involved. Is this referring to the future? Is it a statement about what will happen or is it a general law that applies right now? This indeterminacy is useful for speakers who have the contradictory task of portraying a specific issue and giving a sense of addressing it without actually making clear what this involves.

Hodge and Kress (1979) point to the functional nature of this ambiguity. If we assume that language has the role to deceive as well as inform, then grammar will contain forms that allow us to avoid making certain kinds of distinctions. Modals encode probabilities and certainties, but conceal time and power.

Finally, we can use modals to protect our utterances from criticism:

Teacher: Do you understand this process?

Student: Yes, I think I can. I'm sort of realising it's perhaps the key part of the course.

Hedging

As well as modal verbs, authors can use hedging in order to create a strategic ambiguity within their claims (Wood and Kroger, 2000). Hedging means that a speaker avoids directness or commitment to something, although, as we will see, this can often be used to give the impression of being detailed and precise. Hedging can be used to distance ourselves from what we say and to attempt to dilute the force of our statements and therefore reduce chances of any unwelcome responses. For example, *The Daily Mail* anti-immigration article we looked at previously stated:

Some people say that multiculturalism is outmoded, but, in fact, it is still orthodox thinking.

There is no reason to hedge by 'some people say'. Who these people are and what relevance they have to what has to be said is not clear. And there appears to be no additional benefit by saying 'in fact'. But these structures allow the author to 'dress up' the sentence:

I think multiculturalism is outmoded but it is nevertheless still orthodox thinking.

'Padding' our language in this way softens the impact of the bluntness of an message.

In the same article there is further evidence of hedging through 'sometimes', 'quite often', and 'little':

These incomers sometimes expect everyone to speak to them in their own language, and they quite often make little attempt to integrate themselves into French society or culture.

The sentence could have been written along these lines:

Incomers expect everyone to speak in their own language and make no attempt to integrate themselves into French society or culture.

Adding more vague aggregation, such as 'quite often' and 'little' helps to dilute the force of what is being said.

Sunoo (1998) demonstrates that terms such as 'some', 'many' and 'others' can be used to gloss over lack of concrete evidence by giving the following example:

Corporate universities come in many shapes and sizes. Some, such as Motorola University, have campus locations around the globe. Others, such as Dell University, SunU and Verifone University, have no campus at all. Many have committed to the virtual university model to express their learning philosophy and commitment to continuous learning. (cited in Faber, 2003: 16)

Here, the author of this text aims to justify the virtual university model, but does so through rather vague evidence. Exactly how many universities have committed to this and how many universities have no campus at all?

Tusting et al (2002) gives examples of the way that exchange students distance themselves from the cultural stereotypes they use through hedging. Here the hedging is indicated in italics:

Um, apart from I don't know if it's true but I got the impression that French men are *most* sexist.

It appears that this person states their belief that French men are sexist. But they hedge this statement by using lowered modality, such as 'I don't know if it's true' and 'I got the impression' and through the use of the quantifier 'most'.

Political speeches are full of hedging devices. Here are some examples from Resche (2004). Again, the hedging is indicated in italics:

The American economy, *like all advanced capitalist economies,* is continually in the process of *what Joseph Schumpeter, a number of decades ago, called* 'creative destruction'. *Capital equipment, production processes, financial and labor market infrastructure, and the whole panoply of private institutions that make up a market economy* are always in a state of flux – *in almost all cases evolving into more efficient regimes.*

Resche points out that this could be shortened to:

Though many sectors are being thoroughly affected by creative destruction, our economy will be stronger and more competitive in the end.

Without hedging, however, the speech would lose the elements that serve to soften its contents. Hedges can also serve the important role of giving the impression that the opposite is taking place, that they are increasing the level of explanation and clarification, rather than obfuscating it. In this example, the author hedges the condition of the US economy by saying it is not the only one affected (*like all advanced capitalist economies*). And he 'explains' and legitimises this by reference to a famous economist (*Schumpeter*). No exact date is given so we cannot check exactly what he means (*'a number of decades ago'*).

What we have here is a whole range of hedging features that allow this simple statement to sound more authoritative and persuasive. It allows cushioning from the impact of what is being said and also gives the impression of expertise through technical language. Drawing on the work of Selinker (1979), Rounds (1982), Banks (1994), Dudley-Evans (1994) and Resche (2004), we can identify just what these features are and show how they can be used to hedge the following statement:

> There are many deadlines at this time of year so I was not able to complete my assignments.

- Long noun phrases:

> *A lot of similarly timed deadlines at this time of year all which show a lack of coordination between staff*, prevented successful completion of my assignments.

Here we can see that the actual process of not handing in the assignment has been pushed to the back of the sentence into the subordinate clause behind the long noun phrase. Van Dijk (1993) has shown that this is one grammatical technique for backgrounding information.

- Modal verbs and adverbs such as 'may', 'perhaps' and auxiliary verbs such as 'seems to' and adverbs such as 'especially':

> It *seems to* be the case that a lot of similarly timed deadlines at this time of year *perhaps* all which show a lack of coordination between staff, could have tended to prevent successful completion of my assignments.

Here the speaker lowers the certainty of what they say and hides behind the lowered modality.

- Approximators 'some', 'somewhat' and the compounding of these 'to a somewhat lesser extent':

> *Some* similarly timed deadlines at this time of year perhaps, all which show a lack of coordination between staff, could *somewhat* have tended to prevent successful completion of my assignments.

We can see here that these hedges allow the speaker to conceal exactly how many deadlines fall at the same time and to distance themselves from the commitment to the fact that they did prevent assignment completion.

- Non-factive verbs such as 'report', 'suggest':

Some students seem to be *reporting* that it may be the case that there are a lot of similarly timed deadlines at this time of year, perhaps *suggesting* a lack of coordination between staff, could especially have tended to prevent successful completion of my assignments.

Again, we can see how this allows for a sense of vagueness.

- Comparative forms of adverbs such as *'more* concerned *than* before' suggest precision:

Some students seem to be reporting that it may be the case that there are *more* similarly timed deadlines at this time of year *than before*, perhaps suggesting a lack of coordination between staff, that could have tended to prevent successful completion of my assignments.

Again, here we are given an increased sense of precision and evidence, as comparisons are being made. This can be increased further with the following feature.

- Specific times and referral to history such as 'since last year', 'in 1998', 'previously':

Some students have *on numerous occasions* reported that it may be the case that there are more similarly timed deadlines at this time of year than the *same date last year*, perhaps suggesting less coordination between staff than in *previous years*, that could have tended to prevent successful completion of my *November* assignments.

Here the speaker is able to use times to convey a sense of precision, continuity and a sense that they have an awareness of the broader picture. Mention of history and time in speeches can also suggest wisdom. A speaker might say 'over the last half century', or 'the last two generations have known'.

- Reference to an official body, report, person or expert:

Historically there has been *much better* coordination between staff as regards coordination of essay deadlines *than we now experience. Official departmental documentation appears* to have *traditionally* supported the idea of responding to student *suggestions that might* assist in learning and assessment processes, *especially* where *there might* be an issue of impeding assignment submission. Will *this generation* of students have to tolerate different levels of respect than in this *former age*?

Among the highlighted hedging here we find appeals to history, tradition and also, importantly, 'official departmental documentation', although exactly what evidence this provides is kept vague and could be referring simply to a course handbook or webpage. Politicians especially will even add references to previous kinds of policy or political personalities, although quotes will often be conveniently altered or paraphrased.

> Historically there has been much better coordination between staff as regards coordination of essay deadlines than we now experience. Official departmental documentation appears to have traditionally supported the idea of responding to student suggestions that might assist in learning and assessment processes. Since the times when *Plato* was engaging with his pupils in *ancient Greece*, scholarly thinking has always been based on certain levels of acceptable mutual respect between the taught and the teacher, especially where there might be an issue of impending assignment submission.

Of course, we are entering the realm of the absurd here in terms of the student's excuse for not submitting their essay. But this is in fact not atypical of how politicians use such references.

- Connectors such as 'while', 'although', 'nonetheless', 'moreover' are important to convey that the speaker is covering all the options and alternative explanations. This can be important when speakers are required to appear cautious (Selinker, 1979):

> Some staff might consider it somewhat convenient to place assignment deadlines without attention to broader degree timetable matters as outlined in official University documentation. *Nonetheless*, as Winston Churchill always reminded us, we must be mindful of how history will judge us, and they might therefore want to accept the suggestion that they have been instrumental in damaging the fluency of student essay submission precisely in this last semester.

- Excessive defining of concepts and terms:

> Essay submission deadlines, *that point at which learners are tested on curricula contents*, have been placed around similar dates this semester, *what we might want to call, drawing inspiration from the educationalist Roan Bruner, as 'heavy clustering'*, which has placed a somewhat onerous load on students concerned to submit their work precisely on time, *meaning that date and time specifically documented in individual course material supplied by tutors.*

Resche (2004) also points to the way that hedging can be thought of as simply breaking all the rules of standard use of English:

1 Prefer the familiar word to the far-fetched.
2 Prefer the concrete word to the abstract.
3 Prefer the single word to the circumlocution.
4 Prefer the short word to the long.
5 Prefer the Saxon word to the Romance.

According to Resche, particularly politicians who wish to use hedging will prefer words that sound more sophisticated and learned. For example:

'Facilitate' is preferred to 'allow'

'Necessitate' is preferred to 'require'

'Augment' is preferred to 'increase'

'Envisage' over 'foresee'

'Paucity' rather than 'shortage'

'Cessation' rather than 'end'

Of course the use of all these hedging techniques will depend on the perceived audience.

We can now go back to Resche's example, which we considered earlier on, and show exactly what hedging ingredients are present. This is an example from a speech by Federal Reserve Board Chairman Alan Greenspan.

> The American economy, like all advanced capitalist economies, is con-
> tinually in the process of what Joseph Schumpeter, a number of decades
> ago, called 'creative destruction'. Capital equipment, production proc-
> esses, financial and labor market infrastructure, and the whole panoply
> of private institutions that make up a market economy are always in a
> state of flux – in almost all cases evolving into more efficient regimes.
> (4 September 1998, cited page 731)

First, we are given a comparison 'like all advanced capitalist economies'. This gives a sense of explanation and consideration, yet is vague as to the way in which it is like all capitalist economies. We find reference to expertise and history in 'what Joseph Schumpeter, a number of decades ago' and then speci-fication of concepts in 'creative destruction', none of which really help us to understand what is going on. We then find a very long noun phrase in 'Capital equipment, production processes, financial and labor market infrastruc-ture, and the whole panoply of private institutions that make up a market economy', which suggests wide knowledge and precision, but which in fact stalls over what is actually going to be said. Finally, we find the lowered modality of 'almost', leading into further apparent clarification 'in almost all cases evolving into more efficient regimes'.

As Resche points out, this could have been phrased:

> Though many sectors are being thoroughly affected by creative destruction, our economy will be stronger and more competitive in the end.

What this in fact conveys is that we should not worry so much about job losses and closures of industry, as this is a natural part of capitalism that ultimately leads to a better economy. The use of hedging devices makes it more difficult to pin this down.

Case study 1: Blog comment on knife crime

This first example is from a blog on a newspaper site (*The Daily Mail* – downloaded 1 May 2011) where readers were commenting on the government's response to announced increases in knife crime.

> It concerns me that everyone is so brain washed over the issue of knives. If you're the kind of person who gets angry enough with someone (over something serious like bumping into you!) to want to kill them then the weapon used is irrelevant. You're a loose cannon and a potential murderer, nothing is going to change that. When these groups of youths kill someone then they could just as easily just keep kicking the victim in the head. People seem to think we can just magically change people attitudes about violence (not to mention of course they don't care about the law in the first place).

This statement is characterised by high modality. There is slight hedging in the first sentence with the approximator 'so', but the high modality is something we might expect on such blogs where blunter statements are often made. It could have simply been written:

> It concerns me that everyone is brain washed over the issue of knives.

But for the most part we find certainty:

> If you're the kind of person who gets angry enough with someone [...] to want to kill them then the weapon used is irrelevant.

Here we find high modality using dynamic modality through use of the verb 'is'. Direct causality is used. The writer could have used epistemic modality to say 'I think that if you're the kind of person who...' or lowered dynamic modality: 'If you're the kind of person who gets angry enough with someone [...] to want to kill them then the weapon used may be irrelevant.'

In the next line we find slightly lowered modality:

When these groups of youths kill someone then they could just as easily just keep kicking the victim in the head.

Here the dynamic modality 'could' could have been written as:

When these groups of youths kill someone then they *will* just as easily just keep kicking the victim in the head.

But what we find in language that is designed to be persuasive, as we saw earlier in the example of David Cameron, is that there will be both high levels of certainty and more modest claims in order to present a more considered set of assertions, to sound less arrogant perhaps. Of course the use of 'could' still suggests high probability, but it is slightly more moderate.

Finally, in classic style the views of others are presented as low epistemic modality:

People seem to think we can just magically change people's attitudes about violence.

These people are not represented as 'knowing' or being 'certain', but simply thinking these attitudes can be changed, which implies they are mistaken.

Case study 2: Glossing over the implication of military funding cutbacks

Taken from 'Army cutbacks could lead to housing crisis; Christopher Bellamy, Defence Correspondent, examines the implications of defence cuts', *The Independent*, 19 June 1990.

With the unification of Germany, it seems likely that there will no longer be a need for a full brigade in Berlin. A token presence, perhaps a battalion, might remain. As far as Germany as a whole is concerned, senior Nato planners propose to move over to a structure with multinational covering forces furthest east, then quick reaction forces and, lastly, heavier manoeuvre forces, possibly organised as four corps. These would replace the eight deployed forward in West Germany, of which Britain provides one, accounting for practically all BAOR.

Other forces would be needed to contribute to quick reaction forces (perhaps an air-mobile brigade) and the multinational screening forces, so the overall strength might remain unaltered.

(Continued)

(Continued)

> It seems more likely that Britain might provide, say, an armoured/infantry division, a quick reaction brigade, and maybe a brigade's worth of troops for the covering forces. It is not inconceivable that BAOR's strength might be halved.

What we can observe in this text is the predominance of low dynamic modality. Very little in the text is presented as certain. In fact it is presented as pure speculation. The speaker may of course represent events in this manner, knowing that the events are certain, but use lower modalities as a way of hedging and therefore providing a buffer from the reality of the situation.

> With the unification of Germany, it seems likely that there will no longer be a need for a full brigade in Berlin. A token presence, perhaps a battalion, might remain.

Here it might be the case that the speaker is seeking to create a panic without actually committing himself to any of the statements and presenting them as facts, as in:

> With the unification of Germany there will no longer be a need for a full brigade in Berlin. A token presence of a battalion will remain.

We might argue that journalists should not produce reports in which they are unable to state facts in this manner, although some journalism scholars have observed that much reporting is comprised of high levels of speculation as opposed to actual facts (Jaworski et al., 2003).

> In the next line, we find that Nato 'propose' rather that 'will carry out' changes:

> Nato planners propose to move over to a structure with multinational covering forces furthest east.

Stating that Nato planners 'propose' as opposed to 'will' make the reductions, also softens what is about to happen. It is still not certain that it will happen.

> Towards the end of this extract we find very low dynamic modality in the form of:

> It seems more likely that Britain might provide, say, an armoured/infantry division.

> It is not inconceivable that BAOR's strength might be halved.

> Both of these uses of modality display particularly low levels of commitment.

> In summary, we find that this text consists of very little hard evidence. Although it appears to present a list of facts, they are all delivered with low levels of commitment by the author. Since journalists are rarely held to account on how stories pan out over time, this is not of importance in terms of reporting strategies.

Modality and certainty in visual communication

On page 7 in the Introduction of this book we find an image from *Cosmopolitan* magazine. At first glance, we can see that this is a posed image and not an image of a woman in a naturalistic setting. We can tell this from the iconography and staged nature of the image. Elements have clearly been deliberately placed for the purposes not of everyday activities, but for the purposes of the image. This kind of image is an example of the photograph as a symbolic system rather than as an image that stands on its own, that documents a moment in time. It is also a kind of photograph typical of the era of branding where marketing takes place not so much through describing product details, but through loading the product with certain values. Here the image is used to load the woman's lifestyle magazine with a particular set of values, ideas and identities which can signify women's agency, glamour and fun.

One important quality of such images is the way they are almost 'unreal'. In this case the background is slightly out of focus and appears over-exposed, suffusing it with a feeling of brightness and airiness. In fact, the background in many such images is eliminated altogether, which can be taken to a further level through the reduction of objects and other elements in the image. So a woman will be seen posing in an empty, airy, out-of-focus setting. This kind of decontextualisation allows photographs to be more easily inserted into a variety of contexts, and allows them to acquire a 'conceptual' feel. The world of *Cosmopolitan* is the bright and happy world of 'positive thinking' favoured by contemporary corporate and consumer ideology. It is this 'unrealness' that we are specifically interested in describing in this section.

Kress and van Leeuwen (1996) have pointed out that verisimilitude has never been the only criterion for the truth of images. Scientific diagrams must be truthful, not in the sense that they look like what they represent, but in the sense that they correspond to the underlying nature or 'essence' of what they represent. Scientific diagrams can more faithfully represent something such as the workings of the body, for example, than a detailed photograph which shows unnecessary features and only the surface. Diagrams can get beneath this surface and eliminate needless details.

Another possible validity criterion for images, Kress and van Leeuwen suggest, is their emotive resonance. Here what matters is neither the truth of verisimilitude, as in the photograph, nor the abstract, 'essential' truth of the scientific diagram, but 'sensory truth'. We find this, for example, in impressionist paintings. Also children's toys tend to represent the sensory experience of objects, such as where a toy car has massive wheels to emphasise the 'wheelness' of vehicles. Kress and van Leeuwen call this 'sensory modality'. From the point of view of photographic realism, such 'sensory' images will be less realistic, but this time not because of a reduction, but because of an increase in the use of the means of visual representation: uncannily fine detail, richer colour, extra deep perspective.

In the case of the *Cosmopolitan* image, we find a move towards both the abstract truth, where we cut away unnecessary elements and, at the same time, the sensory, emotive truth, through saturated light, enhanced colour, etc. In doing so they are also increasingly moving *away* from the naturalistic, empirical truth.

We can see this same quality of abstraction and sensory modality on the North Essex Health Trust website homepage on page 99 in Chapter 4. The two participants are seen against a decontextualised background which is suffused with an optimistic light.

In *Language as Ideology*, Hodge and Kress (1979: 127) pointed out that there are ways of expressing modality other than through language. So just as in language we can communicate different levels of commitment to truth through modal verbs such as 'is', 'might be' and 'will be', so in visual communication there are modality markers. As linguists have specified such markers in language, so Kress and van Leeuwen (1996) offered a list of modality markers for visual communication. These can be used as tools to describe different elements, features and qualities of images in order to assess their modality levels and types.

Markers of visual modality

The following means of visual expression are used to indicate modality in images, but they can, in principle, be applied to all forms of visual communication. These are important and useful tools for drawing our attention to the meaning potential of the elements, features and styles of images. As with the linguistic modality markers, they increase our ability to describe what we see.

• Degrees of the articulation of detail

This is the scale from the simplest line drawing to the sharpest and most finely grained photograph. We can see in the *Cosmopolitan* image that details of the woman's skin, her clothing, appear to have been reduced partly through the diffused lighting effect. In this sense, modality has been lowered. In contrast, in the Helmand province photograph in Chapter 2, we can see the details of the clothing of the soldier in the manner had we been there. This image is therefore closer to naturalistic modality in this respect.

There is, in the case of the *Cosmopolitan* image therefore a shift away from naturalistic modality. The woman is not a specific person, but symbolises a type. In such cases, identity is specified by a number of particular deliberate features such as dress, hairstyle, make-up and posture. The woman herself is pretty but unremarkable, and represents a type through her clothes, expression and hair, representative of the generic people who populate such lifestyle magazines and advertising.

What is more interesting is when we find photographs used to illustrate real news stories in lower modality images. For example, we might find a photograph of a person depicted through reduced articulation of detail for an article on knife crime. What does this mean when the news media show us images that do not intend to document specific instances of crime, but rather to symbolise them? Also, we can ask what happens when news stories use graphics and diagrams to represent events such as military strikes. Here we can ask in which instances articulation of detail is most reduced. In graphics which represent military manoeuvres, we might see depictions of soldiers and equipment such as aircraft in higher modality than explosions and targets that are represented by rough icons. In such cases we can ask why the reverse is not the case.

- *Degrees of articulation of the background* – ranging from a blank background, via lightly sketched in or out-of-focus backgrounds, to maximally sharp and detailed backgrounds

In terms of this modality marker, we can see that the background in the North Essex Health Trust image (page 99) is of very low articulation. There is only an indication of green haze in the background, as if suggesting nature. Here we can see the move to abstract truth, communicated through the expressions of the participants. In the *Cosmopolitan* image, modality is reduced only slightly, but more so than in the Helmand province image. What we can see in these images is a continuum of levels from documenting backgrounds to symbolising them.

We might expect branding images to be of a more symbolic nature. But often in the media we find images of soldiers, politicians and criminals in completely decontextualised, low naturalistic settings. Here the aim is not to document particular instances of combat, political decisions or actual criminals, but to symbolise them. We can see this in the case of the Cameron photograph on page 72 in Chapter 3. Here there is no more than a suggestion of a setting. It is not intended, therefore, to document what Cameron did at any one moment, but to symbolise his feelings and reactions. The story depicted Cameron as a man under pressure from rivals in the build-up to the general election in 2010. In the case of the *Cosmopolitan* article, the image symbolises glamour and seduction, which is used to load the text with values that lift it above its mundane content.

- *Degrees of depth articulation* – ranging from the absence of any depth to maximally deep perspective, with other possibilities (e.g. simple overlapping) in between

In the Helmand province photograph we find good depth articulation. This is unlike the North Essex Partnership Health Trust image, where we find virtually none.

Through lowered articulation of details, of background and diminished depth, these images lose their origin in time and space. The image of the person with the knife is not in any particular place and time but simply symbolises knife crime.

What happens is that in images with reduced articulation of details of settings the consequent removal of time and space discourages the viewer from placing such events in actual socio-economic–political contexts and rather indexes typical news frames or discourses about war, health and education, crime, etc. A news item about a school might show an image, or footage, of children in school uniforms sitting behind computers where a teacher points at one screen. These visuals may symbolise 'schooling', but may not help the viewer to conceive the huge waves of changes that have come to grip the education system in terms of funding cuts and privatisation. The world of low modality visuals must lean on well-trodden themes and connotations.

- *Degrees of articulation of light and shadow* – ranging from zero articulation to the maximum number of degrees of 'depth' of shade, with other options in between

This is lowest in the *Cosmopolitan* image. We find rather unnatural patterns of shade and light, whereas in natural settings we do not see scenes saturated with bright light in this way. On the one hand, we can say that this is another shift towards abstraction, but on the other, this increase, the saturation of light, also has a sensory effect. In the case of the *Cosmopolitan* image, this bright suffused light suggests an airy, positive mood.

In the Helmand province image we find naturalistic levels of light and shadow. This is interesting, given that the image itself shows nothing of the military attack described in the text it accompanies. The image, on one level, appears to document a moment in time. But at the same time it documents a moment of calm, showing a soldier patrolling and not the violence depicted in the story. What we showed in Chapter 5 on transitivity demonstrates that the actual violence and effects of the violence are not represented in the story; instead, we find a language that connotes professionalism, military intelligence and precision. The image, too, connotes professionalism. While the image is different from the text, both work together to signify professionalism rather than warmongering. That the image does nothing to illustrate the violence described in the story is partly sidestepped by the use of the high modality image that claims to realistically represent military activity in Helmand province.

On the Essex Health Trust image, light sources appear to be coming from both above and below the participant, thereby reducing the amount of darkness we might normally find. Again, we see the importance of avoiding darker shades in order to signify optimism. We can imagine how the image would have appeared had there been more shadow present. Here, along with the lack of articulation of background, we find a lowered modality image. We might have expected images of real patients and real doctors and nurses located in actual hospital settings. Here we want to ask what is concealed by this use of abstraction. What is backgrounded and recontextualised? In previous sections we have considered the way that these Health Trusts are experiencing new levels of privatisation and a decline of services. Yet what is foregrounded are corporate buzzwords such as 'innovation' and 'communication', and branding processes, which is also evidenced by the use of the symbolic image that does not document the actual practices and locations of the Trust but seeks to load it with values of satisfaction and well-being.

- *Degrees of articulation of tone* – ranging from just two shades of tonal gradation, back and white (or a light and dark version of another colour) to maximum tonal gradation

Again, in the *Cosmopolitan* image we find reduced tonal gradation. We do not find the same tonal patterns we might find in everyday settings. In the Helmand province image we do find levels of articulation of tone that we would find in naturalistic settings. In images we can find extremes of light and dark tones, which can signify extremes of emotion, truth or obscurity. In Western cultures, brightness has metaphorical associations of transparency and truth as opposed to darkness which has associations of concealment, lack of clarity and the unknown.

- *Degrees of colour modulation* – ranging from flat, unmodulated colour to the representation of all the fine nuances of a given colour

In the *Cosmopolitan* image, the colours appear less modulated than we would expect in naturalistic images. This can be seen on the woman's sweater and on the floor where there appears to be only brightness under the table. Reduced modulation brings a sense of simplicity and certainty, whereas full realisation of modulation can make an image appear 'gritty', where all is revealed in its essence. This technique can be used by photographers to connote realism. In adverts, we often find lowered levels of modulation.

- *Degrees of colour saturation* – ranging from black and white to maximally saturated colours

Saturated colours tend to suggest emotional intensity, while more dilute colours suggest something more subtle and measured. In the *Cosmopolitan* image, we find increased degrees of colour saturation. The white of the woman's sweater and the darkness of her hair both appear more saturated than we would normally find. Again, this is typical of the world of advertisements, where it is important to bring a sensory and more emotionally intense view of the world.

Conclusion

In this chapter we have looked at characteristics in language and images that allow us to assess commitment to truth. In language, we have seen that modality can be used by speakers to commit to some things strongly while hedging their commitment to others. We saw how modals can be related to people's own sense of power and authority and how hedging can be used to communicate precision and information while in fact only obscuring and obfuscating. We saw that in the case of images, too, we can look at characteristics where they diverge from naturalistic representations. Analysing these divergences can, as with modals in language, allow us to consider the kinds of identities, values and sequences that are being communicated.

Conclusion: Doing Critical Discourse Analysis and its Discontents

Having presented a range of tools for the multimodal critical analysis of texts in this book, we now want to address a number of criticisms that have been brought forward against this analytical approach. First, however, we will reconsider the method we have used in this book to select, describe and analyse texts critically.

Conducting a CDA analysis often involves the analysis of only a small number of texts, even of just one or two. These are selected according to the interests of the analyst, where perhaps they have observed ideology in operation, where they can then describe the linguistic and grammatical choices used by the author in order to persuasively communicate this ideology. The analysis will, or should, then draw out features in the text not normally obvious to the casual reader. The ideology, buried, or somewhat concealed, in the text will become clear. It is this process of revealing the discourses embedded in texts that is seen as one important step in bringing ideological positions out into the open so that they can be more easily challenged.

The texts considered throughout this book have been analysed in precisely this fashion. As we have shown throughout this book, CDA can certainly increase our ability to describe texts and to document how they communicate.

In CDA, the texts chosen are presented as typical of a particular ideology or discourse. For example, Kress (1985) analysed several texts from school books to show how the ideology of capitalism was presented as neutral. He did not seek to prove that this is the case through a broader study of say 100 school book texts, nor by claiming that the text he analysed constitutes a random sample of a broader collection. While his analysis is compelling, as we learn more about the way such texts work to conceal actual motives and power relations, he provides no evidence to prove that these texts are typical of those we find in all or at least many school books. His chosen examples could therefore in fact be atypical. The same could be said of the texts we have presented throughout this book. To what extent have we proven that the texts taken from women's lifestyle magazines, for example, are characteristic of the discourses normally found in these kinds of magazines?

Often the relevance of a particular text analysed in CDA is made implicitly by researchers by considering them politically interesting enough to be analysed. So a newspaper text that can be shown to be implicitly racist is a reasonable target for analysis, as it is a worthy task to be carrying out. The major academic CDA journals, such as *Discourse & Society*, will contain many papers which analyse lone texts as examples of a particular dominant discourse in a society. This linguistic research is often presented as an important step in the wider quest to critically challenge the uneven power relations in our societies. Throughout the chapters in this book, texts have been chosen which tend to reflect the interests of the powerful and promote particular ideologies. As we saw in Chapter 2, this can take the form of language which seeks to gloss over the consequences of the gradual privatisation of health services in Britain, foregrounding values of 'communication' both visually and linguistically, while backgrounding actual concrete issues of treatment, staffing and facilities that are currently undergoing massive cuts and restructuring in the interests of private investment.

Drawing attention to the strategies by which visual and linguistic semiotic choices are harnessed to conceal this process is one way through which we might reveal the way that this business and neoliberal ideology is being disseminated. But why we are analysing the text, in terms of it being representative of broader trends, has perhaps not been spelled out so clearly.

Analysts may even say that what is found in the texts they analyse is characteristic of broader discourses. For example, in several chapters in this book we have analysed a news story about an event in Afghanistan which sought to portray the actions of British troops deployed there in a positive manner. We could say the ideology in this text is connected to broader pro-war discourses. But what authors do not do is show exactly what these discourses are in any concrete sense. Discourses are often presented as identifiable, yet are never clearly defined. And what we call a 'discourse' may rather be a vaguer and shifting collection of values, ideas, identities and sequences of activity.

CDA methods have come under criticism from various scholars. Some of these are to do with the epistemological question of how the term 'critical' is to be defined. Does being 'critical' simply mean attacking ideas, attitudes and values we do not agree with? And does it mean arbitrarily choosing texts that fit with our analysis? However, most of the criticism concern questions of methodology, as we have indicated above. We first list these and then suggest a number of additional methods that can help improve our own analysis.

Criticisms of CDA have focused on certain inter-related issues which can be summarized as follows:

CDA is not the only 'critical' approach

CDA is an exercise in interpretation, not analysis

CDA for the most part ignores real readers and listeners

CDA does not pay enough attention to text production

CDA is not cognitive enough

CDA is too selective, partial and qualitative

CDA is too ambitious in its quest for social change

All of these challenges can apply equally to Multimodal Critical Discourse Analysis (MCDA).

Toolan (1997: 83), who claims to be 'very much more in favour of CDA than against it', takes issue with the apparent claim of CD analysts that they are the first to 'really see and address the workings of power in discourse' (1997: 87). The study of ideology and language was not started by CDA, of course. The question of the relationship between ideology and language has been debated since Plato and Aristotle, and has been the subject of constructivist theories of language. For example, critical research on language has also been the concern of Voloshinov (1929), whose Marxist theory of language and ideology regards every instance of language use as ideological. Within sociology, there is a broad tradition of work on the social construction of reality (e.g. Berger and Luckmann, 1966). Hammersley (1996), who deals with the philosophical foundations underlying the notion 'critical', charges CDA with reducing relations between people to a relation of domination between oppressors and oppressed. Bhabha (1990) argues that we must not lose sight of the way that people have different and complex relations to different power structures in any society. For example, a woman may find herself in a lesser position of power due to her gender but in a higher position of power due to social class and ethnicity.

As regards MCDA, there has been a wave of literature emerging since the pioneering work of Kress and van Leeuwen (1996) and the rediscovery in this light of the work of O'Toole (1994). Examples of this are Liu and O'Halloran's (2009) work on image–text relations, Baldry and Thibaults' (2006) work on new media, Abousnnouga and Machin's (2009, 2011) work on three-dimensional objects and Jewitt's (2006, 2007) work on the classroom learning environment. This wave of literature appears to claim to be pioneering the critical analysis of the visual mode. Yet this body of research, as exciting as it may be, appears to overlook much research conducted over a century in semiotics, much of which has engaged with the very same problems of seeking out a more systematic way to analyse visual communication.

What is more, since the 1970s traditions in Media Studies, Film Studies, Cultural Studies and Art Studies have been engaging in the analysis of the contribution the visual makes to communicating ideologies (e.g. Hall, 1981, 1990; Arnett, 1994; Malkin et al., 1999). The work of visual designers and film editors themselves appears to be rich in techniques and models useful for visual communication, which has also largely remained ignored, perhaps with the exception of Kress and van Leeuwen (2002), O'Halloran (2004) and Machin and Niblock (2008). The point is that along with CDA, multimodality can often appear to be claiming a critical and analytical position for itself that appears to sideline other significant work being carried out in other fields.

Widdowson (1995, 1998), one of the most outspoken critics of CDA, has taken issue with the central tenets of CDA, maintaining that CDA is not a method of analysis but an exercise in interpretation, in which 'interpretation in support of belief takes precedence over analysis in support of theory' (1995: 159). Moreover, he contends that CDA privileges particular meanings of texts while largely ignoring alternative readings, including how ordinary people read and understand texts. Reactions of real communities to what the analysts deem ideological discourse are rarely taken into account. In this book we have tended to take a negative stance on women's lifestyle magazines, such as *Marie Claire*, for their individualism and aligning of women's agency alongside the interests of consumer capitalism. Yet many women, across countries where these magazines are sold, may feel that they indeed offer new opportunities for them to act outside the burdens of an intensely patriarchal society and to actually celebrate their own sexuality. They may ask what is wrong with the glamorous, stylised world that these magazines represent. They may even find them inspirational and a relief from some of the more mundane aspects of their own everyday lives.

In terms of the way we have analysed the images in this book, we could likewise argue that what has taken place is in fact more interpretation than analysis. We analysed the image of the soldier in Helmand province in several chapters, pointing to things like foregrounding and backgrounding, individualisation and modality as indicators of how real or not the image claims to be. But there are two questions we can ask about this process. First, do people really *look* at such images or are they simply background? They expect to see an image of a soldier and are given one. The image admittedly shows none of the violence reported in the story, but do we need all the technical observations from MCDA in order to work this out? Second, some authors (e.g. Bal, 1991; Dillon, 2006) argue that when we look at images, any part of them might stand out for us. In the Helmand province image we see a civilian in the background and slightly out of focus. We could argue that the civilian seemingly watching passively is evidence for the need of the presence of the soldier who patrols calmly. But other interpretations are also possible. Another viewer might see the civilian as a dangerous militia spy, the soldier as vulnerable and naïve with his back to him. Bal (1991) stressed that we should take care not to place too much emphasis on particular elements or features of images at the expense of others. Why we choose one over another is highly subjective and always a matter of interpretation. Bal (1991: 181) argues that 'the image we see is subordinated to the meanings we know'. In other words, an analysis may always tell us more about the viewer than the image itself.

One way of thinking about Widdowson's criticisms is that the analyses produced by CDA and MCDA are 'post hoc'. Put differently, the analyst looks at the text, makes a decision to analyse it and then uses the CDA tools to demonstrate that this is more than a simple interpretation but rather a systematic and controlled exercise that can be empirically repeated by others. Forceville (1999) has been highly critical of some of the work of Kress and van Leeuwen (1996) in this regard, although it could be argued that he chooses some of the weaker elements in their work to challenge, as does

Machin (2007a). Forceville (1999) suggests that multimodal analysis can constitute of little more than having an idea of what is going on in an image, such as the Helmand province photograph, and then going back to the image as an analyst in order to see multimodal features such as modality and foregrounding, in order to legitimise both the interpretation made and the concepts used to do so. The concepts appear useful since they have been shown to have produced the findings and are not simply the interpretation of the analyst.

It could also be argued that many CDA researchers choose cases that are easier to analyse and which on one level are fairly obvious in terms of what they communicate even without in-depth analysis (Widdowson, 1998). If a newspaper article runs the headline 'Britain swamped by flood of immigrants', do we need linguistic analysis to work out that it is anti-immigration? However, to counter that view we would argue that anyone reading, for example, Kress's (1985) analysis of school books would find it difficult to make the claim that the less than obvious deletion of agents and presentation of power relations through modals is not particularly revealing in terms of the way the world and certain actions and events are portrayed to children.

Yet another significant criticism is that CDA does not pay enough attention to the intentions of text producers. If the main purpose of the analysis is to uncover and challenge the repressive discourse practices of powerful, interested groups, then what needs to be considered are the effects of these practices on ordinary (non-academic) people. With regard to the analysis of media discourse, Richardson (2007) and Verschuren (1985) have both argued that the analysis of the social conditions of text production and consumption in CDA remains an underdeveloped area and that too much discourse analysis ignores 'the structrual and functional properties of the news gathering and reporting process (Verschuren, 1985: vii; quoted in Richardson, 2007: 40). Machin and Niblock (2008) have shown the crucial importance of consulting designers and marketing before drawing conclusions about the images and compositions found in media. Machin and Mayr (2007) show the importance of carrying out interviews with journalists and editors to understand what might appear as a denial of racism in newspapers. We will address this important issue further below.

MCDA has also been criticised for not sufficiently consulting with producers. Bateman, Delin and Henschel (2004) and Machin (2009) argue that much visual or multimodal CDA assumes that the kinds of meanings and interpretations offered by the analyst are to some extent imposed through his or her analysis. In Chapter 8 we carried out an analysis of modality in images. We showed how *Cosmopolitan* magazine uses images that had lowered articulation of detail in the backgrounds. So they had lowered modality on this particular scale. We concluded that this made the image symbolise a set of values for the reader rather than document a particular moment in time. But can we guarantee that readers would encounter the image in this way? Rather than reading the image in terms of visual modality markers, would they not simply see it as one genre of photography? And would the meaning of the image be affected by small details such as articulation of detail? Are readers dealing with such a magazine at a level where they are expecting realism? If the magazine producer used a specific image of a woman, should we not ask them why they do this? What if we offered the analysis of the *Cosmopolitan* image carried out in this book to the editor of the magazine who then told us 'I never wanted to use those kinds of images, but they are very cheap and free of international images rights management'? This would render our multimodal analysis somewhat absurd and invalid if we made the claim that were revealing a specific ideology. It would be rather like you painting your garden shed red as someone gave you some paint they had left over and you had no money to buy the green paint you wanted, and in fact hated the red. Later a multimodal discourse analyst turns up and interprets your ideology on the basis of the hue and saturation of the red you have used.

A criticism linked to the previous one relates to the role of cognition in CDA. Cognition describes the mental processing that is involved in both the reading and understanding of texts and discourse. Adopting a specifically cognitive approach, O'Halloran (2003) addresses two of the key stages in CDA investigations, *interpretation* and *explanation*. O'Halloran argues that CDA has focused mainly on 'explanation-stage analysis', in which it seeks to account for the connections between texts and wider socio-cultural practices at the expense of interpretation. However, as CDA claims to *interpret* texts on behalf of readers who might be unknowingly manipulated, there needs to be an analysis of the relationship between readers and the texts being read and this necessarily involves more focus on cognition. According to O'Halloran, there has been 'relatively little cognitive focus on how text can mystify for readers the events being described'. Similarly, Chilton (2005: 30) points out that CDA, by and large, has not paid enough attention to the question of 'how the human mind works when engaged in social and political action, which is largely, for humans, verbal action'.

Van Dijk (1991, 1993, 2001) has developed a 'socio-cognitive' framework, which theorises the relationship between social systems and individual cognition. His approach for analysing news (particularly the role of the media in the reproduction of racism) is in ways similar to Fairclough's (1989) three-dimensional view of discourse (discourse as text, discourse practice and social practice), but at the same time differs in that his analysis of news production and consumption has a social-psychological emphasis on processes of social cognition. Cognition, according to Van Dijk, is missing from many studies in CDA which fail to show how societal structures influence discourse structures and how these societal structures are in turn enacted, legitimated or challenged by discourse. For example, he argues that racism is both a cognitive and social phenomenon that has the social function of protecting the 'in-group'. More recently, Van Dijk (1996, 1998) has turned to more general questions of power abuse and the reproduction of inequality through ideologies. Unlike Fairclough, Van Dijk argues that no direct link should be made between discourse structures and social structures, because these are mediated by the interface of personal and social cognition.

From within CDA, the 'discourse-historical approach' can be seen as an extension of Van Dijk's socio-cognitive approach. Developed in Vienna by Ruth Wodak and her associates, it is intent on tracing the historical (intertextual) history of phrases and arguments (see, for example, Van Leeuwen and Wodak, 1999). It centres on political issues, such as racism, and attempts to integrate systematically all available background information in the analysis and interpretation of the different layers of a text (see Reisigl and Wodak, 2001; Machin and Mayr, 2007). Developed initially to address the problem of anti-semitic language behaviour in contemporary Austria, the discourse-historical methodology is designed to analyse 'implicit prejudiced utterances, as well as to identify and expose the codes and allusions contained in prejudiced discourse' (Fairclough and Wodak, 1997: 267). The method includes gathering original documents (e.g. Nazi documents on war activities in the Balkans) and ethnographic research about the past (e.g. interviews with war veterans) and then moves on to more wide-ranging data collection in the form of analysing contemporary news reporting, political discourse and lay discourse. One important feature of this approach is the practical relevance of its findings. Wodak (1996) has applied her method also to communication in organisations and to language barriers in courts, schools and hospitals. More recent research has been concerned with the discursive construction of national identities and with the European Union (e.g. Iedema and Wodak, 1999).

Our fourth criticism, that CDA is too selective, partial and qualitative, overlaps with some of the discussion above. The view here is that the analyst selects a text or type of discourse known in advance to be contentious, the confirmation for which is presented through an analysis that in essence only partially addresses certain patterns of language in the text. The linguistic analysis may therefore become a mere supplement to what the analyst has decided a priori about the text (Simpson and Mayr, 2010). Garzone and Santulli (2004: 352) claim that because CDA practitioners are especially preoccupied with sociological and political issues, they 'tend to focus their attention on larger discursive units of text', often at the expense of 'linguistic analysis proper'. They therefore suggest the incorporation of corpus-linguistic tools into a CDA analysis.

As for the criticism that CDA is mainly qualitative, Stubbs (1997), who calls himself 'basically sympathetic' to CDA, challenges CDA's methodological assumptions. He claims that although CDA presents valid arguments about text organisation, its linguistic basis is inadequate. Stubbs questions whether CDA actually adheres to 'standards of careful, rigorous and systematic analysis' (Fairclough and Wodak, 1997: 259). In other words, analysts make generalisations about social representation and social change without the linguistic evidence to support it. There is also no systematic comparison between texts. As a corpus linguist, Stubbs argues that CDA would benefit from using quantitative and comparative methods (see below).

While Stubbs (1997) suggests a quantitative analysis of texts to strengthen CDA's methodology, Widdowson (1998) suggests a more ethnographic approach that would look at how the intended discourse recipients – and not only the discourse analysts – understand and interpret texts. It is precisely because CDA raises important social issues, has an agenda of 'potentially very considerable social significance' (Stubbs, (1997: 114) and 'seeks to reveal how language is used and abused in the exercise of social power and the suppression of human rights' (Widdowson, 1998: 136) that enhancing its methodology should be a priority.

The final criticism concerns the question of how effective CDA is as a method and what it has accomplished in terms of social change and equality. Hammersley (1996) claims that CDA appears too ambitious in aiming for 'social change', which is only vaguely defined in the CDA literature. Because of this, researchers may over-interpret the data, whereby ideological evaluation becomes part and parcel of textual analysis.

This observation corresponds closely to Widdowson's claim that CDA is ideologically committed to a specific form of interpretation of texts. Jones (2007: 366) goes as far as saying that 'despite the good intentions and radical social agenda of its practitioners', CDA as a discipline is invalid. According to Jones, the problem is not with its aims themselves, but with its conception of 'discourse', which may not be helpful in understanding and criticising real-life communicative processes.

Another counter to the idea that CDA is itself ideologically driven, and therefore selective, is that all research is in fact carried out with some conceptualisation of what we should be investigating, of why certain phenomena and not others should be subject to research. Philosophers of science, such as Polanyi (1958), Popper (1934) and Kuhn (1962), all point to the way that what we call scientific investigation and experimentation is always conducted within established paradigms of knowledge that are always arbitrary and culturally bound. These authors suggest that the only true innovation comes by accident, such is the way that paradigms limit our view of the world and how we can investigate it.

Addressing the criticisms

It is important to note that CDA researchers have tackled many of the issues we raise here in recent publications. For instance, Van Dijk (2005) has always integrated cognition in his critical analysis of texts. Similarly, Chouliaraki and Fairclough (1999: 61–2), perhaps in response to Widdowson's critique, acknowledge that CDA should be combined with ethnography which would require 'the systematic presence of the researcher in the context of the practice under study'. Furthermore, ethnography, they continue, can yield 'precisely the sort of knowledge that CDA often extrapolates from text', such as 'the beliefs, values and desires of its participants'. An early example of a CDA analysis that uses an ethnographic approach is Wodak's (1996) participant-observation study of an out-patient clinic in Vienna. In turn, ethnography can benefit from CDA's premise that 'data descriptions should not be regarded as faithful descriptions of the external world', but as particular perspectives of the social world that need to be analysed critically (Chouliaraki and Fairclough, 1999: 62). Wodak makes this clear in the following statement:

> A fully 'critical' account of discourse would . . . require theorization and description of both the social processes and structures which give rise to the production of the text, and of the social structures and processes within which individuals or groups as social historical subjects, create meanings in their interactions with texts. (Wodak, 2001: 3)

Clearly, as Wodak's remarks indicate, there seems to be an increasing awareness by CDA practitioners of the 'discursive scope' that a text can have.

Machin and Niblock (2008) have also taken the step of supporting their visual analysis with interviews with text producers, allowing them to explain visual designs through the processes of marketing strategies. Machin and van Leeuwen (2007), too, carried out MCDA analyses of global magazines and computer games, supporting these with interviews with editors and designers and also by carrying out interviews with readers and users. In this way, they were able to provide links in terms of the ways that discourses are harnessed and used in different levels of semiotic production.

In spite of the interconnected criticisms raised in this chapter, there is no doubt that in the broader context of language study, the practice of CDA has brought to light important issues concerning ideology and power. It has certainly helped to contribute to our understanding, among other things, of the discourses of racism and sexism. Another academic reflex of the CDA method, pointed out by Simpson and Mayr (2010), is that it has encouraged people, especially the young, to interrogate the discourses that surround them in their everyday lives.

We now move on to making suggestions as to how a CDA-style analysis can be extended, enriched and made more rigorous. We restrict ourselves here to two main methods: the corpus approach and the ethnographic approach. Each of the areas will be outlined in turn.

The use of corpus studies in CDA

As we pointed out, one of the criticisms levelled at CDA is its largely qualitative method of inquiry and relative lack of quantitative (and comparative) methods. CDA researchers have traditionally been subjective and to some degree partial in the way they approach the texts (spoken, written, multimodal) they wish to analyse critically. The benefit a quantitative analysis offers is to firm up interpretations made on linguistic evidence. The recent introduction of corpus techniques has been the most marked change in CDA's methodology, with many studies balancing qualitative and quantitative dimensions of textual analysis through a combination of CDA with the methods of Corpus Linguistics (CL). In particular, what can be addressed is 'the problem of the representativeness of the samples of language analysed and the need to check the hypotheses developed in qualitative analysis against empirically verifiable data, chosen on the basis of explicit and objective criteria and collected using rigorous scientific and statistical procedures' (Garzone and Santulli, 2004: 353).

Media discourse, particularly newspaper discourse, offers fertile ground for testing out a combined CDA/CL approach. For example, Baker and McEnery (2005) have used a corpus of newspaper texts, as well as the United Nations High Commissioner for Refugees (UNHCR) website, to examine concordances and collocations of the terms *refugee(s)* and *asylum seeker(s)*, which revealed discourses of such people being framed 'as packages, invaders, pests or water'. Baker et al. (2008) and Gabrielatos and Baker (2008) went on to analyse the discursive construction of refugees and asylum seekers in a corpus of 140 million words of UK press articles between 1996 and 2005 (the RASIM corpus of refugees, asylum seekers, immigrants and migrants). The combined use of CDA and CL, and the use of techniques such as keyword searches, concordance and collocational analyses using specialist corpus software, has been described as a 'useful methodological synergy' by Baker et al. (2008). However, as Gabrielatos and Baker (2008: 33) themselves point out, it is still up to the analyst 'to make sense of the linguistic patterns thrown up via the corpus-based processes'. So although CL might go some way towards making CDA analysis more objective and verifiable, there are still some qualitative and subjective assessments involved in any joint CDA/CL approach.

The use of ethnographic methods in CDA

As we noted, Widdowson contends that what is actually revealed by CDA is no more than the ideology of the analyst, and this has neither legitimacy nor authority (1995: 169). In support of this argument, Widdowson (1996: 60–69) targets a specific analysis by Fairclough which has now come to be known as the 'baby book analysis' (Fairclough, 1992: 169ff). Fairclough analyses two medical texts for pregnant women, with the main focus on *The Baby Book* and some contrastive analysis of the *Pregnancy Book*. What Widdowson was most concerned about was the largely unwarranted claims made by the analyst about the reactions pregnant women might have to these texts.

Widdowson also points out that neither the consumers nor the producers of the texts were consulted. Instead, one could argue, the text was selected as preconceived evidence of the problems *assumed* to exist in it, and the resulting, partial analysis only endorsed this position. For instance, Fairclough argues that a problem with *The Baby Book* is the sense it gives of the text producer writing from a position of 'insider knowledge' (Fairclough, 1992: 173). Yet Simpson and Mayr (2010) suggest that this could be a positive feature of the book, where the insider knowledge of a medic, rather than, say, the speculative commentary of a non-specialist, might offer reassurance to pregnant women.

The latter point appears to have been borne out through an ethnographic study by McFarland (2006) of the *Baby Book* texts. Using questionnaires as well as a range of alternatively worded versions of the relevant texts, McFarland was able to elicit quantitative data through the responses of the 24 members of a group of real mothers. The women's reactions to the texts were different in significant ways to the positions attributed to them by Fairclough. While the survey tended to confirm some of Fairclough's observations about the different 'voices' in the texts, the general attitude of the women to the texts was much more positive and, contrary to Fairclough, they welcomed the texts' attempts to try to 'reassure', 'rationalise' or 'calm' their intended readership (Simpson and Mayr, 2010).

Adding an ethnographic dimension to the analysis of newspaper discourse is especially important. This can mean interviewing editors and journalists or spending some time with news agencies to observe how they work. In this respect, Machin and Mayr's (2007) critical analysis of the *Leicester Mercury* underscores the importance of interviewing its editor about the paper's policies on multiculturalism. It is therefore important to bear in mind that the study of text production and/or consumption can be usefully enriched by an ethnographic approach which investigates the processes that lie behind the production of (newspaper) texts (see Stubbs, 1997).

Similarly, other recent work which has put the study of the reaction to and reception of discourse to the fore is Benwell's (2005) study of male readers' responses to men's magazines and its possible contribution to an understanding of the discourses in and around men's magazines. Benwell's method consisted of unstructured interviews with male men's magazine readers and is therefore an important complement to Benwell's (2002) critical multimodal analysis of men's magazines.

In Chapter 1 of this book we looked at the way that a young woman in a bar used discourses of women's agency that could be related to broader discourses within feminism and which are found recontextualised in women's lifestyle magazines and television programmes. What an ethnographic component in CDA could do is help to connect production and textual analysis to the way that people live their everyday lives. This in turn will allow us to speak more confidently about the nature of the way ideology works and the way that dominant discourses are used by people. In terms of both CDA and MCDA, we will then be able to think about the way that people make, use and reuse semiotic choices. All semiotic materials, language and images, are used in social contexts. It is here in their use that they shape us as we use them (although by using them we shape them too). If we want to reveal ideology and challenge it, we must have a clearer sense of how these semiotic resources are used and reused not only in mass media sites, but in our everyday lives.

Glossary

Abstraction This is where the level of information or concrete details about an event or process are reduced or replaced by generalisations or broader concepts. This can be done in order to conceal certain aspects and foreground others. We can monitor levels of abstraction by looking for the absence of processes and participants or the use of ambiguous concepts or metaphors that distract from the actual micro-processes that took place. For example, in the sentence 'The demonstrators moved forward aggressively and the police reacted,' it is not clear what the police actually did. We can ask why an author might seek to background this process.

Connotation This is the association a word or visual element can bring. So a photograph of a woman depicts or 'denotes' a woman, whereas since she wears a suit and carries a mobile phone, she connotes confidence, independence and success. The word 'independence' in Western culture can connote not lack of responsibility, isolation or selfishness, but confidence and strength. Connotations, therefore, can be deeply ideological.

Critical stance The idea of 'critical' language study is the process of analysing linguistic elements in order to reveal connections between language, power and ideology that are hidden from people. CDA typically analyses news texts, political speeches, advertisements, school books, etc., exposing strategies that appear normal or neutral on the surface, but which may in fact be ideological and seek to shape the representation of events and persons for particular ends. The term 'critical' here therefore means 'denaturalising' the language to reveal the kinds of ideas, absences and taken-for-granted assumptions in [the] texts. This will allow us to reveal the kinds of power interests buried in these texts.

Discourse This is a term that has many wide uses and meanings. In Media Studies, we often find the term 'media discourse', 'television discourse' or even 'American discourse'. In CDA, discourse is used as a particular representation of the world. Discourses comprise participants, values, ideas, settings, times and sequences of activity. So CDA will analyse the details of texts to reveal what kinds of discourses are being presented to readers. A discourse may be communicated by reference to specific social actors which will in turn signify kinds of actions, values and ideas without these being specified. It is difficult to see what might be meant by terms such as 'television discourse' or 'American discourse' and the term 'discourse' can often be found interchangeably with 'genre'. Of course it is a problem to actually define the limits of one particular discourse.

Gender Whereas 'sex' is a biological and physiological category, referring to anatomical differences between women and men, 'gender' is a social construct that refers to the traits that men and women are assigned. These traits are not immutable, but socially and culturally determined and learned.

Genre Discourses can be found or realised in different genres. So the 'war on terror' discourse can be realised in speeches, movies, computer games and play (through plastic war toys). Genres are difficult to define and often blend, but they are characterised by a set of conventions and styles. Genres are also associated with purpose. So a speech can have the aim of persuasion and a movie the purpose of entertainment. News texts can have the purpose of informing, although more tabloid forms may also have the aim of entertaining. Nevertheless, all genres can be means of disseminating the same discourses and ideologies.

Hegemony This is a concept to describe the mechanisms through which dominant groups in society (media, politicians, religious and secular institutions) succeed in persuading subordinate groups to accept the former's moral, political and cultural values. Discourse constructs hegemonic attitude, opinions and beliefs in such a way as to make these appear 'natural' and 'common sense'.

Iconography In the sense in which it is used in this book, iconography is the visual equivalent of lexical analysis. It is the analysis of the visual elements and features of any image, layout, picture or photograph. As with lexical analysis, the aim is to carry out careful descriptive analysis in order to show what discourses are being communicated.

Iconology A term used in art history and the analysis of art, it is a process whereby elements and features of paintings and sculptures are analysed in terms of their symbolic and historical meaning. For example, a statue of a soldier may depict the figure removing his hat. This is associated in Christianity, with bearing one's head before God, and is therefore associated with purity. So too can we consider the origins of meaning of elements and features in contemporary representations.

Ideology Ideologies are simply representations of the world, they are worldviews, views on how society should be organised. Everyone has an ideology, but the analysis of ideology is generally associated with those views of the world that are associated with power and exploitation. In this book, we have considered the ideology of capitalism, which seeks to naturalise the organisation of society for the purposes of the wealthy being able to generate more capital.

Implicature Like presupposition, implicature is a way of delivering information implicitly and leaving it to the hearer to make assumptions about its meaning.

Implicatures depend on the addressee's capacity to draw inferences when the literal meaning of an utterance is not intended. For example, in the exchange

A Are you going to Paul's party?

B I have to work.

B does not say that she is not going to Paul's party but she *implicates* it.

Implicit meanings CDA is often concerned with drawing out the implicit meanings in texts. This means meanings that are not made overtly or explicitly and may need closer analysis to draw out. For example, if a politician says 'British culture is under threat from immigration', they are implicitly saying something like 'All British people are alike and share the same values, which should not change and that non-British cultures are inferior. We can also look for the implicit meanings of images.

Lexical analysis This is simply looking at the kinds of word choices found in texts and their significations. Analysis asks what kind of 'lexical field' is being created. So, for example, if a management letter informing of budget cuts uses terms such as 'opportunity', 'dynamic', 'cooperation', 'new', we can see that they attempt to give a positive spin on the events – to create a lexical field not of waste and damage, but of possibility.

Metaphor This is the means by which we understand one concept in terms of another, through a process which involves a transference or 'mapping' between the two concepts. Common conceptual metaphors are 'Life is a journey', as in 'We are at a crossroads' or 'Don't let anybody stand in your way'. Metaphors can be deliberately persuasive and often conceal underlying power relations (e.g. the use of 'disease metaphors' to describe and augment social problems, as in 'Drugs spread through our communities like an epidemic').

Modality In language, modals are an indication of an author's commitment to the truth of a statement or necessity. Modal verbs are 'will', 'must', 'might' and 'is'. We can see that 'We will go there' indicates a greater commitment than 'We might go there'. There are two main kinds of modality. **Epistemic modality** is about probability, as seen in the previous example. **Deontic modality** is about necessity, as in 'We must go there'. In images, modals characterise a number of scales that can be used to consider the extent to which an image deviates from naturalistic modality, that is, how it would appear were we to simply have been there, although different types of modality can characterise things like scientific diagrams.

Moral panic This is a sporadic episode which makes society worry that the values and principles it upholds may be in jeopardy. Moral panics are usually set in motion by a condition, episode, person or group of people who become defined as a threat to these values (e.g. young people, drug takers, immigrants, football hooligans, paedophiles, etc.). News coverage of moral panics is often disproportionate to the actual social problem.

Multimodal In linguistics, this term came to be associated with the realisation that meaning was communicated not only through the linguistic mode, but by other semiotic modes such as the visual, sound or gesture. In Media Studies and Cultural Studies this might seem a rather obvious discovery, but linguists, with their tradition of more precise observation and description, began to offer useful tools to those outside their field who were interested in other modes of communication.

Nominalisation This is where verb processes are represented in the form of nouns. So the sentence 'Management created a new system of accountability', which contains the verb 'created', could be written as 'the creation of a new system of accountability' using the noun 'creation'. This has a number of important effects. It can be used to conceal agents, simplify complex processes and delete time and place.

Overlexicalisation This is where we find a word or its synonyms 'over-present' in a text (i.e. the word or its synonyms are used more than we would normally expect). This is normally evidence of some kind of moral awkwardness or attempt to over-persuade. For example, if a document from a Human Resources department sent to staff displays an overuse of the word 'opportunity' and its synonyms, we might suspect that there is at least ambiguity of there being any real opportunity present in what is being proposed.

Presupposition This is basically a taken-for-granted assumption found in communication. In fact, all language and communication could be said to rely in presupposition. If a person speaks of a table to you, they have the presupposition that you know what a table is. But in CDA it is important to think about which kinds of concepts are presented as taken for granted and which are contestable. So if a politician speaks of 'French culture being under threat by immigration', there is the presupposition that there is such a clearly identifiable thing as 'French culture'. In fact, if we look at the people who live in France, we find a massive array of ways of living that have long been in flux. Yet politicians can seek to use such presuppositions in order to create a basis for their arguments.

Quoting verbs These are the verbs used to represent the way people speak. For example, 'Jane complained about the food' or 'Jane whinged about the food'. Important here is the fact that both of these are evaluations of what Jane says and one represents her actions and perhaps her identity in very different ways without overtly doing so. We can analyse the kinds of quoting verbs attributed to different speakers.

Recontextualisation This is where language is used to transform events and practices where elements are changed, replaced, removed or simplified. Whenever social actors or events are absent or the micro-processes of an event are simplified or abstracted, we can assume that recontextualisation has taken place. So, for example, an image of a smiling, pretty woman holding a tiny seedling in her hand can be used in the media to represent the fragility of the environment and human responsibility. But what is removed here is who actually does the damage, what is being damaged and what the remedy might be. We might argue that these events have been recontextualised to background the role of global capitalism in the abuse of the world's resources.

Salience In images, there are a number of ways that elements and features can be made to attract our attention or be given importance. In this case, they are given salience. For example, a feature might be foreground, given a brighter colour, or a central position. Different elements and features can be given different kinds of salience to draw attention in different ways and create different hierarchies of importance.

Semiotic resource When humans communicate, they have a range of semiotic resources available to them in term of words, images, sounds, colours, postures. To some extent when we communicate we draw upon a set of shared semiotic resources. CDA and Social Semiotics have been concerned to document the underlying available resources or system of choices so that we can best understand what the meaning potentials of semiotic resources are.

Signification This can simply be the process of a word or visual element giving meaning. So a word such as 'table' signifies the thing, a table. And a word like 'democracy' can signify 'a way of organising society and political power', although, of course, what is signified may mean different things to different people. But we can say that any word, such as 'democracy', or visual element, can be used to signify a whole range of associations, identities, persons or sequences of activity. Signification, therefore, is an important way that discourses can be communicated without them being so overtly stated.

Social actor analysis A set of linguistic categories that can be applied to the analysis of any discourse in which people are evaluated through the way they are named, categorised (either by their occupation or social activity, such as 'teacher', 'immigrant') and/or identified in terms of age, gender, provenance, class, race or religion (e.g. 'a 28-year-old Polish woman'). Newspapers can include, but also exclude, certain social actors to suit their interests. In certain newspapers, we often find negative representations of young people and immigrants in connection with crime, violence and social welfare in many media. Social actor categories can also be applied to visual forms of communications, such as images.

Structural oppositions In representational strategies it may be common to find that one side of an opposition is used to imply its opposite, which is absent from the text. In news texts that represent criminals, their evilness or immorality is emphasised, thus implying the morality and goodness of the rest of the social order. Or a management text may refer to the importance of now being dynamic, innovative, forward thinking. What is not stated is that therefore staff must currently be static, averse to change and thinking only about now and the past.

Suppression This is where social actors or aspects of an event are backgrounded or removed from a representation. For example, in the sentence 'Cuts to the education budget resulted in a drop in standards', who made the cuts has been deleted. In such cases we must ask what ideological work is being done.

Transitivity In CDA, this is the study of social action. It is the study of verbs in order to reveal who is represented as the agent or otherwise in texts. In CDA, this draws for the most part on the verb classification of Halliday (1978), who distinguished between material, behavioural, mental, verbal, existential and relational verbs. Texts can be analysed to see which kinds of verb classifications tend to be used to characterise the actions of certain groups. The same set of categories can be applied visually.

References

Abousnnouga, G. and Machin, D. (2009) 'Analysing the language of war monuments', *Visual Communication*, 9(2): 131–49.

Achugar, M. (2007) 'Between remembering and forgetting: Uruguayan military discourse about human rights (1976–2004)', *Discourse & Society*, 18(3): 521–547.

Arnett, P. (1994) *Live from the Battlefield: From Vietnam to Baghdad, 35 years in the World's War Zones*. New York: Simon & Schuster.

Arnheim, R. (1969) *Visual Thinking*. Berkeley, CA: University of California Press.

Austin, J.L. (1975) *How to Do Things With Words*. Cambridge, MA: Harvard University Press.

Baker, P., Gabrielatos, C., Khosravinik, M., Kryzanowski, M., McEnery, T. and Wodak, R. (2008) 'A useful methodological synergy? Combining critical discourse analysis and corpus linguistics to examine discourses of refugees and asylum seekers in the UK press', *Discourse & Society*, 19(3): 273–306.

Baker, P. and McEnery, T. (2005) 'A corpus-based approach to discourses of refugees and asylum seekers in UN and newspaper texts', *Journal of Language and Politics*, 4 (2): 197–226.

Banks, D. (1994) 'Hedges and how to trim them', in M. Brekke, Ø. Andersen, T. Dahl and J. Myking (eds), *Applications and Implications of Current LSP Research*, Vol. 2. Bergen: Fagbokforlaget, pp. 587–92.

Baldry, A. and Thibault, P. (2006) *Multimodal Transcription and Text Analysis: A Multimodal Toolkit and Coursebook*. London and Oakville: Equinox.

Barthes, R. (1973) *Mythologies*. London: Paladin.

Barthes, R. (1977) *Image, Music, Text*. London: Paladin.

Bateman, J.A., Delin, J. and Henschel, R. (2004) 'Multimodality and empiricism: Preparing for a corpus-based approach to the study of multimodal meaning-making', in E. Ventola, C. Cassily and M. Kaltenbacher (eds), *Perspectives on Multimodality*. Amsterdam: John Benjamins, pp. 65–87.

BBC News, full text: Michael Howard speech, http://news.bbc.co.uk/1/hi/uk_politics/3679618.stm (accessed January 2012).

Bell, P. and van Leeuwen, T. (1994) *The Media Interview: Confession, Contest, Conversation*. Sydney: University of New South Wales Press.

Bennett, L. (2005) *News: The Politics of Illusion*. London: Longman.

Benwell, B. (2002) 'Is there anything "new" about these lads? The textual and visual construction of masculinity in men's magazines', in L. Litosseliti (ed.), *Gender Identity and Discourse Analysis*. Philadelphia, PA: John Benjamins, pp. 149–74.

Benwell, B. (2005) '"Lucky this is anonymous!" Men's magazines and ethnographies of reading: A textual culture approach', *Discourse & Society*, 16(2): 147–172.

Caldas-Coulthard, C. (1994) 'On reporting reporting: The representation of speech in factual and factional narratives', in M. Coulthard (ed.), *Advances in Written Text Analysis*. London: Routledge, pp. 295–308.

Caldas-Coulthard, C. (1997) *News as Social Practice: A Study in Critical Discourse Analysis*. Florianópolis, Brazil: Federal University of Santa Catarina Press.

Cameron, D. (2001) *Good to Talk?* London: Sage.

Cameron, L. (2003) *Metaphor in Educational Discourse*. London: Continuum.

Cameron, L.J. (2007) 'Patterns of metaphor use in reconciliation talk', *Discourse & Society*, 18(2): 197–222.

Charteris-Black, J. (2004) *Corpus Approaches to Critical Metaphor Analysis*. Basingstoke and New York: Palgrave MacMillan.

Charteris-Black, J. (2006) 'Britain as a container: Immigration metaphors in the 2005 election campaign', *Discourse & Society*, 17(6) : 563–81.

Chiapello, E. and Fairclough, N. (2002) 'Understanding the new management ideology: A transdisciplinary contribution from critical discourse analysis and new sociology of capitalism', *Discourse & Society*, 13(2): 185–208.

Chilton, P. (1996) *Security Metaphors: Cold War Discourse from Containment to Common European Home*. Bern and New York: Peter Lang.

Chouliaraki, L. and Fairclough, N. (1999) *Discourse in Late Modernity: Rethinking Critical Discourse Analysis*. Edinburgh: Edinburgh University Press.

Clark, K. (1992) 'The linguistics of blame: Representations of women in *The Sun*'s reporting of crimes of sexual violence', in M. Toolan (ed.), *Language, Text and Context: Essays in Stylistics*. London and New York: Routledge, pp. 208–226.

Dillon, G.L. (2006) 'Writing with images. Introduction: Imagetext multiples and other mixed modes', available at: http://courses.washington.edu/hypertxt/cgi-bin/book/wordsimages/wordsimages.html.

Duerr, H. (1985) *Dreamtime: Concerning the Boundary between Wilderness and Civilization*. London: Powell's Books.

Eriksson, K. and Aronsson, K. (2005) '"We're really lucky": Co-creating "us" and the "Other" in school booktalk', *Discourse & Society*, 16(5): 719–738.

Faber, B. (2003) 'Creating rhetorical stability in corporate university discourse technologies and change', *Written Communciation*, 20(4): 391–425.

Fairclough, N. (1989) *Language and Power* (2nd edition, 2001). London: Longman.

Fairclough, N. (1992) *Discourse and Social Change*. Cambridge: Polity Press.

Fairclough, N. (1994) 'Conversationalisation of public discourse and the authority of the consumer', in R. Keat, N. Whitely and N. Abercrombie (eds), *The Authority of the Consumer*. London: Routledge, pp. 253–68.

Fairclough, N. (1995a) *Critical Discourse Analysis: The Critical Study of Language*. London: Longman.

Fairclough, N. (1995b) *Media Discourse*. London: Arnold.

Fairclough, N. (2000) *New Labour, New Language*. London: Routledge.

Fairclough, N. (2003) *Analysing Discourse: Textual Analysis for Social Research*. London: Routledge.

Fairclough, N. and Wodak, R. (1997) 'Critical discourse analysis', in T. van Dijk (ed.), *Discourse as Social Interaction*. London: Sage, pp. 258–85.

Fishman, M. (1980) *Manufacturing the News*. Austin, TX: University of Texas Press.

Forceville, C. (1999) 'Educating the eye? Kress and van Leeuwen's *Reading Images: The Grammar of Visual Design* (1996)', *Language and Literature*, 8(2): 163–78.

Fowler, R. (1991) *Language in the News*. London: Routledge.

Fowler, R., Hodge, R., Kress, G. and Trew, T. (1979) *Language and Control*. London: Routledge.

Gabrielatos, C. and Baker, P. (2008) 'Fleeing, sneaking, flooding: a corpus analysis of discursive constructions of refugees and asylum seekers in the UK press, 1996–2005', *Journal of English Linguistics*, 36(1): 5–38.

Gee, J.P. (1990) *Social Linguistics and Literacies: Ideology in Discourses. Critical Perspectives on Literacy and Education*. London: Falmer Press.

Gellner, E. (1983) *Nations and Nationalism*. Ithaca, NY: Cornell University Press.

Goatly, A. (1997) *The Language of Metaphors*. London: Routledge.

Graham, P., Keenan, T. and Dowd, A.M. (2004) 'A call to arms at the end of history: A discourse-historical analysis of George W. Bush's declaration of war on terror', *Discourse & Society*, 15(2–3): 199–221.

Gramsci, A. (1971) *Selections from the Prison Notebooks*. Ed. and trans. Q. Hoare and G. Nowell-Smith. London: Lawrence & Wishart.

Guardian, full text: Tony Blair's speech, www.guardian.co.uk/politics/2003/mar/18/foreignpolicy.iraq1 (accessed January 2012).

Hall, S. (1973) *Encoding and Decoding in the Television Discourse*. Birmingham: Centre for Cultural Studies, University of Birmingham.

Hall, S. (1990) 'The whites of their eyes', in M. Alvarado and J.O. Thompson (eds), *The Media Reader*. London: British Film Institute, pp. 7–23.

Hall, S. (1997) *Representation: Cultural Representations and Signifying Practices*. Milton Keynes: Open University Press.

Halliday, M.A.K. (1978) *Language as Social Semiotic: The Social Interpretation of Language and Meaning*. London: Edward Arnold.

Halliday, M.A.K. (1985) *Introduction to Functional Grammar*. (2nd edition, 1994) London: Edward Arnold.

Hammersley, M. (1996) 'On the foundations of critical discourse analysis', *Language and Communication*, 17(3): 327–48.

Hart, C. (2008) 'Critical discourse analysis and metaphor: Toward a theoretical framework', *Critical Discourse Studies*, 5(2): 91–106.

Hawkes, G. (1996) *A Sociology of Sex and Sexuality*. London and Philadelphia, PA: Open University Press/McGraw-Hill.

Hobsbawm, E. (1983) 'Mass producing traditions', in E. Hobsbawm and T. Ranger, (eds), *The Invention of Tradition*. Cambridge: Cambridge University Press, pp. 263–308.

Hodge, R. and Kress, G. (1979/1993) *Language and Ideology*. London: Routledge.

Hodge, R. and Kress, G. (1988) *Social Semiotics*. Cambridge: Polity Press.

Iedema, R. and Wodak, R. (1999) 'Introduction: Organizational discourses and practices', *Discourse & Society*, 10(1): 5–19.

Irigaray, L. (1985) *The Sex which is Not One*. Ithaca, NY: Cornell University Press.

Jaworski, A., Fitzgerald, R. and Morris, D. (2003) 'Certainty and speculation in broadcast news reporting of the future: The execution of Timothy McVeigh', *Discourse Studies*, 5(1): 33–4.

Jeffries, L. (2007) *Textual Construction of the Female Body: A Critical Discourse Approach*. Basingstoke: Palgrave Macmillan.

Jewitt, C. (2006) *Technology, Literacy and Learning: A Multimodal Approach*. London: Routledge.

Jewitt, C. (2007) 'A multimodal perspective on textuality and contexts', *Pedagogy and Culture*, 15(3): 275–90.

Jewkes, Y. (2011) *Media and Crime*. London: Sage.

Jones, P. (2007) 'Why there is no such thing as "critical discourse analysis"', *Language and Communication*, 27: 337–368.

Kitzinger, J. (2004) 'Audience and readership research', in J. Downing, D. McQuail, P. Schlesinger and E. Wartella (eds), *Handbook of Media Studies*. London: Sage, pp. 167–81.

Kitzinger, S. (2005) *The Politics of Childbirth*. China: Elsevier.

Kress, G. (1985) 'Ideological structures in discourse', in T. van Dijk (ed.), *Handbook of Discourse Analysis*. London: Academic Press, pp. 27–42.

Kress, G. (1989) *Linguistic Processes in Sociocultural Practice*. Melbourne, Vic.: Deakin University Press.

Kress, G. (2010) *Multimodality: A Social Semiotic Approach to Contemporary Communication*. London: Routledge.

Kress, G. and van Leeuwen, T. (1996) *Reading Images: The Grammar of Visual Design*. London: Routledge.

Kress, G. and van Leeuwen, T. (2001) *Multimodal Discourse: The Modes and Media of Contemporary Communication*. London: Arnold.

Kress, G. and van Leeuwen, T. (2002) 'Colour as a semiotic mode: Notes for a grammar of colour', *Visual Communication*, 1(3): 343–68.

Kuhn, T.S. (1962) *The Structure of Scientific Revolutions*. Chicago: University of Chicago Press.

Lakoff, G. (1993) 'The contemporary theory of metaphor', in A. Ortony (ed.), *Metaphor and Thought*. Cambridge: Cambridge University Press, pp. 202–51.

Lakoff, G. and Núñez, R. (1997) 'The metaphorical structure of mathematics: sketching out cognitive foundations for a mind-based mathematics', in L. English (ed.), *Mathematical Reasoning Analogies, Metaphors and Images*. Mahwah, NJ: Lawrence Erlbaum Associates, pp. 21–89.

Lakoff, G. and Johnson, M. (1980) *Metaphors We Live By*. Chicago: University of Chicago Press.

Leach, E. (1964) 'Animal categories and verbal abuse', in E.H. Lenneberg (ed.), *New Directions in the Study of Language*. Cambridge MA: MIT Press, p. 34.

Leitner, G. (1980) 'BBC English and Deutsche Rundfunksprache: A comparative and historical analysis of the language of radio', *International Journal of the Sociology of Language*, 26: 75–100.

Levinson, S. (1983) *Pragmatics*. Cambridge: Cambridge University Press.

Levitas, R. (2005) *The Inclusive Society: Social Exclusion and New Labour*. London: Macmillan.

Liu, Y. and O'Halloran, K.L. (2009) 'Intersemiotic texture: Analyzing cohesive devices between language and images', *Social Semiotics*, 19(4): 367–88.

Lu, L.W. and Ahrens, K. (2008) 'Ideological influence on building metaphors in Taiwanese presidential speeches', *Discourse & Society*, 19(3): 383–408.

Lutz, C.A. and Collins, J.L. (1993) *Reading National Geographic*. Chicago: University of Chicago Press.

Machin, D. (2007a) *Introduction to Multimodal Analysis*. London: Arnold.

Machin, D. (2007b) 'Visual discourses of war: multimodal analysis of photographs of the Iraq occupation', in A. Hodges and C. Nilep (eds), *Discourse, War and Terrorism*, London: John Benjamins, pp. 123–42.

Machin, D. and Mayr, A. (2007) 'Antiracism in the British government's model regional newspaper: The "talking cure"', *Discourse & Society*, 18(4): 453–78.

Machin, D. and Niblock, S. (2008) 'Branding newspapers: Visual texts as social practice', *Journalism Studies*, 9(2): 244–59.

Machin, D. and Thornborrow, J. (2003) 'Branding and discourse: The case of *Cosmopolitan*', *Discourse & Society*, 14(4): 453–473.

Machin, D. and Thornborrow, J. (2006) 'Lifestyle and the depoliticisation of agency: Sex as power in women's magazines', *Social Semiotics*, 16(1): 173–88.

Machin, D. and van Leeuwen, T. (2005) 'Language style and lifestyle: The case of a global magazine', *Media, Culture & Society*, 27(4): 577–600.

Machin, D. and van Leeuwen, T. (2007) *Global Media Discourse*. London: Routledge.

Manning, P. (ed.) (2007a) *Drugs and Popular Culture*. Cullompton: Willan Publishing.

Manning, P. (2007b) 'The symbolic framing of drug use in the news: Ecstasy and volatile substance abuse in newspapers', in P. Manning (ed.), *Drugs and Popular Culture*. Cullompton: Willan Publishing, pp. 150–67.

Marx, K. (1933) *The German Ideology*. Ed. and trans. S. Ryazanskaya. London: Lawrence and Wishart.

Mayr, A. and Machin, D. (2012) *The Language of Crime and Deviance: An Introduction to Critical Linguistic Analysis in Media and Popular Culture*. London: Continuum.

McClintock, M. (2002) *Instruments of Statecraft: US Guerilla Warfare, Counterinsurgency and Counterterrorism 1940–1990*. New York: Pantheon.

McConnell, J. (2001) The counterterrorists at the Fletcher School: The Reagan administration's new terrorism policy', *Boston Review*, October/November.

McFarland, K. (2006) 'Strengthening Critical Discourse Analysis: *The Babybook* Revisited', available at http://cw.routledge.com/textbooks/reli/resources/LAP_McFarland_2006.pdf (accessed 15 October, 2011).

Morley, D. (1980) *The 'Nationwide' Audience: Structure and Decoding*. London: British Film Institute.

Newman, J. (2001) *Modernising Governance: New Labour, Policy and Society*. London: Sage.

Oktar, L. (2001) 'The ideological organization of representational processes in the presentation of us and them', *Discourse & Society*, 12(3): 313–346.

O'Halloran, K.L. (2004) 'Visual semiosis in film', in K.L. O'Halloran (ed.), *Multimodal Discourse Analysis*. London: Continuum, pp. 109–30.

O'Toole, M. (1994) *The Language of Displayed Art*. Leicester: Leicester University Press.

Panofsky, E. (1972) *Studies in Iconology: Humanistic Themes in the Art of the Renaissance Book*. Boulder, CO: Westview Press.

Parker, H., Aldridge, J. and Measham, F. (1998) *Illegal Leisure: The Normalization of Adolescent Recreational Drug Use*. London: Routledge.

Parker, H., Williams, L. and Aldridge, J. (2002) 'The normalization of "sensible" recreational drug use: Further evidence from the North West England Longitudinal Study', *Sociology*, 36: 941–64.

Polanyi, M. (1958) *Personal Knowledge: Towards a Post-Critical Philosophy*. Chicago: University of Chicago Press.

Pollock, A. (2006) *NHS plc: The Privatisation of Our Health Care*. London: Verso.

Poole, E. and Richardson, J.E. (2006) 'Introduction', in E. Poole and J E Richardson (eds), *Muslims and the News Media*. London: I.B. Tauris pp. 1–11.

Popper, K. (2005) *The Logic of Scientific Discovery*. London, Routledge.

Reisigl, M. and Wodak, R. (2001) *Discourse and Discrimination: Rhetorics of Racism and Antisemitism*. London: Routledge.

Resche, C. (2004) 'Investigating "Greenspanese": From hedging to "fuzzy transparency"', *Discourse & Society*, 15(6): 723–44.

Richardson, J.E. (2007) *Analysing Newspapers*. London: Macmillan.

Rogers, R. (ed.) (2004) *An Introduction to Critical Discourse Analysis in Education*. Mahwah, NJ, and London: Lawrence Erlbaum Associates.

Ryder, M.E. (1999) 'Smoke and mirrors: Event patterns in the discourse structure of a romance novel', *Journal of Pragmatics*, 31: 1067–80.

Sapir, E. (1929) 'The status of linguistics as a science', in E. Sapir (1958), *Culture, Language and Personality* (ed. D.G. Mandelbaum). Berkeley, CA: University of California Press, pp. 160–6.

Saussure, de Ferdinand ([1916] 1983) *Course in General Linguistics*. Trans. Roy Harris. London: Duckworth.

Scammel, A. (2011) 'Risk in midwifery talk and practice'. Paper presented at City University and British Sociology Association Risk Study Group one-day conference on 'Risk Policy and Decision Making', City University, February.

Scannell, P. and Cardiff, D. (1991) *A Social History of British Broadcasting*. Oxford: Blackwell.

Schegloff, E. (1997) 'Whose text? Whose context?', *Discourse & Society*, 8(2): 165–87.

Scollon, R. (1998) *Mediated Discourse as Social Interaction: A Study of News Discourse*. London: Longman.

Scraton, P. (1997) *Power, Conflict and Criminalisation*. London: Routledge.

Seddon, T. (2008) 'Drugs, crime and social exclusion: Social context and social theory in British drugs–crime research', *British Journal of Criminology*, 46(4): 680–703.

Semino, E. (2008) *Metaphor in Discourse*. London: Sage.

Simpson, P. and Mayr, A. (2010) *Language and Power: A Resource Book for Students*. London: Routledge.

Stubbs, M. (1997) 'Whorf's children: Critical comments on critical discourse analysis (CDA)', in A. Rayan and A. Wray (eds), *Evolving Models of Language*. Clevedon: Multilingual Matters, pp. 100–116.

Sunoo, B.P. (1998) 'Measuring technology-based training', *Workforce*, 77(7): 17–18.

Teo, P. (2000) 'Racism in the news: A critical discourse analysis of news reporting in two Australian newspapers', *Discourse & Society*, 11: 7–49.

Tuchman, G. (1978) *Making News: A Study in the Construction of Reality*. New York: Free Press.

Van Dijk, T. (1991) *Racism and the Press*. London: Routledge.

Van Dijk, T. (1993) *Discourse and Elite Racism*. London: Sage.

Van Dijk, T. (1995) 'Discourse analysis as ideology analysis', in C. Schäffner and A. Wenden (eds), *Language and Pace*. Aldershot: Dartmouth, pp. 17–33.

Van Dijk, T. (1996) 'Discourse, power and access', in C.R. Caldas-Coulthard and M. Coulthard (eds), *Texts and Practices: Readings in Critical Discourse Analysis*. London: Routledge, pp. 84–104.

Van Dijk, T.A. (1998) *Ideology*. London: Sage.

Van Dijk, T.A. (2000) 'Parliamentary debates', in R. Wodak and T.A. van Dijk (eds), *Racism at the Top. Parliamentary Discourses on Ethnic Issues in Six European States*. Klagenfurt, Austria: Drava Verlag, pp. 45–78.

Van Dijk, T. (2001) 'Multidisciplinary CDA: A pleas for diversity', in R. Wodak and M. Meyer (eds), *Methods of Critical Discourse Analysis*. London: Sage, pp. 95–120.

Van Dijk, T.A. (2008) *Discourse and Power*. Basingstoke: Palgrave: Macmillan.

Van Leeuwen, T. (1996a) 'The representations of social actors', in C.R. Caldas-Coulthard and M. Coulthard (eds), *Texts and Practices: Readings in Critical Discourse Analysis*. London: Routledge, pp. 32–70.

Van Leeuwen, T. (1996b) 'Representing Social Action', in *Discourse & Society* 6(1) 81–106.

Van Leeuwen, T. (2000) 'Semiotics and Iconography', in T. van Leeuwen and C. Jewitt (eds), *Handbook of Visual Analysis*. London: Sage, pp. 92–118.

Van Leeuwen, T. (2005) *Introducing Social Semiotics*. London: Routledge.

Van Leeuwen, T. (2008) *Discourse and Practice: New Tools for Critical Discourse Analysis*. Oxford: Oxford University Press.

Van Leeuwen, T. and Wodak, R. (1999) 'Legitimizing immigration control: A discourse-historical analysis', *Discourse Studies*, 1(1): 83–118.

Voloshinov, V. (1929) *Marxism and the Philosophy of Language*. New York: Seminar Press.

Widdowson, H. (1995) 'Discourse analysis: A critical view', *Language and Literature*, 4(3): 157–72.

Widdowson, H. (1996) 'Reply to Fairclough: Discourse and interpretation: Conjectures and refutations', *Language & Literature*, 5(1): 57–69.

Widdowson, H. (1998) 'The theory and practice of critical discourse analysis', *Applied Linguistics*, 19(1): 136–51.

Wodak, R. (1989) *Language, Power and Ideology: Studies in Political Discourse*. London and Amsterdam: Benjamin.

Wodak, R. (1996) *Disorders of Discourse*. London: Longman.

Wodak, R. (2001) 'The discourse-historical approach', in R. Wodak and M. Meyer (eds), *Methods of Critical Discourse Analysis*. London: Sage, pp. 87–122.

Wodak, R. and Meyer, M. (eds) (2001) *Methods of Critical Discourse Analysis*. London: Sage.

Wood, L.A. and Kroger, R.O. (2000) *Doing Discourse Analysis: Methods for Studying Action in Talk and Text*. Thousand Oaks, CA: Sage.

Wykes, M. (2001) *News, Crime and Culture*. London: Pluto Press.

Zeynep, A. (2007) 'News coverage of violence against women', *Feminist Media Studies*, 6(3): 295–314.

Index